The Joy of SOX

The Joy of SOX

Why Sarbanes-Oxley and Service-Oriented Architecture May Be the Best Thing That Ever Happened to You

Hugh Taylor

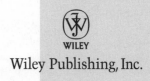

Wiley Publishing, Inc.

The Joy of SOX: Why Sarbanes-Oxley and Service-Oriented Architecture May Be the Best Thing That Ever Happened to You

Published by
Wiley Publishing, Inc.
10475 Crosspoint Boulevard
Indianapolis, IN 46256
www.wiley.com

ISBN-13: 978-0-471-77274-3
ISBN-10: 0-471-77274-7

Manufactured in the United States of America

10 9 8 7 6 5 4 3 2 1

1B/RT/QT/QW/IN

For general information on our other products and services or to obtain technical support, please contact our Customer Care Department within the U.S. at (800) 762-2974, outside the U.S. at (317) 572-3993 or fax (317) 572-4002.

Library of Congress Cataloging-in-Publication Data

Taylor, Hugh, 1965–
  The joy of Sox : why Sarbanes-Oxley and service oriented architecture may be the best thing that ever happened to you / Hugh Taylor.
     p. cm.
  Includes bibliographical references and index.
  ISBN-13: 978-0-471-77274-3 (pbk. : alk. paper)
  ISBN-10: 0-471-77274-7 (pbk. : alk. paper)
  1. Management information systems—United States. 2. Corporate governance—United States. 3. Corporations—Accounting—Law and legislation—United States. 4. United States. Sarbanes-Oxley Act of 2002. I. Title.
  HD30.213.T397 2006
  657 .320973—dc22

                        2006000879

*To my wife, Rachel. For your support and encouragement
I am eternally grateful.*

About the Author

Hugh Taylor is Vice President of Marketing at SOA Software, the leading provider of management and security solutions for enterprise service-oriented architecture. He is the co-author, with Eric Pulier, of Understanding Enterprise SOA (Manning, 2005). The author of more than a dozen articles and papers on the subject of web services and service-oriented architecture, Taylor is an authority on business process management, SOA, and compliance issues. Taylor received his B.A. degree, Magna Cum Laude from Harvard College in 1988 and his M.B.A. degree from Harvard Business School in 1992. He lives in Los Angeles.

Credits

Executive Editor
Bob Elliott
Carol Long
Chris Webb

Senior Acquisitions Editor
Jim Minatel

Development Editor
Ed Connor

Production Editor
Kathryn Duggan

Copy Editor
Michael Koch

Editorial Manager
Mary Beth Wakefield

Production Manager
Tim Tate

Vice President and Executive Group Publisher
Richard Swadley

Vice President and Executive Publisher
Joseph B. Wikert

Project Coordinator
Ryan Steffen

Graphics and Production Specialists
Lauren Goddard
Brooke Graczyk
DennyHager
Stephanie D. Jumper

Quality Control Technician
John Greenough

Proofreading and Indexing
TECHBOOKS Production Services

Contents

Acknowledgements

A book that integrates the disciplines of information technology, accounting, and business management will necessarily involve the author with experts in each of these areas. I am deeply indebted to a number of people who helped me through the process of researching and writing this book. In particular, I want to acknowledge the following individuals: Scott Royster, Debbie Cowan, Leslie Bauer, Daniel Henriquez, Derek Wimmer, Luis Puncel, Tom Flocco, Don Goldstein, Larry Russell, Susan Kimes, Kris Krishnan, and Kieran Brennan. Don Sanders gave me the benefit of his extensive knowledge of COBIT. Finally, I owe a special thank you to Sonia Luna, CPA, and President of SOX Solutions, who helped immeasurably with her contribution of audit industry insights and specific knowledge.

At Wiley, I am indebted to the professional expertise of Carol Long, Acquisitions Editor, Ed Connor, Development Editor and, Kathryn Duggan, Production Editor.

Introduction

We choose to go to the moon. We choose to go to the moon in this decade and do the other things, not because they are easy, but because they are hard, because that goal will serve to organize and measure the best of our energies and skills, because that challenge is one that we are willing to accept, one we are unwilling to postpone, and one which we intend to win, and the others, too.
PRESIDENT JOHN F. KENNEDY, 1962

These are the words that inspired a generation of Americans to undertake one of the greatest achievements in human history. In today's culture of "what's in it for me?" Kennedy's exhortation to do the hard work and reap the benefits seems quaint, corny even. Yet, even in our present, frenetic MTV reality of overloaded Blackberries, virtual meetings round the clock and fast approaching earnings reports, perhaps we too can find inspiration in the idea that the hard challenges are the ones worth doing.

I have found that the most worthwhile tasks are often the hardest. However, when I tell my friends that I am writing a book about how businesses can prosper by complying with the Sarbanes Oxley Act (SOX), they give me an incredulous look. How can adherence to such a set of rules—in their opinion dreamt up by Congress to enforce honesty in American business—have anything to do with actually running a business? My response, channeling Kennedy: How do we turn adversity into advantage? It's about making choices. I'd rather find the opportunity to benefit from a challenge than complain about it.

I recognize that there is a certain perversity to the position I take in this book. While most executives—sensibly, perhaps—view SOX as a set of regulatory hoops that they must pay experts to help them jump through, I am advocating that we look at SOX as a pretext for increasing our effective control over business operations. I own the perversity of this book. Essentially, I am an odd-ball, forever looking at different ways of doing things, much to people's intrigue or derision, depending on the circumstances. This does not make sense to everyone, but not everyone has my eccentric but auspicious background for the task of looking at the upside of SOX through the lens of information technology. I am not an auditor, or a compliance consultant. I have worked in several different industries, and have had experiences ranging from great to horrific. My background and experiences, however, continually motivate me to look at the opportunity that is present in every challenge.

I have come to see that SOX actually has the potential to be a driver of positive change in business. Innovation is one of the great traditions and strengths of American business. In the spirit of adaptation and vision, I encourage you to look at the regulatory requirements of our age as potential catalyst for positive change in tightening operational control while maintaining strategic flexibility. My goal with this book is to show you how this might be possible for you and your business. At a high level, my hope is that this book will help you make sense of the epoch-making changes that are occurring around you in the corporate world.

Perhaps we should take our cue from Kennedy. We choose to do the right thing with SOX, not because it is easy, but because it is hard, because SOX will serve to organize and measure the best of our energies and skills, because that challenge is one that we are willing to accept, one we are unwilling to postpone.

The Challenge and Opportunity of Sarbanes Oxley

2005 has been a year of reckoning for past corporate excess. In the last decade, we have witnessed an amazing whirlwind of boom, bust, and atonement. Investors were defrauded out of billions. Institutions that the public trusted have been revealed to be compromised by conflicts of interest, poor management, and outright criminality. With Dennis Kozlowsky, Bernard Ebbers, and John Rigas all sentenced to prison for breaking the law in pursuit of excessive business returns or enriching themselves at the expense of shareholders, the era of accountability has arrived.

Yet, amidst this remarkable backdrop of comeuppance and judicial threat, the loudest voices are those whining about the hassle and expense of complying with the Sarbanes Oxley Act (SOX), the major vehicle of accountability. American public companies are groaning under the requirement that they comply with the new law, especially Section 404. *The New York Times* reported that companies were " ... complaining that the costs of carrying it out [SOX 404] have outweighed the benefits" (*New York Times*, December 1, 2005).

The whiners do have a point. American business is projected to spend $6 billion in 2006 (and $6 billion in 2005, as well) on SOX compliance efforts, and the guidelines for SOX call for annual reporting, so the outlays are likely to continue. What does a company get for this hefty investment in compliance? Aside from avoiding embarrassment, fines, and the potential for a primetime "perp walk" by the CFO, not too much. SOX does not increase revenue or earnings. SOX compliance appears to be a big money pit with little positive justification and a great deal of negative potential.

What is SOX, anyway? It depends who you ask. In objective terms, SOX is a Federal Law that gives the Securities and Exchange Commission (SEC) more power to force publicly traded companies to stand by the accuracy of their financial statements. The act is comprised of multiple sections, each of which attempts to improve the reliability of financial statements used by investors to evaluate the performance and value of a publicly traded company.

Congress enacted SOX in the wake of scandals at Enron, WorldCom, and others, to assure a worried investing public that the financial markets could be relied up on to deliver valid performance data and accurate stock valuations. The primary innovation of SOX is its insistence that individual business leaders personally attest to the validity of the financial reporting they are presenting to shareholders, with the threat of personal criminal liability hanging over theirs head for non-compliance. No wonder the law has received such laser sharp focus from top managers.

In this book, we will concentrate primarily on Section 404 of the Sarbanes Oxley Act, which requires public companies to establish rigorous internal controls, document them, and then attest to their effectiveness. Internal controls are processes designed by management to provide reasonable assurance regarding the reliability of financial reporting. They also assure the reliability of the preparation of financial statements for external purposes in accordance with generally accepted accounting principles (GAAP). Internal controls attempt to guarantee that each activity at a business produces the actual financial result that is booked in the accounting records.

For example, proper internal controls in a business would dictate that a sales representative should not be allowed to take possession of inventory, receive funds for it from a customer, and enter the transaction in the accounting system. Proper controls would dictate that more than one person have responsibility for this chain of activities. If not, the sales representative might have the ability to steal money or merchandise (or lose it by mistake) without anyone being able to reconcile revenue and cash received to inventory. At a high level, controls provide confidence to investors and management that a business is functioning properly. Most well-run businesses have controls, but their effectiveness varies depending on a myriad number of factors.

With SOX, however, these controls are now a matter for public attestation. Under the threat of criminal prosecution, the top executives of a firm must now declare that their internal controls are adequate to guarantee materially sound financial statements. The effect of this has been a big increase in spending on the development of controls, their documentation, and enforcement. Specialized consultants, often working with dedicated software packages, can generate a compliance program that meets the criteria of the Sarbanes Oxley Act.

You might be asking yourself, "Haven't corporations always had internal controls?" (The answer, which is maybe, might come as a surprise to you.) Shouldn't a CFO want to know what's going on at his or her business? I thought about this recently as I sped down a Los Angeles freeway. As I slowed down, I thought, yes, I want to be in compliance with the traffic laws, but that's not why I was tapping the brakes. I wanted be alive. I didn't want to wreck my car, or hurt anyone. That's the reason to slow down. Complying with the law is probably the least compelling reason to drive the speed limit.

So it is with Sarbanes Oxley. A lot of executives are aggrieved over the government pushing them around and forcing them to comply with the securities laws. Like a sensible driver, however, perhaps they ought to look at the benefits of complying with the law, rather than just the specific burdens of compliance. In corporate terms, compliance should mean that your business is well run, and that your financials are accurate. Isn't that what a good business manager wants?

The drama over SOX has arisen because, unfortunately, as we are seeing in case after highly publicized case, a lot of internal controls aren't that good, or well enforced, and a lot of big, well-known companies often have a rather poor true understanding of what's going on within their walls on a day to day basis.

In the past, senior executives might have comfortably delegated reporting and compliance detail to accounting executives and outside auditors. The experience in the good/bad old days was that financial reports from multiple divisions and operating companies would be consolidated and validated after the close of a reporting period. Auditors would catch any bad guys, and any problems wouldn't be that severe, and if they were then the company would work it out with the SEC or the lawyers would handle it, and so on. Things would work out well and senior executives would be spared any grand inquisitions. But not anymore.

SOX means that managers of public companies can no longer operate with loose, verbal, undocumented controls. They have to sign on the dotted line and attest that their businesses operate with effective internal controls. Specifically, compliance with Section 404 of Sarbanes Oxley means that a company has designed and implemented sufficient internal controls that will not surprise investors with fraud or errors that might materially affect the accuracy of its financial reports. For this to have a chance of working, internal controls must be tight. So far so good, right? Effective controls are tight controls and tight controls mean accurate financial statements. It is fine, except it isn't playing very well in 2005.

Now, I don't want to be accused of maligning the accounting profession. There are many proven and excellent ways for an auditor to help a publicly held company achieve compliance with SOX. The COSO framework (from the Committee of Sponsoring Organizations of the Treadway Commission), for example, provides a flexible, holistic approach to determining controls that can be quite effective if implemented properly.

The "if" in the previous paragraph, however, can he be a fatal flaw in SOX compliance. The biggest problem with SOX and COSO, which I have observed in my role in the enterprise information technology (IT) field, is that it assumes a relatively static mode of business operations, and today, to be static is to be dead. Those tight controls that SOX 404 mandates are typically difficult to change. Or, even if an auditor outlines a change-friendly control set based on the COSO framework, the day-to-day reality of managing the change process might render the control ineffective. We operate in a business environment of virtually perpetual change. How can we manage SOX and still remain dynamic enough to compete?

Management seems to have three choices in this matter, one worse than the next. You can have few or poor control, meaningless paper-based controls that everyone ignores, or overly rigid controls. Choose your poison. In the first case, with few controls or poorly designed ones, your business may or may not perform well, but you will be quite vulnerable to SOX violations and other legal challenges if things go wrong.

If your aim is to comply on paper but not get too involved in actually implementing your Section 404 compliance program, you will have gained some credibility in compliance if the authorities come knocking on your door. In reality you will have done almost nothing except spend a lot of money on consultants. Writing vast unread policy tomes that are gleefully ignored by all but those in the accounting and legal profession tasked with their development is the corporate equivalent of "In case of fire, walk to the nearest exit." It's a great idea, but most people don't put theory into practice.

Finally, if you roll up your sleeves and design and implement overly rigid controls, you will be compliant but paralyzed. From the perspective of strategic vision and operational management, SOX can be a toxic formula. SOX calls for minute documentation of business processes, but how can a company be expected to operate effectively in today's rapidly shifting marketplace and still diligently document every internal control that might affect the accuracy of financial results? Thus, SOX is decried as a straitjacket for corporate managers who face increasing shareholder pressure to create value through a dynamic growth strategy and agile operations—an objective that appears to be entirely at odds with the restrictive modalities of SOX compliance.

With all of these unfortunate scenarios in mind, you may be tempted to ignore SOX. The reality today is that the law is poorly understood by almost everyone in the business world, and an exact, tested definition of compliance, as well as the actual pattern of enforcement, remains somewhat vague as of 2005. Perhaps we should just let the auditors sweat the details and phone in some lukewarm compliance efforts as a sop to what business leaders decry as overzealous government regulators. Let the bean counters deal with it and get on with your career. I think this would be a mistake.

Maybe, you'll even dream, SOX will go away on its own. Certainly, impressive lobbying dollars are being spent with this purpose in mind. And, the law itself may disappear or be so watered down that it becomes a moribund artifact of a scandal-prone era. That is false comfort, in my opinion. The public, as represented by both the government and the legal profession, are onto us, and we better get moving or our businesses will suffer greatly from non-compliance with the new mode of accountability in business, SOX or no SOX.

Even if SOX goes away, there are still a number of comparable threats to American business that remain in force. If SOX is repealed, or watered down, there will still be dozens of federal and state laws concerning corporate fraud to contend with, as well as a variety of SEC rules that serve the same purpose. And if all of those laws fail to check corporate malfeasance and errors, a swarm of securities class action litigators eagerly await your next misstep.

So where does that leave all of us? There is a fourth way, which is to use the tight controls demanded by SOX as a pretext for improving the operations of your business. SOX can be a catalyst for change in your business. After all, who among us wants a business that is less well controlled than it could be? I think we all know deep down, what matters in corporate life is not compliance with arcane SEC rules, but compliance with sound business practices, regardless of what the law says. There are ample punishments for not complying with sound business practices. The market, the consumer, and the lawyers all have the ability to crush those who lose money, steal, or act incompetently. Bad business is bad for business. No Senate subcommittee is needed to validate that law of nature.

On this point, however, I have also been advised that SOX is about accuracy in financial statements and nothing else—that SOX has nothing to do with operations. I disagree. What is a financial statement if not a reflection of a set of operations? To look at SOX only in the narrowest possible terms, which is as a law to assure accurate financial statements only and ignore the reality that business operations generate those financial statements is to miss the point, in my opinion.

Our challenge, then, if we choose to accept it, is to look at a law that most of us have considered a nuisance, or even a threat to our existence, as an opportunity. This is a leap of thought for some of us, but a leap that I would recommend making. SOX has the potential to give us a chance to get better at what we do. If we reflect on the past history of business, we will see that this is a lesson we have learned before.

American companies have grumbled mightily in the past over a variety of reforms that have turned out, in the long run, to be good for business. In the last century, American businesses resisted labor organization and workplace entitlements, only to discover that modern labor practices and diversity programs created long-term loyalty among employees and helped build strong brands. In the 70s, industry lobbied against environmental regulations, subsequently to find that the pressure to conform to the new regulations gave them a much needed rationale to adopt numerically-controlled, high tolerance manufacturing and other high-tech fabrication processes that resulted in quantum leaps in production quality.

In this spirit, SOX can provide the catalyst for American businesses to cross the new frontier of management: profitable business that is as highly dynamic as it is tightly controlled. We can use SOX as the driver of business processes that are flexible enough to change with market and operating conditions, but also constantly visible to upper management and auditors. SOX can provide the impetus for making this revolutionary version of your business a reality. Rather than being a straitjacket on corporate growth and flexibility, SOX could be your business lifejacket. My suggestion, then, is to look at SOX, and its equivalents in Federal Law, State Law, and private litigation, as a new mandate to tighten control over business processes while remaining agile enough to be dynamic and competitive in the face of constant change. This is not an easy thing to do, but it may just be the most important challenge you've ever undertaken in your business. It will not be painless, but it will likely deliver results in management effectiveness that will pay for themselves many times over as you march forward into the future.

On a Practical Level, This Concerns IT

Although SOX compliance is assumed to be province of accountants and lawyers, on a practical level, it has a lot to do with information technology (IT). Although many internal controls are manual in nature, a great number of them involve manual interfaces with accounting or other operational software. Others still are solely concerned with accounting or software packages such as enterprise resource planning (ERP). And, some of the manual internal controls either should be automated on computers, or management wants them to be so. Therefore, when we talk about SOX 404 compliance, we're often talking about IT.

In this book, when I describe using SOX as a catalyst for improving business operations, I mostly mean improving the alignment between IT and business processes and objectives. Using SOX for business improvement has to do with mastering IT. Throughout this book, we are going to look at the interrelationships between IT and business, people, organizational issues, compliance, operations, and strategy. As you have probably seen in your business career, for virtually every business strategy and set of operational tactics, there is a mirror set of IT strategies and tactics. Little happens in an American business today without a correlated IT initiative or set of procedures in full effect.

When we look at establishing, documenting, and enforcing internal controls, we need to keep our attention focused as much on the underlying IT processes as on the actual business processes that are the subject of that control. The IT systems that support business processes are needed to record business transactions in the general ledger. IT also needs to give us visibility into operations, even if they are far-flung and difficult to monitor in person.

To address the importance of the link between IT and operations, the tech industry has come up with several approaches to corporate IT that attempt to confer control, change management, agility, and visibility for operations. You may see these approaches given various names, such as Enterprise Application Integration (EAI), Business Process Management (BPM), or Enterprise Architecture Planning (EAP). Collectively, these related technology disciplines blend operational management with enterprise software to provide top managers with holistic control over business processes. These technology approaches are, in theory at least, a tremendous boon to those who would create value for shareholders through dynamic management. They give executives the ability to monitor, change, and implement optimal business processes in a time cycle that confers competitive advantage.

Unfortunately, more than a few EAI and BPM efforts have foundered because of technological complexities inherent in large enterprises. In many cases, corporations dismiss these kinds of initiatives as being too costly and complicated. Lacking easily visible ROI, ambitious IT solutions for holistic management wind up in the nice-to-have column of requests for proposals—the IT equivalent of taking one's sister to the prom.

The problem is that IT, including EAI and BPM, is not known for being particularly flexible. Restricted by conflicting islands of proprietary technologies, IT doesn't change easily, although this foundation of corporate life is itself beginning to change. An emerging set of standards-based interoperability technologies, web services and the service-oriented architecture (SOA), have the potential to make it easier to design IT systems that can adapt to changes in the enterprise. As such, they can be deployed in the service of SOX 404 internal controls but still be flexible enough to keep up with changes in the corporate operational environment.

At this point, I feel I must issue a disclaimer. I work for a company that produces security software for web services and SOA. I am a passionate believer in the potential of web services and SOA as a technology that can transform enterprise computing, yet I have also seen the limits of the technology. There is nothing about an SOA that would inherently improve your ability to monitor business processes and gain compliance. In fact, if poorly deployed, an SOA might just make your company less agile and compliant. I will explore this problem in greater depth later in this book, in the section called "Even a Magic Bullet Can Kill You." In the same vein, when I discuss EAI and BPM, I am referring to the general concept of EAI and BPM, not any particular software vendor or consultant's construct of these technologies. My goal in this book is to be as agnostic as possible about specific technologies.

The distinction between SOA and other technologies may be irrelevant anyway. The entire software industry is remaking itself into a set of SOA providers, as they did in the 1990s with the Internet. As we move into 2006 and beyond, almost every major player in the IT industry will be calling itself an SOA company. Overall, I believe that there are many different ways to use IT to realize the goal of agile business process management and dynamic operational efficiency. Some of these approaches utilize SOA, while others do not. What matters is the effectiveness of the solution, distinguished by its design and implementation, not its technological makeup.

How This Book Is Organized

This book is meant to give you a practical look at how you might be able to use SOX as a catalyst for performance-enhancing change in your business. It is not a cookbook or how-to guide. It is meant to inspire a thought process, to get you to ask questions within a framework of ideas around agility and compliance. The actual steps you might take to make your business agile and compliant could vary widely depending on numerous factors unique to your company, industry, and organizational culture.

I have tried to depict as realistic as possible examples of business situations to illustrate my points. In this, I am trying to counter what I perceive to be an unfortunate tendency toward abstraction in the compliance industry. You may find yourself at a seminar, staring at a slide like the one depicted in Figure I-1, a vague graphic of business that I like to call an Abstractagon.

In my experience, the Abstractagon, when accompanied by a scintillating lecture, is momentarily inspirational. Then, when you get to the parking lot, you can't remember exactly how to implement the concept. When you return to the office, you can't explain it to anyone. It remains inert on your desk until the recycle bin inevitably claims it. Beware consultants selling overly abstract paradigms and enterprise compliance packages. Of course, you might need that package, but you also need to think through what your business actually requires and match it up with the compliance scheme.

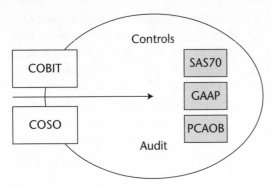

Figure I-1 The Abstractagon

To save you from the perils of abstraction, I have attempted to build the core of this book around the case study of a fictitious but realistic company called DexCo. A maker and distributor of computer gear, Dexco finds itself struggling both with compliance issues as well as day-to-day control over operations. My intent with the DexCo case is to keep us focused on pragmatic, results-oriented processes.

A reasonable amount of basic information about Sarbanes Oxley, IT, and accounting is also layered into the text in various places. In my experience, you can't have a productive conversation about a complex issue without first working through some essential knowledge and definitions. In Part I, "The SOX Paradox," I will look at DexCo's troubles and see how the company's lack of agility is causing trouble in its operations and financial performance. Along the way, I will explore how the Sarbanes Oxley process works, what the law requires, and how the accounting and IT professions work toward making a company compliant.

DexCo is performing adequately, although the CEO and shareholders expect it to do better. Some good things are happening in the business, but a number of potentially bad problems are festering under the surface, invisible to upper management, including the potential for fraud. DexCo's management, like that of so many companies, is sitting atop a virtual box of live grenades.

I will look at the challenges DexCo faces as it attempts to get into compliance with Section 404 of Sarbanes Oxley. This will include a look at some of the company's most pressing categories of risk, most of which will need to be mitigated to assure compliance with the law, as well as provide better protection for the business itself. Part I concludes with an examination of the ways that DexCo is constrained from adapting both to SOX and to shifting business needs due to its inflexible IT systems.

I will look at DexCo management's options as they relate to compliance. Reading through Part I, you may conclude that DexCo doesn't have many good options. I will touch on the pain of SOX in Chapter 7 and take a hard look at how complex and challenging it can be to attain agility and compliance.

In Part II, "The Joy of SOX," I will look at what DexCo could be like if it were more agile and compliant at the same time. I will look at the alignment between DexCo's IT and its operations. I will explore ways that DexCo can take advantage of SOX's mandate for compliance as a catalyst for implementing business and IT solutions that will help the company manage its business better in addition to complying with the Sarbanes Oxley law.

Part II will go into depth on the technological and organizational aspects of achieving agile compliance. Both areas are critical to the attainment of the goal. I will also walk you through what agile compliance might look like at DexCo, and explore the real pay-off in dollars for the company's investment in agile compliance.

Part III, "Actually Doing It—For Real," focuses on a practical process for identifying places in the company where managers can most effectively deploy solutions for agile compliance. One cannot attack everywhere at once, nor would one want to. We will lay out a reasonable methodology for finding the areas in the business where it is most vulnerable to compliance and operational problems and then establish how those problems can be mitigated through a combination of IT and internal controls. Overall, we will attempt to look at the situation on multiple layers, including business strategy, the market, operational needs, technology, as well as personalities and politics.

Who Should Read this Book

This book is written for the general business reader, especially one who is dealing with a Sarbanes Oxley effort at a public company. Although there is a fair amount of accounting and information technology detail contained within it, I do not assume that anyone reading this book is expert in either field. My hope is that if you are an accountant, you might find the exploration of business process management and IT helpful and stimulating. If you are in the IT field, as I am, I believe you will find the discussions about business processes and accounting to be highly informative.

You may not need or want to read this book all the way through. If you are already conversant with the specifics of internal controls, Sarbanes Oxley, and COBIT, you might want to read Chapter 1 and then skip to Chapter 7.

Summary

Is SOX a straitjacket or a lifejacket for your business? This book may give you the answer, or at least a fresh way to look at the question. Looking at the DexCo case study, which starts in Chapter 1, you will see how a company can work through its issues and find the path towards both agility and compliance. It is far from easy for DexCo's management team, but they rise to the occasion. My hope is that the story I tell in this book will help give you some insight into how to better use the realities of our age—strict and burdensome compliance laws and a rugged competitive climate—to your advantage in making your business as successful as it can possibly be.

The SOX Paradox

In Part I of this book, you will be introduced to DexCo, a company that has struggled with Sarbanes Oxley (SOX) compliance, as well as a variety of operational and control issues. DexCo will be the case study vehicle that I will use to show you the tension that can arise between a company's need for compliance and the marketplace's demand for agility. DexCo will also help you understand the deep connections that exist between Information Technology, controls, and operations.

This part also doubles as a primer on Sarbanes Oxley, internal controls, and the specific accounting, regulatory, and technological domains that affect a public company's SOX compliance. These in-depth looks at specific compliance topics are not meant as digressions, but rather as a way to establish a baseline of knowledge so that I can discuss the issues in depth.

Part I also will delve into the SOX Paradox, a situation where the need for compliance and internal controls can reduce the ability of a public company to be agile and dynamic in the marketplace. This scenario is paradoxical because the internal controls that must be documented under SOX are meant to help a company perform well and meet its financial goals. However, in reality, these controls can strangle a business. And, the burden of documenting them for SOX compliance can further compound the strictures wrought by internal controls.

This part will take you through a series of discussions, using DexCo as an example, of how problematic true Sarbanes Oxley compliance can be. It will set the stage for Parts II and III, which will explore how these problems can be solved.

The Trouble with DexCo

Ed Tait, CEO of DexCo, grabs his pen and signs certification documents that attest to the existence of strong internal controls at his company. He is required to sign these certifications in order to comply with the Sarbanes Oxley Act (SOX), but he is uneasy about the whole process. Seated opposite him are Linda Fuller, his CFO, and Sebastian Perkins, his CIO. These two executives have just spent the better part of a year, and over a million dollars, going through a torturous process of documenting and testing the company's internal controls.

A good judge of character and emotion, Ed can tell that Linda and Sebastian are fed up with working together on this project. Although he tries not to get involved in politics of this kind, Ed has heard that Linda and Sebastian have been at each other's throats for months. An endless, thankless game of finger pointing and task shuffling between their respective departments in the SOX process has left everyone with raw nerves. At least, Ed thinks, they have complied with SOX this year. He hopes that next year will be simpler, and cheaper.

This is how our story begins. I use a story to frame a discussion of SOX compliance and Information Technology (IT) because a story is the best way to communicate a complex business and technology situation. This method works well in business school case studies, and I have had the additional experience of telling stories for a living at one point in my career.

When I worked in the television movie business, it was my job to find true stories that could be made into highly rated movies of the week. Often, however, the stories as they existed did not have all the right elements to be perfect movies. So, we would modify the story and present it to the network as "inspired by actual events." So it is with DexCo.

There is no DexCo in real life. It's a fictitious amalgam of actual companies. The issues faced by DexCo, the struggle of its management to achieve better controls and comply with Sarbanes Oxley, are all inspired by true events.

I love a good mystery, and like a mystery author, I have placed some clues in the story of DexCo that might prompt you to wonder, "What's really going on here?" See if you find the compliance issues that threaten DexCo. I will discuss each of them throughout the book, but in this chapter, you can play detective and see if you can figure out what is happening in this fictitious business. My hope is that you will recognize your own business in DexCo. If you cannot, then you are either involved in an enterprise of exceeding excellence in every sphere or blind to potential trouble lurking beneath the surface at your company.

The Curse of the Adequate Performer

To put my story in perspective, you need to get some background on DexCo. DexCo is in the business of computers, software, and related accessories. The company publishes a mail order catalog and operates a direct retail web site and a chain of outlet stores. However, only about 12 percent of its $2 billion in revenues come from retail sales. The bulk of the company's business comes from wholesaling to retailers in North America and distributing electronic components to manufacturers worldwide. DexCo sources most of its product from contract manufacturers in Asia as well as liquidators throughout the world. The company owns no manufacturing facilities, although it operates two large distribution centers in the United States.

DexCo is a bit of a chimera. For retail consumers, DexCo is a bargain-brand resource for reliable PC products and special offers. For corporate clients, the company is regarded as a low-cost, diversified resource for computer products of all kinds. For yet another group of business customers, DexCo is the source of Original Equipment Manufacturer (OEM) components that anonymously fill the insides of many different electronics products. The DexCo catalog changes from month to month. Although certain staples of the catalog are constant, such as the firm's 17-inch monitor or PC Tower product, any given day will see such special offers available to retailers as five-cent CD-R disks (10,000 unit minimum order) or last year's laptop computer for $299.99.

DexCo's eclectic (some would say patchy) image stems partly from the company's history. DexCo came into existence in 1996 through the merger of three promising computer retail and distribution companies. PC Stores operated a mail order PC business and a chain of 200 computer specialty stores throughout the United States. U.S. Electronics was a narrowly focused distributor of electronic components and parts for computers and other electronic goods. Hsing Technology Imports was a successful wholesaler of low-cost PCs and computer products from Taiwan and other manufacturing sectors in Asia. The three companies had combined revenues of a billion dollars and a cash flow of almost one hundred million when the combined entity went public to much fanfare.

The idea behind the merger was to leverage the synergy between the retail segment and the wholesale importer. Respected, specialized U.S. Electronics was seen as a generator of brand credibility by the investment bankers who put the deal together. The market, however, was not kind to DexCo. The advent of computer superstores forced the closure of a quarter of the PC Stores. The wholesale import business suffered from volatility in Asian currencies. The OEM business never faltered, but its margins had always been flat and unlikely to grow.

Financially, DexCo is doing okay, but not great. Although the Y2K scare and dot.com boom drove revenue and earnings up in the late 1990s, the synergy of the merger never materialized. After two disastrous years in 2001 and 2002, DexCo has been profitable for the last two years. 2004 revenues were up 15 percent over 2003, but down 10 percent in the first half of 2005. The company is profitable, with earnings of $40 million in 2004. However, despite the growth in revenue, earnings rose just 2 percent in the same year. 2005 looks as if it will be a break-even year. Once a darling of Wall Street in the late 1990s, DexCo stock now trades at 10 times its earnings, which is low for the industry. For several quarters in a row, DexCo has failed to meet or exceed its earnings projections, and analysts frequently express the opinion that the company should be more profitable for its level of revenue.

A Functioning Mess

Operationally, DexCo is a functioning mess. Like so many corporations that were formed through mergers (and how many have not been affected by M and A?), DexCo still retains some of the character of its former selves. As shown in Figure 1-1, each business unit operates with a fair degree of autonomy. Each unit has its own General Manager, who has profit-and-loss (P&L) responsibility. The business units have a moderate degree of cohesion when it comes to sharing resources and financial reporting processes, although the organization seems to most insiders as if it were stitched together Frankenstein-style.

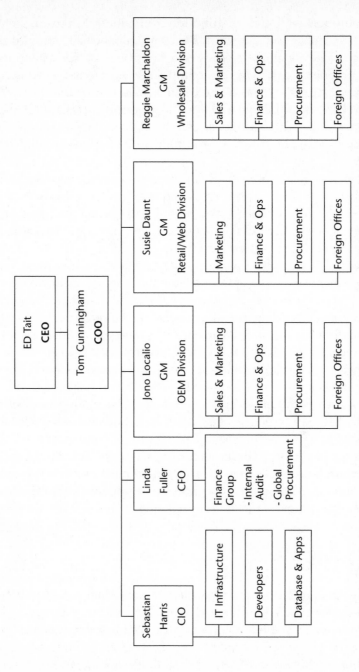

Figure 1-1 Organization chart of DexCo, showing silos of activity and reporting for each operating division

DexCo's management team comprises executives who have never really had to work together with much seriousness. Ed Tait, the CEO, previously ran the American sales operations of Hsing Imports. He is a salesman, and the company has a strong sales culture. Tom Cunningham, the COO, held the same position at U.S. Electronics. Known for his hands-off style, he prefers to let his divisional GMs select their teams and work toward P&L targets. The firm's CFO, Linda Fuller, had been the CFO of PC Stores. Although she is experienced in accounting for retail, her experience in international business is somewhat limited. She has always relied on DexCo's audit firm to help her with the company's extensive international procurement business. Sebastian Harris, the CIO, is a recent addition to DexCo. He was recruited from a global system integrator a year before the time period described in this book. None of the three divisional General Managers served with the former operating companies that came together to form DexCo.

Each division of DexCo has its own Sales & Marketing department. A VP of Sales manages a team of sales representatives that specializes in the division's particular line of business. CEO Tait provides sales leadership at the top, and often uses his relationships with major retail chains to help close business. However, most of the sales and marketing activities of the company are planned, budgeted, executed, and paid for at the divisional level.

DexCo is known as a competitive, up-or-out company where base pay is low and incentives can be quite generous to those who perform. Sales representatives receive high commissions and bonuses for reaching and exceeding quotas. Each divisional GM receives a bonus based on revenue growth; earnings growth has no upper limit.

Although they now share a common financial system, each division has its own finance and operations staff. This is also true of procurement. Because each division has such specific procurement needs, and the relationships with suppliers are so specialized and subjective, various attempts over the years to create a centralized procurement group have failed. In theory, CFO Linda Fuller has oversight over procurement, and she has coordinated efforts to standardize procurement processes. The day-to-day task of buying the goods that DexCo sells is a matter of divisional discretion. DexCo's procurement processes are also influenced by the company's distributed international character.

DexCo operates on three continents. Headquartered in Chicago, the company has four manufacturing management and procurement offices in Asia (China, Japan, Taiwan, and Singapore) and distribution centers in Los Angeles, North Carolina, and Germany. The company operates data centers in Taiwan, Arizona, Maine, and Germany. Each division makes its own arrangements for customer support. The OEM division contracts with an outsourced customer support call center in Iowa. The retail and wholesale division each operates its own separate call center, the former in Kansas City, the latter in India. DexCo outsources logistics and warehousing of goods to Asia. Figure 1-2 shows how DexCo's operations span the globe.

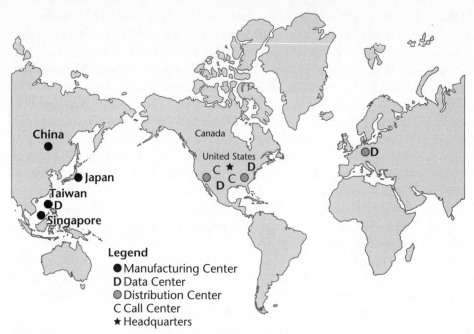

Figure 1-2   DexCo has operations in Asia, the United States, and Europe.

Although procurement for each division is managed from the home office in Chicago, the local offices in Asia play a key role in sourcing the best deals on manufactured items and closeouts on parts and other supplies. Each of the company's Asian offices has a separate department for each operating division within it. Despite the fact that there are over a hundred people involved in procurement in Asia, each division's contingent in an Asian office is known as a *desk*. The desks have some degree of autonomy to act on their own, without minute-by-minute input from the home office. For example, a Chicago-based procurement staffer might phone or e-mail the Taiwan desk and request the sourcing of DRAM chips. Another time, the Singapore desk might find a great deal on PC motherboards and take the procurement all the way to contract before notifying the home office of the acquisition.

The somewhat haphazard nature of the Asian procurement process is caused by two basic underlying factors. In the Asian spot market for electronics and computer goods, it is necessary for procurement staffers to act quickly or risk losing the opportunity to make the buy. Furthermore, the company has done well, generally, by allowing knowledgeable domain specialists to operate on their gut instincts.

In terms of IT to manage operations, the company maintains two separate Enterprise Resource Planning (ERP) systems. The retail and wholesale divisions share a mainframe-based ERP system while the OEM division uses a mini-computer (see Figure 1-3). The retail division also has a network of point-of-sale terminals that link to a centralized mini-computer. The retail web site, which was built more recently than the ERP systems, uses a J2EE application on the windows platform. The OEM division manages a Value-Added Network (VAN) for EDI communication with selected vendors.

Corporate headquarters maintains DexCo's overall general ledger and financial reporting system, which is a modern J2EE application running on Sun Solaris equipment. Two sets of custom-developed interfaces connect the two main ERP systems with the financial system. In this way, DexCo can consolidate its financial reports from its operating divisions and create its monthly, quarterly, and annual financial statements.

DexCo has three Customer Resource Management (CRM) systems that track contact information, sales projections, and customer service issues for company clients. Each call center has access to the CRM system that it needs to work with its relevant client group. The CRM systems are neither connected to one another nor with the ERP systems. Each call center and CRM operation prepares weekly reports on returns, complaints, and problems that are faxed to division GMs.

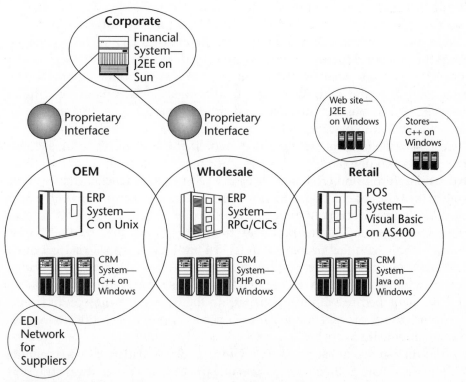

Figure 1-3   DexCo's existing Enterprise IT architecture

DexCo is evolving toward a single integrated ERP and CRM system that will govern all procurement, customer service, sales projection, logistics, and financial reporting. This massive system, code-named Future Applications and Systems for Transactions or FAST, is envisioned as a total management solution for the business. The system is dependent on the deployment of Enterprise Application Integration (EAI) hubs that will connect DexCo's existing legacy architecture of mainframes, mini-computers, and Windows-based servers.

With FAST, DexCo's top management will be able to access an Enterprise Dashboard that will show all pending sales transactions, procurements, sales projections, customer service issues, pending returns, and financial reports, in real time. FAST has built-in currency converters that are indexed in real time to financial markets. FAST will create an enterprise portal that will enable each division to access its ERP and CRM systems on demand using a browser. Similarly, FAST will make available customer web sites that will enable wholesale and OEM clients to order goods directly over the Web. At the same time, FAST will provide supplier hubs that will allow procurement to be done in real time online within full view of top management.

FAST is being implemented by a global, multibillion dollar technology provider. The development of this integrated system has been underway for two years, and the original 18-month timeframe for its completion has been extended to 36 months. The functional requirements for FAST have changed twice, and the working requirements are considered to be *drafts* by all major stakeholders in the project. FAST is projected to cost $14 million by the time it is completed. To date, the project has incurred fees of $2 million for requirements gathering, business analysis, and enterprise architecture planning. Figure 1-4 provides an overview of the FAST IT architecture.

Corporate policy dictates that all procurement and logistics transactions must be booked onto an ERP system at the time of their completion. All sales, expenses, returns, and credits must be booked on the financial system at the time of the transaction. This kind of rule is a prominent component of the SOX internal controls documentation process. DexCo's staff complies with these policies, and the company produces financial reports that routinely pass through audit with few problems. In its last audit cycle, DexCo's accounting firm developed the procurement business process shown in Figure 1-5. (However, moving forward, they will not be able to be so involved in the workings of their client, because of recent changes in the rules governing audit firms.) According to the process chart, the CFO has to approve each division's sales and procurement plan prior to its execution. Subsequently, upon the presentation of a final merchandising plan, the Global Procurement staff, which reports to the CFO, is to negotiate the best possible prices with each vendor and issue purchase orders. Division staff then reconciles incoming invoices and handles logistics and sales.

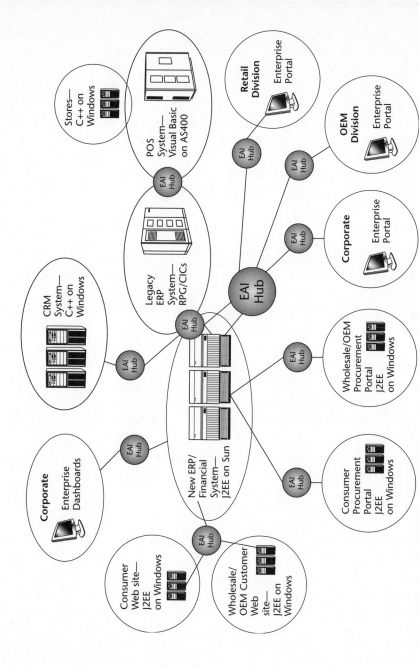

Figure 1-4 The FAST IT architecture, now a work in progress. Each globe represents an Enterprise Application Integration (EAI) hub between the major systems.

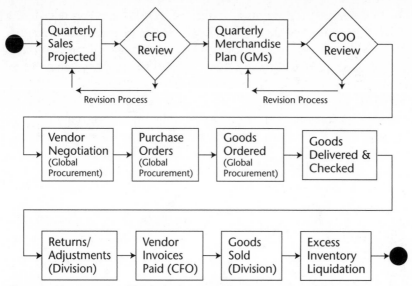

Figure 1-5 DexCo's official, documented business process for procurement and sale of goods

However, the reporting from the core systems does not fully describe the operations of the business. Each division has its own offline back channel of communication regarding procurement and sales. For the OEM division, it is a set of spreadsheets that float around in e-mails. The OEM spreadsheet contains all pending procurements, sales transactions, likely discounts to major customers, and probability of closing sales. The divisional GM sees the spreadsheet as it evolves throughout a given quarter. Senior DexCo management, however, does not know that the spreadsheet exists.

The wholesale division relies almost exclusively on Instant Messaging (IM) technology to communicate procurement and sales information. The wholesale division's General Manager (GM) issues informal approvals of procurements and sales terms using Instant Messaging many times during the day. The GM has an informal agreement with his direct reports: Any deal less than $100,000 does not need his direct approval. All deals over $100,000 require his input. Working this way, and using the pretext that IM is the quickest way to communicate, the wholesale division executes millions of dollars of procurement and sales activity on the backchannel, and then books the transactions into the ERP and financial systems once the terms of each deal are solidified by the divisional GM or his direct reports.

The actual process for procurement involves the divisional GM working through an internal forecast to hit a pre-determined earnings target (see Figure 1-6). After the GM has determined the Merchandise plan, his or her staff works with vendors to arrange procurement. After the goods have been ordered informally, Global Procurement is notified of the terms of each procurement. Global Procurement, which has a staff of four to manage all procurement worldwide, inputs the transactions into the ERP and financial systems based on the information received from each division.

As the quarter progresses and goods are received and sold, the division may return merchandise or consign it to local liquidators without notifying the corporate office or entering the transactions into the ERP or financial systems. Although the amounts involved may be significant, the division staff and their vendors, as well as the liquidators, have a long track record and history of trust. They are able to operate on a handshake. Any problematic deals can typically be made good in subsequent periods.

At the end of the period, when the GM is satisfied that the earnings target has been reached, he or she will formalize the major procurement transactions. Similarly, as the OEM and wholesale divisions close sales orders with major clients, they may offer discounts to push the transactions into the next quarter in order to manage revenue and earnings growth.

Part of the feud between Linda and Sebastian in their SOX duties had to do with their respective departments' failures to acknowledge and work through the differences between the official policy and the actual practice. Both IT and Accounting were not prepared to start documenting what was really going on. Instead, they worked with what they thought was supposed to be going on.

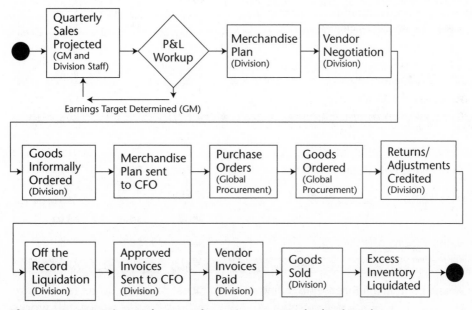

Figure 1-6   DexCo's actual process for procurement and sale of goods

Financials

DexCo's numbers tell a story of uneven performance. The sector itself is somewhat volatile, but even by computer retailing standards, DexCo's financials are unpredictable. Table 1-1 shows DexCo's income statement for the last three quarters, as well as Cost of Goods Sold (COGS) and Marketing expense by division as a percent of revenue. Finally, the table shows the calculation of each division's GM bonus, which is based on revenue and earnings growth, as well as overall corporate profitability.

Table 1-1   DexCo's Income Statements and Divisional General Manager Bonus Calculation for the Last Three Quarters

INCOME STATEMENT (000S)	Q3 2004	Q4 2004	Q1 2005
REVENUE			
OEM	$125	$130	$132
Wholesale	$445	$460	$455
Retail	$80	$81	$85
Total	**$650**	**$671**	**$672**
COGS—OEM			
Division S, G, and A Expense (including IT)	$25	$25	$25
Division Marketing Expense	$13	$13	$13
COGS	$75	$85	$87
Total	$113	$123	$125
Gross Margin—OEM	$13	$8	$7
COGS—WHOLESALE			
Division S, G, and A Expense (including IT)	$65	$65	$65
Division Marketing Expense	$67	$69	$68
COGS	**$276**	**$271**	**$287**
Total	**$408**	**$405**	**$420**
Gross Margin—Wholesale	**$37**	**$55**	**$35**
COGS—RETAIL			
Division S, G, and A Expense (including IT)	$8	$8	$8
Division Marketing Expense	$15	$15	$7
COGS	**$64**	**$62**	**$67**

Table 1-1 *(continued)*

INCOME STATEMENT (000S)	Q3 2004	Q4 2004	Q1 2005
COGS–RETAIL			
Total	**$87**	**$85**	**$82**
Gross Margin–Retail	**$(7)**	**$(4)**	**$3**
Total Gross Margin	$43	$58	$45
CORPORATE EXPENSE			
Information Technology	$5	$5	$5
S, G, and A	$15	$15	$15
Total	$20	$20	$20
Pretax Income	$23	$38	$25
AS A % OF REVENUE			
Revenue–OEM	**19%**	**19%**	**20%**
Revenue–Wholesale	**68%**	**69%**	**68%**
Revenue–Retail	**12%**	**12%**	**13%**
Total Revenue	**100%**	**100%**	**100%**
COGS–OEM (As % of Revenue)	**60%**	**65%**	**66%**
COGS–Wholesale (As % of Revenue)	**62%**	**59%**	**63%**
COGS–Retail (As % of Revenue)	**80%**	**77%**	**79%**
Total COGS (As % of Revenue)	**64%**	**62%**	**66%**
Marketing–OEM (As % of Revenue)	**10%**	**10%**	**10%**
Marketing–Wholesale (As % of Revenue)	**15%**	**15%**	**15%**
Marketing–Retail (As % of Revenue)	**19%**	**19%**	**8%**
Total Marketing (As % of Revenue)	**15%**	**14%**	**13%**
BONUS CALCULATION			
Revenue Growth			
OEM		$5	$2
Wholesale		$15	$(5)
Retail		$1	$4
Gross Margin Growth			
OEM		$(5)	$(1)

(continued)

Table 1-1   *(continued)*

INCOME STATEMENT (000S)	Q3 2004	Q4 2004	Q1 2005
BONUS CALCULATION			
Wholesale		$17	$(20)
Retail		$3	$7
GM Bonus			
OEM		$0.036	$0.030
Wholesale		$0.290	$(0.038)
Retail		$0.041	$0.071

Of concern to shareholders, as well as the board, is the company's uneven performance. Revenue growth in the first quarter was flat, despite leaping forward in the fourth quarter. Pretax income was down, and fluctuations in COGS seem to make each line of business look like a gambling proposition.

Hidden Time Bombs

If you're good at finding hidden clues in a mystery, perhaps you spotted a few things going on with DexCo that don't seem quite right. Although the company is making money, there's quite a lot wrong with DexCo. Some of the company's problems bear on compliance and risk management. I won't name names or spill all the beans yet, but watch out for the following hidden time bombs as I move ahead with my analysis of DexCo.

There are several areas where internal control weaknesses threaten integrity of DexCo's financial reporting. In other areas, deficient controls give executives the ability to play games with their bonuses. Even if they are not actually doing so, the potential for executives to use the levers of control at his or her disposal, such as marketing expense variability, informal procurement dealings, and liquidation of excess inventory outside of regular channels, makes for highly questionable SOX certifications. In another area, there is out-and-out fraud going on completely undetected by the company's internal audit processes.

Each of these situations is a potential snare for Sarbanes Oxley compliance. In all probability, the revelation of improper activities would bring indictments, inquiries from tax authorities, or even shareholder lawsuits. At the very least, DexCo's already underperforming stock would be hammered mercilessly by even the mere accusation of impropriety. The Sarbanes Oxley Act was enacted to provide investors with a level of assurance that a company like

DexCo should have sufficient internal controls to detect and prevent operating risks, safeguard company assets that are exposed to a significant level of risk by the misconduct of key executives, and produce reliable financial statements. However, as you can see even in this preliminary view, DexCo's internal controls are not adequate to this task. In the next chapter, I will explore why this is really just the beginning of a much more complex set of problems for the company.

Summary

This chapter introduces DexCo, a fictitious company that has just completed its first Sarbanes Oxley certification. The SOX process has been quite difficult and costly, resulting in a great deal of tension between the company's CFO, Linda Fuller, and its CIO, Sebastian Perkins.

DexCo is an electronics and computer supplies and components business with a mediocre performance history on the stock market. It was formed through the merger of three companies that were never fully integrated. The three firms still operate as essentially autonomous divisions.

The company functions, but not well. Each division has its own way of doing things, and the financial statements often do not reflect the exact state of affairs within each division. Controls are loose and deficient. Official policies for procurement and revenue are not followed consistently.

In terms of IT, the company has many systems that operate without sound integration. An ambitious, costly application integration plan is in the works, but its completion is some years off.

DexCo's lack of well-managed operations and controls creates several problems for Sarbanes Oxley compliance. There is the potential for errors in financial statements due to poor controls. In addition, several areas of the company are so loosely governed that executives there have the ability to manipulate results and boost their bonuses. Elsewhere, there is actual fraud going on. As DexCo goes into its second year of Sarbanes Oxley, it will have to contend with these serious issues.

CHAPTER

2

Agility: The Do or Die Mandate

DexCo's board of directors and largest shareholders had put significant pressure on management to shake the image of being an adequate performer and move the business back into the ranks of growth companies. First quarter results for 2005 were not impressive, so DexCo's board met in the second quarter of 2005 and faced a tough decision. The time had come to replace Ed Tait as CEO. With the understanding that his departure might also mean the end for COO Tom Cunningham and other key members of the team, the board nonetheless resolved to ask Tait to leave. Tait took the news as well as he could, and agreed to stay on through a transitional period while a replacement was sought. The move was not a surprise for him. In a way, it was almost a relief.

Within a few months, the board identified a promising candidate, Jim Wilde, who had spent the last five years building a hugely successful travel web site that had just been sold for several billion dollars. Wilde, a self-described "cowboy" who "doesn't need the money anymore but loves a good challenge," accepted the board's offer to take over DexCo. His deal provided him with millions of options. At the time of his contract signing, DexCo was trading at $4 a share. If Wilde could get DexCo into alignment with the kind of price-to-earnings (P/E) ratios common for electronics wholesale businesses he stood to make $50 million in his first year on the job. (The stock jumped a dollar a share based only on the press release announcing his appointment.) He could earn even more in subsequent years based on similar bonus programs built into his agreement.

New Blood, New Operating Environment

Although every generation of business leaders faces its challenges, it is not a hyperbolic statement to note that today's managers face an unprecedented level of uncertainty and rapidity of change in their business-operating environment. For Jim Wilde, turning DexCo around is going to involve some extremely adept maneuvers to put the company on track for both growth and change. And, he's going to have to do it while working within the Sarbanes Oxley Act, a compliance environment of unprecedented complexity and stringency.

DexCo's problems are not unique, nor are the causes of its circumstances. The company exists in a corporate climate where rapid change is expected and necessary, and where focus on short-term results dominates. To put DexCo in context, think about how much the business world has changed over the last few decades.

In 1980, you would have been hard pressed to find a category of business in which to place DexCo. At that time, Microsoft was a relatively small player in an industry dominated in every imaginable way by IBM. One could buy an Apple or Radio Shack computer, a machine of miniscule computer power but with a high price tag. The IBM PC was a year away from its debut. In 1982, my father's business purchased a 20MB hard drive for $25,000. It was 14 inches wide.

By 1990, there was a robust market for PCs and related products. Dell, which was started in 1984, was emerging as a leader in the field. Microsoft was one of the world's largest and most influential companies. In 1991, I saw a demonstration of the Internet on a $10,000 Sun SPARCstation. It took 5 minutes to download a graphic. In 1998, I bought a 63GB Micronet RAID drive for $30,000. It weighed 80 pounds.

In 2005, I sold the Micronet RAID drive for $10 on eBay, which didn't even exist in 1990. My $1,200 laptop has a 60GB hard drive. I could go to Best Buy and buy a 2 GHz PC for $399. I have a DSL line in my house. I get e-mail on my cell phone. In 1990, I didn't have e-mail or a cell phone. They were for big shots.

What I'm getting at is the way change has defined American business. Of course, the computer industry is a particularly good example of that, but the velocity of the business cycle has affected many different sectors. Today, I can apply for a home equity loan over the phone and get nearly instant approval. I can track an express shipment on my cell phone while sitting on a boat. The cable TV company wants to sell me Internet service. The Internet service provider wants to sell me phone service. Airbus is the world's largest aircraft manufacturer. My son's toys contain more microchips than Apollo 11. I have to keep 15 secret passwords in my head at all times. (How many passwords did you have to remember in 1980?) The world's fastest growing capitalist economy is (Communist) China. My next car is going to be a hybrid. You get the idea.

Moving Targets

Jim Wilde is taking over a business that must cope with a volatile operating environment where rapid, unpredictable change is a worrisome constant. To succeed, he will have to devise a plan that manages rapidly moving markets, shortening cycle times for marketing and manufacturing, the growth in out-sourcing and virtualization, and mergers and acquisitions. As you look at the challenges he faces, think about the further complication involved in staying compliant as he keeps up with changing industry factors.

Today, markets change at a rapid pace in almost every key dimension. The size and definitions of markets change quickly in the present day. For example, the market for electronic pagers, quite hot a few years ago, is now stagnant in terms of growth. Cell phones replaced pagers as the growth segment, but now Personal Digital Assistants (PDAs) and smart phones are eclipsing simple cell phones. Overall, the worldwide adoption of cell phones (1.7 billion in use as of 2005) would have stunned even a bullish market analyst a decade ago.

If you are in the cellular field, the answer to the most basic question—"What business are you in?"—would have changed at least twice in the last 15 years. Originally, you might have answered, "car phones," then "cell phones and pagers," and now "wireless devices." The question, "What kind of customer do you serve?" would also have produced a radically different answer over the years since 1990. Back then, you might have said, "We serve business pro-fessionals." Today, my housekeeper has a cell phone, and so does her ten-year-old daughter, who speaks to her as she skateboards around town. If I had told you in 1980 that a ten year old would have had his or her own portable phone for $9.99 a month, you would have probably told me I was insane.

Geographic market definitions are changing rapidly, as well as the methods by which they can be serviced. The U.S. market is a moving target. There are almost two million people living in Las Vegas, a city that had 450,000 residents in 1980. In the same period of time, Philadelphia has lost 170,000 people. Regional buying power is on the move today, and any long-term success strategy must take these trends into account. And despite the existence of new distribution processes and technologies, which make servicing shifting geo-graphical markets easier, a business must plan to put these kinds of processes into effect.

The situation gets more complex when you look at the pace of change glob-ally. Constitutional difficulties notwithstanding, Europe is now an economic unit of vast proportions. And it continues to grow, absorbing (at least concep-tually) the Middle East and former Eastern Bloc nations. Any serious global company needs to have a strategy for dealing with the constantly growing and changing European market.

Asia, too, is an evolving puzzle that encompasses both marketing and sup-ply chain challenges. Japan, once perceived as the singular force to deal with in that region, is now just part of an overall picture that includes Taiwan, South

Korea, Singapore, and of course, China. When Ross Perot warned of the "giant sucking sound" from Mexico, depleting the United States of jobs and capital, he was right, but his sense of direction was off. China is the awakening giant of the economic world.

Jim Wilde is also taking the helm of a company that plays in an ever-changing competitive landscape. Like so many other industries, the household names of earlier times are no more. American business was never static, but by the standards of a generation ago, companies today cannot seem to figure out what they want to be when they grow up. The era of conglomeration has crested and ebbed. The drive for core competencies has run out of gas. Today, a lot of companies appear to be grasping at something that they think will drive growth. IBM is out of the PC business that it helped create. Apple sees part of its future in the music device market. Computer specialty retailers must now compete with office superstores and discount warehouses. How will Jim Wilde play in the computer retailing business when his customers can put a PC into a shopping cart at Wal-Mart and buy it for less than he pays to manufacture it? How does he play in the wholesale computer business when his customer base has been eroded by unparalleled consolidation in the retailing sector?

Partnerships

Entering into partnerships with other companies is an approach to revenue growth that has become popular in the last decade. Partnering has now become a standard practice. Today, we consider it normal to receive airline miles as an inducement to buy a cell phone plan, or reward points for free merchandise as an incentive to use a particular credit card. Or, we can save the whales with our Mastercards, and so on. In-store partnerships, too, have become increasingly sophisticated. That cell phone display at the office superstore is the front piece of an elaborate partnering structure. Two companies find that they can attract more customers by working together. That's a fact of life for any modern business.

Rapid Market Cycles

Every type of business cycle time is also decreasing with each passing year. Product life cycles no longer are what they used to be, especially in the electronics industry. Items such as hard drives, memory chips, CPUs, and printers routinely make their debut and find themselves superseded by a new model within months. Manufacturers, distributors, and retailers must plan their product development, supply chain, marketing, and sales plans based on carrying just the right amount of inventory of a product before it becomes obsolete. Poor planning, development, implementation, and lack of subsequent assessment can bring financial problems.

Time to market has thus also become compressed. The elapsed time between the development of a product and its introduction to customers has shrunk noticeably in many sectors. One sensible response to this challenge has been the growth of fast manufacturing cycles, or even on-demand manufacturing, where inventory is reduced to virtually nothing. Factories build goods to order. This is a complex process to manage, but the alternative of building goods that no one may want to buy is far less desirable.

Whole market life cycles have become reduced. Markets for product categories, which used to be measured in decades (or centuries) are now down to years. For example, if you look at the evolution of the market for television sets, you would see a fairly standard twentieth century trend: A product appears in the 1940s. It is expensive, but eventually gains a massive acceptance in the broad market place. Improvements such as color, stereo speakers, and improved picture tubes continue to enable consumer upgrades through the 1990s, at which time the traditional television set begins to be eclipsed by replacement technologies such as the LCD flat panel display. As shown in Figure 2-1, the plasma screen market is growing, although it will probably peak shortly and be replaced by another display technology. Yet, one can still spend handsomely on a traditional cathode ray tube television set. The television set market, now in its maturity and fade-to-sunset mode, has been around for about 60 years.

Contrast the television set market with that for portable music players. The Sony Walkman debuted in the early 1980s. It caught on as a popular way for people to listen to music while out and about. However, unlike television sets, which enjoyed a 50-year run before being phased out in favor of improved technologies, the Walkman has experienced a rapid decline—twice. First, we saw the introduction of the DiscMan, a portable CD player, which effectively ruined the market for portable tape players. You can still buy a portable tape player at the drug store for $19.99 but you probably wouldn't want to. Yet, the DiscMan and its ilk have also been replaced by the iPod and similar digital music players.

Market change and definition is much faster than it used to be. The Walkman-DiscMan-iPod transition is typical of the product life cycle trend in the current era, which shows no sign of abating. The mode is one of "Chasm," "Tornado," rapid peaking, and replacement. Author Geoffrey Moore has popularized this concept in his books *Crossing the Chasm* and *Surviving the Tornado*. Figure 2-2 shows the effect of this rapid product life cycle. Early adopters begin to show interest in a new product, such as the Walkman, but large-scale public demand lags as consumers wait for prices to fall and the product to improve. Then, there is a massive increase in demand, characterized by Moore as a tornado of consumer interest, production, supply chain tension, and competitive marketing. Within a few years, a new replacement product has arrived on the scene, tested by early adopters and ready for its own journey across the chasm.

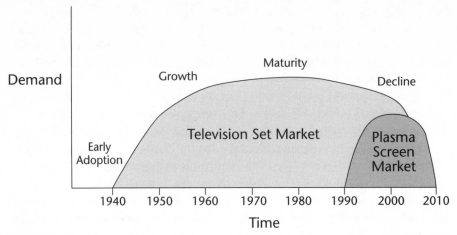

Figure 2-1   The traditional market life cycle, as shown in the example of the television set industry

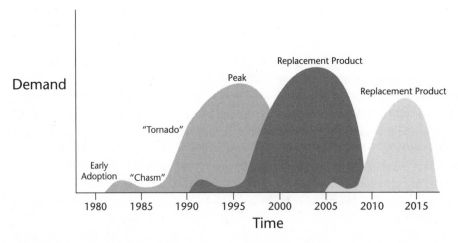

Figure 2-2   The current mode of product life cycles—chasm, tornado, rapid peak, and arrival of a replacement product

The question is: What would you do about it, if you were running a large company that competed in one of these industries? If you were Sir Howard Stringer, Chairman of Sony, how would you respond to the relatively rapid demise of a key product category (the DiscMan) in favor of its replacement, the Apple iPod? How much would you invest in a competitive response? If Sony were to attempt to unseat the iPod with an improved technology, what kind of product life cycle would that marketplace gambit expect to enjoy? One thing is fairly certain—whatever it is won't have a 60-year shelf life.

Technology Shifts

Technology shift is the inevitable culprit in many of these truncated market life spans. The iPod exists because of a shift toward digital recording and distribution of music. Or, in another example, Java and Linux, two technologies that didn't even exist in 1990, have become pillars of the computing world. Giants such as IBM and Microsoft now build their strategies around either competing with or changing their products to work with Java and Linux, both of which are free.

Technology-driven market shifts affect many industries. For example, a generation ago it would have been hard to imagine that service-oriented businesses could operate call centers halfway around the world. We don't give a moment's thought today to the remarkable fact that the person answering the phone for a car rental company or airline might be in Barbados, Ireland, or India. Technology has had a major impact on service industries.

Another great example of technology causing rapid disruption in an industry is the current state of the photo industry. For nearly 100 years, the industry had experienced relatively stable growth and a sound business model. Customers bought cameras and film, and had their film processed by large central laboratories. Over the years, the industry introduced incremental innovations, such componentized camera systems, where photographers could buy accessories over time and expand their equipment set, color film, instant cameras, one-hour labs, and so on. The major players, such as Kodak and Fuji, found their core business of selling film, photographic paper, and chemicals to be competitive but manageable.

In the 1990s, the photo industry found itself in a grave crisis driven largely by technology change and unforeseen consequences of seemingly good marketing decisions. Camera manufacturers had, in the words of one of its leading executives, "sewn the seeds of its own destruction" by introducing the point and shoot camera, which effectively killed the component-based product lines. Widespread creation of one-hour labs, originally seen as a new marketing channel for Kodak and Fuji paper products, had led to the erosion of Kodak and Fuji's core paper and film business as most independent one-hour labs opted for a lower-cost brand of paper. In response, Kodak and Fuji went on an aggressive campaign to win back the film processing business by subsidizing one-hour labs inside major drugstore and discount chains. If you are a picture-taking person, you might recall seeing double-print film processing for $6.99 on Kodak paper while you wait at the drugstore while the mom-and-pop one-hour lab down the street offered the same service for $12.99 on Mitsubishi paper. Guess who went out of business?

Before the major players could exult in their triumph, disaster struck in the form of digital photography. Digital cameras use no film, and while it is possible to order prints from a digital camera, many digital photographers have opted to share photos electronically or print them out at home using low-cost color inkjet printers that weren't even considered within the consumer's price range even a few years earlier. Indeed the color inkjet printer is a product category that has experienced one of the most dramatic increases in functionality and drops in retail cost of any product ever invented.

To respond to the digital photography threat, the major players in the photo industry banded together to introduce a film format called *Advanced Photo System* or APS (marketed as Advantix by Kodak). APS, which was supposed to provide a cartridge technology for film-based photographers to scan photos into computers easily, has essentially been a flop. Then, each player has introduced a succession of digital cameras, with mixed financial results. Kodak and Fuji now find themselves competing with companies like Sony in the camera market, which has increasingly become a consumer electronics category.

The photo industry crisis, which has mugged a century-old line of business in about ten years, is a great example of how contemporary companies must deal with unprecedented and challenging change in short periods of time. Basically everyone has lost money on digital cameras. The local one-hour photo lab is an institution of the past in most areas. Polaroid went into bankruptcy and only recently emerged. Kodak and Fuji, two of the world's most respected brand names, struggle to find profitable, long-term lines of business.

There are many examples of the type of rapid shift that I describe here. VCRs, DVD players, cell phones, Internet-connected PCs, and on and on. In some instances, company, and even industry life cycles follow this giddy course. Some product life cycles force a company into an incremental change in focus, while others may necessitate a complete change in direction and alliances.

M&A

The other major factor in the present business environment that creates a harrowing set of moving targets for managers is the pace and scope of merger and acquisition (M&A) activity. As far as a potential wrecker of sales and marketing channels, customers, supply chains, and competitive fields, M&A is perhaps the most potent force that today's top executives face. Thinking through whether one wants his or her company to be an acquirer or a takeover target is enough to swallow a good chunk of a chief executive's time. Figuring out how to respond to radical shifts in the industry due to M&A activities might absorb the rest of the schedule.

If you look at the computer field, you will see that a host of computer-related firms that dominated the markets and news in 1990 are no longer in business. In the last five years, HP bought Compaq (which had purchased Digital Equipment Corp, which had purchased Data General). Oracle has absorbed PeopleSoft, Siebel, and JD Edwards. Several other firms, once considered invulnerable bulwarks of the industry, are rumored to be in play.

Retail Consolidation

The retail arena has seen a massive shift toward the dominance of one firm, Wal-Mart, and the demise of numerous competitors. Sears, JC Penney, and K-Mart have had no end of trouble in recent years. Thousands of small merchants have been marginalized by giants such as Wal-Mart and Home Depot. With massive purchasing power, these firms can buy at unprecedented low prices, forcing competitors to take extreme measures or go under.

Regulatory Shift

In some cases, changes in the regulatory environment can provide the basis for company-destroying change. The broadcasting industry, for example, has been transformed by M&A activities that stem from changes in regulations. For many years, it was forbidden for television networks to own more than a limited percentage of the programs they broadcast. Similarly, the networks were restricted to owning a certain number of television stations. Then, the industry regulations were relaxed. Suddenly, Disney bought ABC, the WB and UPN networks were launched, Fox bought two dozen stations, Viacom bought CBS, everyone bought cable networks, and on and on. Myriad independent production entities and television stations disappeared within a period of two or three years. A massive, parallel consolidation took place in radio at the same time.

Betting the Company

The changes wrought by such shifts in regulation and M&A recall the great geopolitical saw, "If the rock falls on the egg, woe is the egg. If the egg falls on the rock, woe is the egg." Indeed, what, if anything can a manager do if the industry is hurtling in a direction that he or she cannot find a successful strategy for survival? One strategy is to avoid making big investments that might turn sour if conditions go wrong.

If you look at the telecom industry, you will see an example of a mature industry facing negative consequences of making big investments in an uncertain time. As the Internet boomed in the 1990s, the marketplace seemed to scream for faster access and broadband. Many of the large telecom companies built huge fiber optic networks that were completed just in time for the Internet bubble to burst. A lot of this "dark fiber" was eventually put to use, but not before causing financial carnage across the industry and in dependent fields of business such as phone equipment. The scandals at Enron, Global Crossing, and WorldCom actually stem at least in part from speculation on fiber optic networks. We are still living with several after-effects of the fiber cataclysm: low-cost phone rates and the jump in off-shore outsourcing are both results of the huge, unneeded increase in telecom wire capacity fueled by the Internet boom.

All of this reminds me of one of my favorite misunderstood concepts from my business school days. As we reviewed case studies of brave entrepreneurial CEOs who had invested in their vision, we often said, in awe, that they had "bet the company" on their ideas. Many of us wanted to grow up to become that kind of brass-knuckled, heavy-hitting, money-flinging chief executive who had the guts to "bet the company" on our visions. Yet, as we saw in the 1990s, betting the company was just that, a bet. And who wins all bets? Not anyone I know. "Bet the company" is what the effort is called when it succeeds. When it fails, it's called a Chapter 7 filing.

Outsourcing

One can mitigate market cycle risks. One approach that has proven effective in recent years is the trend toward outsourcing, off-shoring, and virtualization. By farming out non-core business processes such as customer service and manufacturing, a company can reduce its overhead and enhance its ability to weather unforeseen downturns in the market without having an overly negative impact on earnings. Yet, like many solutions, outsourcing also can create problems. Inconsistent staff training and capacity management can be problematic with outsourcing. More insidious, however, is the potential loss of critical business competencies to competitors that the outsourcer accidentally finances. Looking at IBM's bargain sale of its PC business to Lenovo, the Chinese contract manufacturer that actually assembled the machines for Big Blue, one can see the perils of shipping an entire business process to a low-cost provider. That low-cost provider eventually becomes your low-cost competitor and you're better off sprinting for the exit door.

Conversely, if you happen to have the fortune/misfortune of seeing your business change from being a primary player to an outsourced vendor, you'll experience the whipsaw of market cycles. What is the best strategy for coping with serving at the whim of your virtual partner? Well, you can turn your employees into contractors, which makes them an outsourced commodity of their own. You can get rid of them and rehire as demand dictates. Sounds great, until it happens to you.

So what does this mean to you? You're probably either ready to run off to circus school or saying something like, "I'm in butane refining. I don't bet my company. My business is fine, thank you very much!" Perhaps you are, perhaps you are not. The lesson to focus on is how high the stakes have become in today's business world and how you can best position your company to succeed—and still stay in compliance with the law.

We work in a business era of increasingly fast and evasive moving targets. This may not be big news to you, but I wanted to underscore just how complex it can be to navigate the management of a large enterprise in uncertain times. The ultimate conception of effective business management that makes sense today is the idea of agility. Agility refers to the capacity of a business to react to change without compromising strategy or earnings. Agility means having the ability to make strategic and operational moves quickly to take advantage of profitable trends without having a negative impact on long-term earnings viability. Agility is the do or die mandate of business in the twenty-first century. Companies that are agile are best suited to survival and success. Those that lack agility are exposed to great risk, and may not make it in the coming years.

Agility for DexCo

Agility was the driving force behind Jim Wilde's first 100 days at DexCo. Wilde arrived at DexCo and proceeded to spend two weeks in lengthy meetings with each of the key executives of the company. After reviewing the strategic and operating plans, as well as performance results, of each division and corporate department, he disappeared for a week, taking his private jet to his Idaho ranch with a group of ex-McKinsey and Bain advisors that the current DexCo team privately nicknamed his posse or simply, "The Wilde Bunch."

Upon his return, referred to as "Black Monday" by the old timers at DexCo, Wilde convened an all-day executive meeting during which he attempted to use a browbeating variation on the Socratic method to diagnose what DexCo needed to thrive in the marketplace. Wilde opened the meeting by digging into what he considered DexCo's major problems.

Why was DexCo always a follower, not a leader, Wilde asked a room of silent executives, most of whom were trying to avoid eye contact with their new boss. Could it never get ahead of the curve? Ask 20 people in the business about what we do and you'll get 20 answers, Wilde stated in amazement. Who are we and what do we do for a living? Why are we so fixated on this haphazard bargain-of-the-week style of business? What's DexCo's source of sustainable strategic advantage? What does this company want to be when it grows up?

Eventually, several executives spoke. Size was a factor, they contended. The company, as a distributor, was in essence always following the marketing. And as a smaller player, it could not gain the kind of cost advantages needed to secure long-term strategic advantage.

"Okay, fine," Wilde said. "Fair enough. We're not big, and we're not going to be big for a while. How do we manage that?" Someone in the back of the room muttered, "Second prize is a set of steak knives. Third prize is 'you're fired.'" Wilde then proceeded to the white board and started to lay out categories for discussion.

Product Mix was his next focus area. What could the company do to find a mix of product offerings that would position it for higher and more sustainable earnings growth? Indeed, he asked, was there even such a thing in such a fast moving business as the PC and peripherals field? Should the company expand its own proprietary product lines? And if so, what should it be? Should they focus on PCs or some specialized line of peripherals? Could we be the king of products that use Universal Serial Bus (USB)? Maybe DexCo should be the low-cost supplier of all things USB. The executives nodded in vague approval.

Next came the marketplace itself. Should DexCo expand its direct consumer web site or drop it? What was the long-term play in the wholesale field now that the customer base was consolidating so much? DexCo had a relationship with Wal-Mart, but the big retailer was so unprofitable to work with, perhaps they ought to abandon the whole effort. The OEM business was an enigma, Wilde declared. What was the upside, he asked, in being the invisible ingredient in someone else's business? Sure we make money today, but we are building no brand equity with the OEM stuff.

As for the supply chain, Wilde wanted to know how DexCo was going to create permanent strategic advantage through its current sourcing process, which to him appeared to be like "shooting at the broadside of a barn." He said, "You go to Taiwan, see what's for sale. You buy it. You ship it here. Maybe it sells, and maybe it doesn't. What the hell kind of supply chain strategy is that?"

Finally, one of the executives said, "We're making money today." Wilde responded, "True—I know we're making money, and believe me, I know the situation here could be a lot worse. However, I believe in shaking the tree to see what falls out. I'm just asking questions. Nothing is definitive." Everyone seemed somewhat relieved by Wilde's change in attitude. "Everything at this company is up for grabs—strategy, tactics, marketing choices, product mix, alliance, and so on," he said. "The main thing I want is to be able to move where we need to move when we need to move there. I want us to be agile. We need to be agile to survive."

The Wilde Plan

Discussions went on all day. After another week of private review, Wilde summoned another management meeting and set out a sweeping set of changes that he planned to implement at DexCo over the coming year. First off, Tom Cunningham announced his resignation effective at the end of the quarter. His replacement was Dale Steyer, a former Army Major and partner from a global management consulting firm.

Wielding a massive PowerPoint deck, Wilde proceeded to lay out a plan for turning DexCo around. His goals were impressive: Doubling of revenue within two years. Tripling market cap in earnings in the same time period. Increasing earnings growth every quarter. His methods were straight out of the modern CEO playbook.

New markets were the key, Wilde said. To grow and establish itself in sustainable growth mode, DexCo would need to venture into new market segments. In his opinion, for example, wireless was the wave of the future, and he was willing to bet the company that DexCo could leverage its core competencies in sourcing, marketing, and distribution of technology goods to become a major player in the wireless space. Of course, he had many other new market segments that he planned to enter, but first he wanted everyone to buy into a complete re-engineering of the company. Only a holistic overhaul could enable the changes that Wilde had in mind.

Over the next year, Wilde predicted, as it entered new market segments and exited others, DexCo would develop many new product lines. The company would initiate relationships with new suppliers, and drop others. It would rethink its supply chain in entirety. DexCo would revamp its distribution system, including the possibility of outsourcing all outbound logistics and inventory management. Wilde wanted to look into the potential cost savings of working exclusively with rack jobbers who contract to fill retail shelf space to complete the wholesale channel delivery process.

Wilde planned to consolidate the three operations groups from the three existing business units. "No offense," he said. "But there's a lot of lard in the stew here." The immediate plan was to centralize all procurement, sales and marketing, and logistical management into one office at company headquarters. Redundant staff would be laid off. "This isn't easy, I know," Wilde said. "But this is business. Sometimes we have to make tough choices." Each divisional General Manager would stay in place as a head of his or her line of business, but with a generalized set of support staff reporting to them, rather than a dedicated division. In addition, Wilde planned to outsource all non-core functions such as Information Technology, Human Resources, and customer support that weren't already outsourced.

"We've got to be nimble, agile . . ." Wilde said again. "We've got to be able to turn on a dime, and reinvent ourselves as we go along." Specifically, he meant that DexCo would need to be able to enter into partnerships with other companies in a "quick and dirty fashion," as he put it, assuming adequate due diligence, of course. "I want to be able to OEM a new kind of smart phone chip from Samsung, build a brand for it, and sell it in the American Airlines magazine with frequent flyer miles as a bonus for signing up for a service plan that we resell through Verizon; maybe market it through a drug store chain—and I know they want to be in the wireless business too, boy do they ever!—and then be ready to do it again six months later with another product like a car fax machine and market it through General Motors with a co-op arrangement from Pep Boys. I call this flex-acturing."

Big executive incentives were to be part of the mix, Wilde indicated. "It's going to be like it's your own business. The more we make, the more you make. It's that simple. You bring home the bacon, you take home the bacon. That's the way I work. I want you guys to get rich, as long as I get rich, too." Mild laughter ensued. With that, he yielded the floor to Dale Steyer, the new COO.

"A whole new way of working," that's how Dale described the new organization chart shown in Figure 2-3. Instead of divisions with their own P&Ls, DexCo would comprise Strategic Business Units (SBUs), each of which would be evaluated based on gross profit contribution and revenue growth. The divisional marketing, procurement, foreign desks, finance, and operational departments would be fundamentally reorganized. All marketing would be centralized, with matrixed teams providing marketing services to each SBU as needed. Marketing would report to an as yet unnamed executive. The CFO Linda Fuller would now have the full accounting, procurement, and contract manufacturing management staff reporting to her directly.

There would be more SBUs created over time, Steyer assured. To maintain constant market leadership, DexCo was going to establish a permanent EVP of Synergy, who would continually evaluate the company's core competencies in the context of the evolving market environment. Reporting directly to the EVP of Synergy would be a group of strategic planners who would form what Steyer called the "Synergy and Competency Operational Center." In a nod to his military background, Steyer dubbed his new creation the *SynCompOpCent*.

Sebastian Perkins, who had been taking in Steyer's presentation with a feeling of absolute dread, scribbled "Nincompoop Central" on a piece of paper and handed it to Linda Fuller, who smiled at him. It was the first light moment the two had shared in months.

Specifics of the reorganization plan would be forthcoming, but in the meantime, Steyer asked that everyone continue with business as usual.

"What about IT?" someone asked.

"What about it?" Steyer replied.

"Well, it looks like you're going to have to revamp a lot of your systems if you're going to shake up the whole company like that."

"Okay," Steyer replied. "We're so ready to get going with a major IT services firm. We're going to just push it all through and make it work. I'm a can-do kind of guy. I get things done."

"What about Sarbanes Oxley?" another voice muttered from the back of the room. "We just went through a whole 404 audit."

"That's great," Steyer said. "We were wondering where DexCo was with all of that SOX stuff."

"No," the objector continued. "If we do your plan, we're going to have to redo the whole 404 process and whatever we've certified will have to be recertified."

"Whatever," Steyer said. "We have the auditors coming in next week. They'll take care of it."

"They can't," Linda Fuller said urgently. "Sarbanes Oxley precludes our audit firm from helping us with this kind of thing now. The law prohibits them from auditing their own work. We're on our own." Dale didn't know what to say. He was beginning to see, however, that this SOX matter was a lot more involved than he had been led to believe.

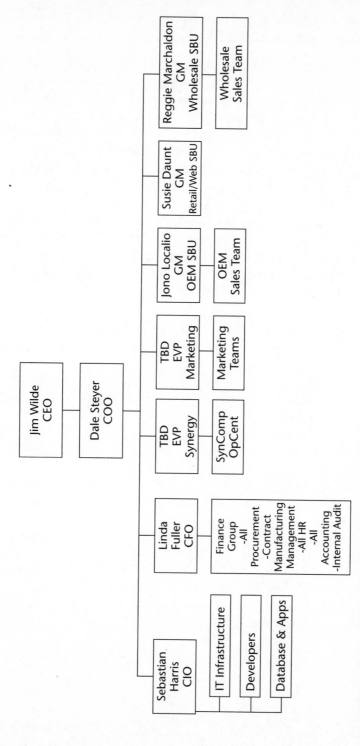

Figure 2-3 Proposed new organization chart for DexCo

Summary

Faced with disappointed shareholders, DexCo replaces its CEO and brings in an ambitious outsider named Jim Wilde. Wilde faces a marketplace where agility is an absolute do-or-die mandate for DexCo. He must get the company on track and enable it to change rapidly as it moves forward.

He is not alone. Over the last 20 years, American businesses have had to contend with an unprecedented level of change and challenge. Fast changes in market conditions, technology shifts, retail consolidation, mergers and acquisitions, and regulatory shifts are but a few of the major issues that Wilde will have to contend with as he puts DexCo on the path to growth.

Jim Wilde has a plan to reorganize DexCo's business operations and strategy. He wants to consolidate several operating groups and reduce the autonomy of DexCo's divisional General Managers. While these may be sound business ideas, they will cause disruption in operations and a concurrent set of problems in Sarbanes Oxley compliance.

CHAPTER 3

Ramifications of SOX 404

Linda Fuller tendered her resignation as CFO of DexCo the day after Jim Wilde's presentation of his ambitious management plan for the company. Although she said that her mind was made up, she agreed to sit down and hold an extended conversation with her new boss about her apparently rash move. While he assumed that her decision to leave was motivated by distaste for his management style, discomfort with change, or a strategy for increasing her salary, her comments truly surprised him.

"I don't want to be overly alarmist," she said. "But if we follow your plan, we might wind up in major hot water with the SEC or even getting delisted from the exchange due to financial disclosure problems and restatements. Or, we could get sued by shareholders. I don't feel like sticking around for that trouble."

"Whoa!" Jim said. "What are you talking about?"

"We're in a whole new world today," she replied. "I just spent an entire year and a solid million bucks complying with the Sarbanes Oxley Act. Now, with what you want to do, we're going to have to do it all over again and there's no guarantee we'll get it right. If we get it wrong, there could be serious consequences."

Jim was surprised, even though he had just had an earful from Sebastian Perkins, his CIO, who had come to him earlier to complain about the lack of cooperation he got from the CFO and her department on the firm's SOX efforts. He regarded his departing CFO in a stunned silence—and he was not a man who usually lacked for words. Finally, he spoke. He pleaded with her to stay on for six months and work with him to keep the company compliant while they began to phase in his new plan for strategy and operations. To his further surprise, she agreed. Apparently, being listened to had made a big difference in her opinion. Jim realized, however, that in addition to all of his other responsibilities and plans, he might need to take a closer look at all the hullabaloo over the Sarbanes Oxley act.

SOX 404—Definition and Context

Ms. Fuller's threatened resignation notwithstanding, DexCo's new management team is very much ready to march forward with their sprawling plans for change. Is their glib brushing aside of concerns about Sarbanes Oxley legitimate, or are they courting trouble? To answer this question, let's take a step back and look at what Sarbanes Oxley, and especially Section 404 of the Act, actually means for a public company.

If you're reading this book you are probably not a professional auditor. Let's be honest. This is a bewildering subject. I have run businesses, have an M.B.A. degree, and specialize in information technology, yet I could barely make sense of this when I got started. Poring over a phonebook-sized set of accountings rules isn't going to help much either, unless you're a serious masochist.

I'm not going to make any assumptions about what anyone knows or does not know about the overall compliance and reporting process. I feel it is necessary to provide a context for SOX before plunging into detailed discussion. Too many conversations and articles about SOX and compliance assume a general understanding of the entire Securities and Exchange Commission (SEC) reporting process and guess what? Few people have a very good understanding of it. A lot of people think they do. Others still pretend they do. Entering a discussion about SOX can be like walking into a movie halfway through—everyone seems to know the plot, but you're lost.

To understand Sarbanes Oxley, you really have to go back to the beginning and get a general idea of why we have securities laws in this country as well as the enforcement body known as the Securities and Exchange Commission. In 1933 and 1934, which came after the great stock market crash of 1929, in which the Dow Jones Industrial lost more than 30 percent of its value in two days, the Federal Government founded the SEC as a practical step to regulate the securities markets.

The crash of 1929 had many causes, including unregulated stock trading on margin, but the collapse of the financial markets also showed the perils to investors when there is uncontrolled fraudulent activity amongst corporations owned by the public. Something had to be done about reining in crooked business practices and establishing confidence in the stock market. The SEC was formed to monitor financial markets and enforce new securities laws that were aimed at maintaining the transparency and integrity of securities markets. The assumption made at the time, which was generally valid, was that where fraud is pervasive, or at least suspected, and investors can never be sure what they are getting, capital markets will suffer.

Over the years, the government has updated the 1934 securities laws, but the process remains essentially unchanged. Whereas before 1934, publicly traded companies had quite wide latitude in financial reporting and little supervision or penalties for unscrupulous activities, after the formation of the SEC and the enacting of the 1934 securities laws, publicly traded companies have been obligated to file periodic reports to the SEC that state various audited measures of financial performance. The 10K and 10Q reports that we see online today are the electronic editions of a practice that has been in place for 70 years.

The securities laws of the Depression also gave new prominence to the field known as public accounting. The management of a public company is responsible for creating financial statements, and independent Certified Public Accountants must audit those financials and provide an opinion as to whether the financials are presented fairly in all material respects, and that they represent the financial condition of the company and comply with Generally Accepted Accounting Principles (GAAP). GAAP is like the Bible of the accounting world. If the auditor believes the financial statements are not accurate, or if they consider the methods by which the statements were prepared to be subject to weaknesses, then the auditor is expected to state that opinion in their opinion letter.

The SEC reporting and audit system has worked well, in general, since its inception, although there have been some spectacular breakdowns in its proper functioning over the years. In 1985, a wave of corporate financial scandals lead to the formation of a body known as the Treadway Commission, or National Commission on Fraudulent Financial Reporting. James Treadway, the group's leader, had served as Commissioner of the SEC previously. The Treadway Commission was an independent group that looked at the underlying causes of fraudulent financial reporting and made recommendations for improved processes to detect fraud among public companies and their independent auditors.

The Treadway Commission brought together five separate accounting organizations to develop new accounting practices and guidelines for the detection and prevention of fraud. These five organizations—Financial Executives International (FEI), the American Accounting Association (AAA), the American Institute of Certified Public Accountants (AICPA), the Institute of Internal Auditors (IIA), and the Institute of Management Accountants (IMA)—became known as the Committee of Sponsoring Organizations of the Treadway Commission (COSO).

If you're involved in SOX issues, you will have no doubt heard about COSO. I mention its provenance here because in many senses SOX is a direct offshoot of COSO. The premise of the Treadway Commission was that improvements in internal business controls could reduce fraud. The internal controls framework most commonly used to achieve SOX 404 compliance is the COSO *Integrated Control-Integrated Framework*. When people talk about the role of COSO in Sarbanes Oxley Section 404 matters, they are typically referring to the Integrated Control-Integrated Framework. More on this later in the chapter.

Jump ahead to 2002. Enron, Global Crossing, Worldcom, Adelphia, and others imploded amidst breathtaking levels of fraud. The venerable Arthur Andersen accounting firm self-destructed over allegations that it both missed the Enron fraud and then covered up its own trail of culpability. Public outcries over billions in investor losses (while very wealthy top executives appeared to dance away unscathed) led Congress and the Bush administration to create further enhancements to the existing securities laws. They passed the Sarbanes Oxley Act, which contains numerous provisions to improve corporate accountability, governance, and accuracy of financial statements. The Sarbanes Oxley Act also led to the creation of yet another organization, the Public Company Accounting Oversight Board (PCAOB), which is charged with overseeing the accounting firms that audit publicly traded businesses.

In a broader context, you should understand that you are involved in the classic agency problem that arises in the modern, publicly traded company. Whereas in the old days, a business owner might finance, manage, and profit single-handedly from his or her business, today, most of us work for owners, also known as shareholders, who are myriad and completely abstract from our daily work lives. You may be a product manager at a large company, and in practical terms, you may think you work for the head of product marketing. Not so! In reality, and by law, you actually work for the shareholders. You are an agent of the shareholders. In your agency, you are given certain authorities and responsibilities to act on behalf of the shareholders by spending or investing their money. The extent to which you do your job properly for them defines the quality of your agency. Good agents are good for shareholders because they interpret their role of agent to mean acting in the best interest of the shareholder. Bad agents, such as John Rigas or Dennis Koslowski, act in their own best interest and shirk their responsibility as agents of shareholders. I bring this up because the Sarbanes Oxley act, in its essence is meant to be a tool to be wielded in the hands of shareholders to make sure their agents—that would be you—are acting in their best interests. (A tool, I might also add, that includes the possibility of jail and heavy fines.)

Thus, Sarbanes Oxley, while new, is actually just the latest tentacle of a complex set of government regulations that have existed since the 1930s. The difference is, today, your role in the process has changed. Compliance is no longer just a matter for the professionals. If you are a business manager, the world of SOX has enabled you (or forced you) to join a once esoteric cluster of professionals, agencies, outside firms, and organizations that is responsible for generating accurate financial statements for filing with the SEC as well as complying with a host of other securities laws, including SOX.

If you are a business manager, the matter that connects you with this rarefied world, is the burden of complying with section 404 of the Sarbanes Oxley Act. SOX has numerous sections, some of which deal with issues such as auditor independence, filing requirements, and so on. We will not address these other sections in this book. We will deal with Section 404, which mandates that top management attest to the existence of effective internal controls at a business that will result in accurate financial statements. Specifically, Section 404 calls for the audit and certification of policies and procedures at a public company that support internal controls, which in turn support sound financial reporting. Section 404 says:

...each annual report [required by the Securities Exchange Act of 1934] contain an internal control report, which shall--

(1) state the responsibility of management for establishing and maintaining an adequate internal control structure and procedures for financial reporting; and

(2) contain an assessment, as of the end of the most recent fiscal year of the issuer, of the effectiveness of the internal control structure and procedures of the issuer for financial reporting.

(b) INTERNAL CONTROL EVALUATION AND REPORTING- With respect to the internal control assessment required by subsection (a), each registered public accounting firm that prepares or issues the audit report for the issuer shall attest to, and report on, the assessment made by the management of the issuer. An attestation made under this subsection shall be made in accordance with standards for attestation engagements issued or adopted by the Board. Any such attestation shall not be the subject of a separate engagement.

SOX 404 is based on the premise that the production of accurate financial statements depends on the existence of effective internal controls. A company's financial reporting processes must be subject to controls that prevent and detect potential misstatements of financial results because of errors, omissions, or fraudulent activities.

A quick definition of internal controls is in order. The PCAOB defines an internal control as, "A process designed by, or under the supervision of, the company's principal executive or principal financial officers, or persons performing similar functions, and effected by the company's board of directors, management, and other personnel, to provide reasonable assurance regarding the reliability of financial reporting and the preparation of financial statements for external purposes in accordance with generally accepted accounting principles."

Got That? Let me put it in terms that might make more sense to someone who actually runs a business for a living. Imagine that your business has a cash register. The amount of cash in the drawer at the end of the business day represents your revenue. If the amount of cash in the drawer is less than it should be, you will be understating your revenue due either to theft or error. To guard against this problem, you may want to institute some controls over the use of the cash register.

There are two general types of internal controls. A *preventive control* prevents theft or error from taking place. A lock or password to protect the cash drawer is a preventive control. It stops accidental or intentional opening of the drawer for improper purposes.

A *detective control* is a process or device (or software) that management can use to detect errors or frauds in their operations and resulting financial statements. The reconciliation of the cash register tape to the contents of the cash drawer is a detective control. If the tape total matches the cash in the drawer, then the manager can be confident that the revenue reported from the cash register has not been subject to error or fraud. Of course, someone could still be stealing merchandise, and there would have to be other internal controls to catch those activities. Yet, the cash register would be under control. If Sarbanes Oxley discussions seem complex or esoteric, just remember the cash register and you will be fine.

If a company has sound internal controls, then its financial statements are more likely to be correct, or at least lacking material misstatements. SOX 404 puts the onus on a company's management to assure shareholders that financial reporting is accurate by forcing them to attest to the existence of robust internal controls. In the next section, we will look at today's standard process for complying with SOX 404.

SOX 404 and the Audit Process

At this point, you may still be thinking, "This can't possibly be my problem." Audits, controls, SEC filings—that's the accountant's role, right? Yes and no. SOX forces us to ask ourselves what a reasonable perspective might be on all of this. There is the universe of auditors, of Generally Accepted Accounting Principles (GAAP), of Statements on Auditing Standards (SAS), and the Financial Accounting Standards Board (FASB). It's a perfectly nice universe. It's just not a universe that you or I go to much, if at all. It exists in its own sphere. As does IT. Yet, SOX changes that. Now, we all have to understand each other.

Perhaps the biggest change that SOX has wrought is the new expectation that a company's management team is responsible, on its own and without the help of their audit firm, for the definition and documentation of internal controls. To assure the integrity and independence of the auditor, SOX restricts the ability of audit firms from participating in non-audit business consulting. Under SOX, the auditor's job is to test and evaluate their client's controls. To make it fair to the shareholders, who expect the audit to be unbiased, the auditor may not develop those same controls that they are testing. It makes sense, but it's a big shift in the way things have been done for decades.

Let's take a quick look at the process that a publicly traded company must go through to comply with SOX 404. Of course, the actual process and structure of activities at your particular business may be different from what follows, but this outline should give you a good general overview of what's involved in putting together a 404 effort.

Structurally, a SOX 404 process involves three distinct groups of people:

- **The management team:** Usually, this means the Chief Financial Officer and his or her staff, and perhaps an Internal Audit department. Often, there will be an individual executive, or team of people that is given the specific assignment of complying with SOX 404.

- **The audit committee:** This group of outside Directors from the company's board represents the company's shareholders in the SOX 404 as well the overall SEC reporting process.

- **The outside auditor:** For most large public companies, the outside auditor will be one of the Big Four firms: Deloitte, Ernst & Young, Price-Waterhouse-Coopers, and KPMG.

If you are lucky (or unlucky) enough to be given the SOX 404 responsibility at your firm, you will likely go through something like the following process to attain your compliance:

1. Working on your own, or with the help of an outside consultant that is not your auditor, you develop an internal controls framework. In most cases, that means using the guidelines set out in the COSO Integrated Framework as discussed previously. For the purposes of this book, you can assume that COSO is the standard framework to be used for SOX 404.

2. You prepare your list of controls, and then document each control. Management must also test controls, identify control weaknesses (which they will hopefully remediate), and issue its own report on internal control.

3. The audit firm reviews your controls documentation and tests various internal controls, based on its own framework. Depending on the outcome of the test, the audit firm attests to the strength of the controls or reports weaknesses, ranging from minor to material.

4. Your firm submits a report to the SEC as part of its 10Q and 10K reports that attests to the existence and soundness of your internal controls under SOX 404. (A quick note on SOX 302. Section 302 is the sister provision of SOX 404. 302 is the actual certification process in the annual report. In this sense, when people talk about SOX 302, they really mean the final paperwork involved in wrapping up a 404 process.)

5. Serious deficiencies noted by the auditor need to be remediated under SOX 404 remediation (*remediation* is a $64 word for "fixing the problem").

6. Depending on the SOX 404 filing, auditor's opinion, or other information, the SEC may investigate your firm if it determines that weaknesses in internal controls could have an impact on the accuracy of your financial reporting. In any event, the SEC will evaluate your firm every three years.

Both management and the auditor must do enough work on their own to be able to render an opinion on the company's internal control. Management may not rely at all on the work of the auditor. The auditor may rely on management's work to some extent, based on some very proscriptive guidelines, but must do most of the work himself or herself to support his or her opinion.

At the end of the cycle, there are three reports: Management issues a report on its internal controls over financial reporting. The auditor issues a report on management's assessment process and also reports on the company's internal controls over financial reporting. (The auditor also reports on whether the company has materially stated its financial statements.)

Depending on the results of the audit, the auditor may identify deficiencies in your internal controls. The PCAOB defines a significant deficiency in internal controls as, "A control deficiency, or combination of control deficiencies, that adversely affects the company's ability to initiate, authorize, record, process, or report external financial data in accordance with generally accepted accounting principles such that there is more than a remote likelihood that a misstatement of the company's annual or interim financial statements that is more than inconsequential will not be prevented or detected."

The severity of these deficiencies is related to both the potential scale of financial misstatement resulting from the control deficiency and the likelihood of a control failure occurring. The most problematic internal control deficiency that can be noted by an outside auditor is known as a "material weakness." Figure 3-1 shows a matrix by which an auditor can determine whether a deficiency in internal controls represents a material weakness or not. Material weaknesses can have an adverse impact on a company's reputation and stock price. (Although especially relevant under SOX, material weaknesses have been a part of the SEC disclosure process for many years.) Typically, management works hard to remediate a material weakness in the next accounting period after the auditor's letter identifying them has been released. As a point of reference, American auditors noted 550 material weaknesses in public companies in the first two quarters of 2005.

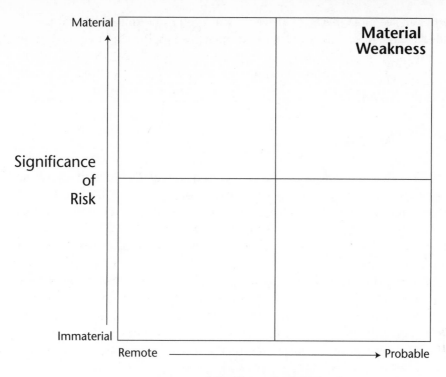

Figure 3-1   Evaluation of material weaknesses in internal controls
(From Section 404 Compliance in the Annual Report by Michael Ramos. *Journal of Accountancy* 2004)

If you're curious about what this process feels like at a real company, here's an account of the SOX 404 effort at RadioOne, a broadcasting company. According to Accounting VP Debby Cowan:

After just kind of laying out the structure, the architecture, the hoops and mile-stones, whatever you want to call it, the framework, the project management template, whatever, we looked at basically 80-some odd project tasks with people's names assigned, and due dates and timeframes. We just kind of soldiered our way through it. We matrixed the organization, realizing that I certainly couldn't do it all by myself. I didn't own enough people in resources to do it. We matrixed the organization internally, assigned subject matter experts to fly over the right spaces. For example, we can now enter the market to take ownership of our revenue cycle. That's where the sales people are. They're experts at it. Guess what? You own this process.

And we just punched our way through the architecture. It was hard. It was very intense, took a lot of resources. It cost a lot of money. We had to go further outside the company to a resource bank here, just in terms of arms and legs to get it done.

As you can see, SOX 404 is hard work, and costly in terms of time and dollars. Indeed AMR Research estimates that businesses will spend over $6 billion on SOX compliance in 2005, and comparable outlays are likely to continue in the future. At the rate of about $4 million for the average SOX effort, let's look at why it can be so expensive to put the COSO process into practice.

COSO at DexCo

Warning: There's some serious accounting jargon ahead. It's necessary, because when you start talking about COSO and controls, you're in the domain of accountants, and when you're in the domain of accountants, you better understand what they're talking about. Putting the COSO Integrated Framework into action is about realizing a set of control objectives through the use of analytical processes known as control components. A discussion of COSO necessarily revolves around the interplay between the control components and how they will help management and the auditors assess the most potentially material risks to the control objectives. Put another way, we're talking about ways in which we help the company assure its stockholders that: 1) their financial reports are complete, accurate, and presented in accordance with GAAP; and 2) that the net assets truly exist and are owned by the company.

Control Objectives

To provide a context for the implementation of its integrated framework, COSO sets out three control objectives for the management and auditors of the public company:

- **Operations:** Assuring that the company is operating effectively as a business and most importantly, protecting the assets of the shareholders.

- **Financial reporting:** Assuring that the financial statements of the company are produced in accordance with Generally Accepted Accounting Principles (GAAP).

- **Compliance:** Assuring that the company is in compliance with relevant laws and regulations, including SEC rules, health and safety laws, and tax laws.

Technically speaking, only one of these three, Financial Reporting, is in scope for a SOX 404 audit. However, I wanted you to see all three because discussions of COSO tend to be broad and you may hear about the other two in your SOX travels.

Control Components

To make sure that the company is meeting the control objectives, COSO sets out five essential control components for use by company management and auditors. It is worth noting that COSO is assumed to be a dynamic process, or applied set of frameworks, rather than a narrowly focused set of instructions. There is a great deal of variability built into the framework on purpose. The COSO creators recognized that every industry, company, and management team is different. As a result, COSO recommends evaluating the optimal application of the control components in the subjective context of the specific company in question. With that in mind, let's look at COSO's five interrelated control components.

Control Environment

The control environment refers to the overall tone or culture of the organization as it concerns control. Accounting professionals view the control environment, despite being perhaps the most subjective of the five control components, as being the foundation for other aspects of internal control. The control environment includes consideration of such facets of the company's culture as integrity and ethical values; commitment to competence; participation by the board of directors or audit committee in the internal controls process; management's philosophy and operating style; organizational structure; assignment of authority and responsibility; and human resource policies and practices.

For DexCo's Linda Fuller, one of her greatest problems with the radical shift in operational plans, as well as management team members, was the impact it was going to have on her assessment of the control environment. Fuller had just spent a year (and a great deal of money) on the company's Sarbanes Oxley compliance effort. As part of the process, she had developed a report on the company's control environment, which had actually taken a fairly honest look at some of the issues and challenges inherent in achieving effective control at a decentralized, incentive-oriented company such as DexCo. She had presented the assessment to the company's auditors, and it had become a central part of the SOX 404 evaluation. Now, with the Wilde Plan coming into effect, Fuller feared that she would have to start over again, and work blind for at least another year.

Risk Assessment

Risk assessment is the core issue in SOX compliance and COSO. Risk assessment and risk management are the common denominators of audit, IT, and SOX. SOX 404 makes you attest that your internal controls can mitigate against financial misstatements arising from poorly managed risk. If you learn nothing else from this book, I hope you will retain this one critical concept. SOX 404 compliance is always asking, in essence, what is it about your business that creates risk of financial misstatements? What has been done, what can be done, to control those risks? Everything else is just jargon, rules, and esoterica.

The standard COSO risk assessment process calls for the identification of risks according to a standard definition of the way a business typically earns revenue and manages expenses. That is, the risk assessment should follow the specific company's value chain of activities that it employs to make money through its business. (For a very thorough explication of this approach to risk, please see *Manager's Guide to the Sarbanes Oxley Act* by Scott Green).

The value chain will vary depending on the company. For a retailer, the value chain involves acquiring products, carrying them in inventory, and selling them to the public. For an oil refiner, the value chain means acquiring a commodity, processing it in accordance with some assessment of market conditions, and selling it to wholesale customers. A manufacturer's value chain calls for the acquisition of raw materials or sub-assemblies, carrying inventory, creating finished goods that are of sufficient quality to sell, carrying a finished goods inventory, selling to customers, and collecting money.

Each stage of the value chain contains risks to the business. For example, the oil refiner faces risks in acquiring the commodity. It may not arrive on time; it may not be suitable for refining; it may explode. The oil refiner also faces market risks. The refiner may acquire oil based on the assumption that gasoline will sell for $2.50 per gallon, only to find that prices have slumped to $2.00 during the time it executed the value chain steps of acquiring the commodity and processing it. The internal controls framework and control components for the oil refiner need to factor in these specific risks.

Like any business, DexCo faces a number of risks, some generic, some specific to DexCo's industry. Linda Fuller's team has compiled a lengthy report on the company's risks, including the following:

- **Inventory risk:** DexCo has substantial inventory risk. The company is constantly betting that certain items will sell according to a projection. If the item does not sell, it must be marked down or sold off to a liquidator for a fraction of its cost.

- **Trade channel risk:** The company works with channel resellers in its wholesale and OEM businesses. DexCo bears a risk that a trade channel will not resell its products as promised, a situation that can result in unexpected returns and reduced earnings.

- **Subcontractor practices:** DexCo makes use of many outside companies to complete its value chain. Examples include the call centers, logistics vendors, and advertising agencies. The practices and operations of these subcontractors pose both tangible and intangible risks to DexCo. Tangible risks from subcontractors include errors, fraud, and theft of data. Intangible risks include loss of reputation or damage to client relationships at the hands of improperly trained contractors.

- **Import/Export risks:** As a company operating in numerous countries, DexCo faces risks from international import and export considerations. The company could risk losing money unexpectedly if tariffs or trade rules change. Alternatively, the company has little recourse if a foreign competitor decides to engage in dumping products in the U.S. market at a price lower than manufacturing cost, a practice that is illegal but difficult to prevent.

- **Credit risk:** In its wholesale and OEM business, DexCo relies on credit to collect payment for delivery of goods to its customers. With several large customers accounting for a high percentage of its revenue, DexCo has exposure to credit risk if one or more of its customers develops financial problems and cannot pay its bills.

- **Currency risk:** With its international dealings, DexCo has exposure to currency risk. If the company cannot manage currency exchange rate fluctuations, then it may find itself paying more than it anticipated for its products and even runs the risk of taking a loss on certain transactions.

- **Technology risk:** Given the nature of its business, DexCo is vulnerable to shifts in technology. As an OEM supplier to the electronics industry, it may find certain clients declining if their particular technologies are replaced as advances in technology make their lines obsolete. Similarly, with the rapidly escalating performance of technology, DexCo runs the risk of carrying obsolete inventory that it will have to liquidate.

- **Trade risk:** DexCo has risk from the way it buys close-outs in Asia. The company runs the risk that by allowing too much discretion to the individual buyer it may end up with excessive inventory that it cannot sell at a profit.

- **Validation risk:** With its far-flung operations, outsourced functions, and overly independent divisions, the company has a risk that it may not be able to check to ensure that inbound orders have been completed and paid for and that outbound purchases have been delivered. DexCo needs internal controls to validate its transactions.

- **Regulatory (FCC, UL, EPA, OSHA):** As a purveyor of electronic components, computers, and computer parts, DexCo faces risk that its business may be affected by changes in regulations. For example, the Underwriter's Laboratory (UL) could change its rules and render some of DexCo's products ineligible for import. The FCC, EPA, or OSHA regulations could also have an impact on the marketability of DexCo's products. A change in marketability could have a negative effect on the company's future earnings potential. (Technically, this last category is not in scope for SOX 404, but in the spirit of identifying risks to operations that have an impact on financials. I wanted you to be aware of it.)

Linda Fuller's team has performed an evaluation of the levels of these various risk categories. By emulating the process shown in Figure 3-1, they have determined that certain risks are not likely to cause material problems in financial controls. For example, although regulatory or currency issues may arise from time to time, the risk that either type of risk will result in a material misstatement of financial results is low. Alternatively, her examination of the company's inventory controls, credit granting guidelines, and transaction validation has produced some worrisome results. In those areas, Fuller has recommended strong control procedures.

Control Procedures

Control procedures (also known as control practices) refer to a set of practices, corporate policies, software settings, and other procedural guidelines that are put into place by management to reduce the risk of fraud or error that can result in financial misstatements. In general, each control procedure matches a specific type of risk. Stated another way, the control procedure is the action taken by management to mitigate the risk that a control objective will not be realized. For this reason, you will typically see matched sets of control objectives, risks, and control procedures. A specific set of control procedures provides a level of assurance that a specific set of control objective will not be subject to a given set of risks. That is the theory, at least.

In a typical Sarbanes Oxley 404 compliance effort, a company may identify dozens of risk areas that require control procedures for mitigation. DexCo has pages of such objective/risk/procedure pairings. As many companies do, DexCo has divided most of its internal control issues into *inbound* and *outbound* transaction categories. Inbound transactions are those that involve sourcing of components and services from vendors. Outbound transactions involve selling goods and services to customers. In both inbound and outbound transactions, DexCo can define how its control objective of safeguarding its assets can be subject to risk and require control procedures for risk management.

Linda Fuller's team prepared a three-column table to define its pairings of control objectives, risks, and control procedures. Table 3-1 shows several examples of these pairings for inbound transactions.

Table 3-1   Example of Paired Control Objectives, Risks, and Control Procedures for Inbound Transactions

CONTROL OBJECTIVE	RISK	CONTROL PROCEDURE
Only pre-approved suppliers can be used to meet price, service level, and quality specifications	Suppliers or their products may be incapable of meeting DexCo's needs	Establish an approved supplier list and set up periodic review of prices, quality parameters, and service levels.
All sourcing costs are booked into the correct accounting period	Improper cut off of purchase records at the end of the period	Establish proper cut off procedures at the end of the month for all purchase orders

Source: Nagel, Karl. *Disclosure/Internal Control Primer 2003*

As Table 3-1 illustrates, each identified risk to a control objective can be mitigated, at least theoretically, through the enactment of a control procedure. In our example of inbound transactions, DexCo has identified the selection of appropriate vendors as a control objective because vendor selection has a potential impact on DexCo's entire value chain. If the company works with the wrong vendors (meaning a low-quality, inconsistently priced vendor with unreliable service), then the company faces the risk that it will lose money on transactions, carry low-quality merchandise, or even lose clients. To mitigate these risks, DexCo has established a control procedure that calls for DexCo's sourcing staff to work only with an approved vendor list and periodically update the standing of the vendors on the list.

Table 3-2 shows a comparable set of paired control objective/risk/procedures for outbound transactions. As with the inbound transactions, the outbound business also creates risks to the control objectives. If not transacted properly, the company runs the risk of booking sales orders that will either not be paid or require costly revision. Either case could negatively affect earnings. If a very large order were subject to problems, it could make a material difference in a period's financial results. Furthermore, poorly managed risks in inbound transactions could expose DexCo to fraud. For example, if the duties of order entry, sales, and credit record keeping are not segregated properly, the company faces the risk that a dishonest employee could authorize bogus sales of merchandise to dummy accounts and profit personally from the sale of the stolen goods.

Table 3-2   Example of Paired Control Objectives, Risks, and Control Procedures for Outbound Transactions

CONTROL OBJECTIVE	RISK	CONTROL PROCEDURE
Process only valid and approved customer orders	Customer order may not be authorized	Customer order approval is verified with sales and credit personnel
Process orders accurately and expeditiously	Customer order information may be unclear, inaccurate or incomplete	Customer order information is verified with sales personnel or confirmed directly with customer
Safeguard order entry files and related accounting records	Inadequate physical security (or data security) over credit and order entry documents	Order entry is independent of sales and credit record keeping functions

Source: Nagel, Karl. *Disclosure/Internal Control Primer 2003*

These paired control objective/risk/procedure sets are the essence of Sarbanes Oxley 404 compliance. To comply with the law, a company must satisfy its auditor that it has identified its relevant control objectives and the attendant risks to attaining those objectives, and then implemented control procedures to ensure that those risks are being properly managed. Viewed collectively with information, communication, and monitoring, this process forms the internal controls specified in the Sarbanes Oxley Act.

Information and Communication

Information and communication, the fourth of the five control components of the COSO framework, calls for a company to establish procedures that will generate information about the state of its internal controls and communicate this information to the appropriate managers. This makes sense. After all, what good would it do for internal controls to exist in an opaque place where their activities could not be viewed? Therefore, a properly designed internal control must not only work to mitigate a risk to the control objectives, it must be able to provide information about its performance that can be communicated to management. COSO requires management to monitor its internal controls.

Monitoring

Monitoring, COSO's final control component, requires that management periodically look at the state of their internal controls. Again, this is a logical extension of the entire COSO framework. If a company is going to establish controls, it ought to monitor them on a regular basis, right? You'd be amazed how it often doesn't quite happen that way. However, according to COSO, management needs to keep an eye on how its internal controls are functioning. As we will explore in great detail throughout the rest of this book, the information, communication, and monitoring aspects of COSO have a great deal to do with information technology.

These are the five Control Components of COSO. As you can see, there is a lot of latitude in their design. Actual implementation of COSO varies greatly from one company to another.

Why Linda Is Freaking Out

If you've read this far in the book, you might start to see why Linda Fuller is freaking out and wants to quit. The COSO process is labor intensive and costly. And, unfortunately, it is not particularly friendly to rapid change. Linda fears that all of her work at establishing controls, which she has just completed and barely begun to put into action, will now become obsolete—a situation that presents serious problems for the company in legal and operational terms, and is also a major hassle. As we move forward with our story, we will see just how problematic some of these issues can be.

Summary

Linda Fuller, CFO of DexCo, tells Jim Wilde that she plans to resign in the wake of his announced changes in the company's organization, operations, and strategy. Having just spent a year on Sarbanes Oxley, she fears that his radical changes will ruin DexCo's ability to be compliant and place the company in jeopardy of SEC investigations.

To help us understand where Linda is coming from, this chapter then describes the origins of Sarbanes Oxley, starting with its roots in earlier SEC regulations that govern public companies. SOX is the latest addition to a set of laws that help make public companies accountable in their financial disclosures to the markets.

The core of Sarbanes Oxley Section 404, which is the most costly and worrisome aspect of the law, is the requirement that public companies attest to the existence of effective internal controls. Using a framework known as COSO, a public company is supposed to go through a process of identifying risks to financial misstatements due to error or fraud and then create, implement, and document internal controls to mitigate against those risks.

A public company's auditor is supposed to audit those internal controls and supply management and shareholders with its opinion of those controls. If the controls are deficient, the auditor may identify problems with the internal controls, ranking in serious from deficiencies to material weaknesses. Material weaknesses in internal controls identified under SOX must be remediated (fixed) or the company will face SEC penalties of various kinds.

Control deficiencies are a serious matter for a public company. Because of the complexity and hard work involved in internal controls, Linda Fuller feels that she cannot do her job properly and assure effective controls at DexCo with the pace and scale of change being planned by her new boss.

4

Between SOX and a Hard-Coded Place

Linda Fuller, Sebastian Perkins, the division general managers and the entire Sarbanes Oxley team pulled up in cabs in front of Jim Wilde's faux log cabin ranch house in Montana. After their initial conversation, Wilde had suggested that they hold a retreat off site to delve into the SOX matter. Dale Steyer, the new Chief Operating Officer, would be there as well. Jim said he always focused better when he could look out the window and watch his horses grazing under the big sky.

"I just don't see," Wilde began, "why we can't do what we want to do and stay compliant?"

"Well," Fuller replied. "It depends on what you mean by 'stay compliant.' If we really want to comply with SOX Section 404—and I think that is a very valid goal for many reasons—then we really have to be careful about how our strategic shifts and operational changes affect our internal controls. Internal controls are fragile and easily broken."

"So what?" Wilde asked. "We have an auditor. They tell us how to set up our books. At the end of the year, they bless our numbers and we're off to the races."

"Not anymore," Fuller said. "The world has changed after Enron and Worldcom. Our auditor is trying to be a lot more objective about what they see in our controls and records. We have to make sure that our internal controls work properly on our own. The auditor is going to look critically at how we are set up."

"What you're saying," Wilde muttered, "is that SOX is going to hurt our ability to be agile."

"No," Fuller replied. "What I'm saying is that we need to be circumspect about how our plans affect controls. Let's do a deep dive into the issue and see if we can understand it better." With that, she and her team proceeded to unwrap portable whiteboards and easel pads and lay out the tricky interconnections between controls, IT, business process, and compliance.

Internal Controls and Business Processes

As a starting example, Fuller's team outlined the paired objective/risk/control set shown in Table 4-1. Although it is just one of many inbound controls identified by Fuller's SOX team, this particular issue is potentially material for DexCo because of the company's reliance on clever sourcing as a key factor in its earnings strategy. Both the SOX consultant hired by Fuller and the company's audit firm had noted the importance of controlling the booking of sourcing costs in the correct period.

There were several reasons for their emphasis on this issue. Because so much of the company's business revolves around the buying and selling of merchandise in unpredictable patterns, the consultants and auditors felt there was a real possibility that material errors could be made in the processing of the many different purchase orders (POs). For the sake of accuracy and control, everyone wanted procedures for handling sourcing to be tightened up quite a bit. In addition, there was an uncomfortable feel that some individuals involved in the process could be gaming the system and manipulating purchase orders and payables in order to rig the earnings growth numbers. If this were actually happening, then DexCo could be in for serious problems with the SEC and shareholders.

Table 4-1   Objective/Risk/Control Pairing for Ensuring Sourcing Costs Are Booked into the Correct Accounting Period

CONTROL OBJECTIVE	RISK	CONTROL PROCEDURE
DexCo needs to be reasonably sure that its sourcing costs are booked into the correct accounting period.	DexCo faces a risk of material misstatement of financial results if sourcing costs are not booked in the correct period. The company has risk if there are improper cutoffs of purchase records at the end of the period.	Establishing and maintaining policies to ensure proper cutoff for all purchase orders at period end date.

To create an internal control that would "Establish proper cutoff procedures at the end of the month for all purchase orders," it is necessary to understand the overall business process that is taking place in the sourcing and procurement operation. Figure 4-1 illustrates the official business process outlined by the Global Procurement (GP) department for the sourcing or goods. By following the process described in the flow chart, DexCo management can attest to the existence of sound internal controls over financial reporting. Expenses and payables for the sourcing of goods in a given month can be accurately stated because the process is designed to cut off purchase orders at the end of each month.

Table 4-2 shows the process steps and financial reporting results for the official process. Linda says, "Of course, this could change as we move forward." Sebastian interjects, "Yes, of course it could change. Just do the courtesy of giving me enough time to assemble a team to make the change." The two exchange another hostile look that does not go unnoticed by Dale Steyer.

Linda ignores the jibe and continues. Remember, she says, that each of DexCo's divisions does a lot of its own purchasing but also coordinates the deals it makes with vendors with DexCo's Global Procurement department— at least in theory. Throughout the month, she explains, Division, Global Procurement department, and the vendor are in continuous communication about the status of an order. Global Procurement is able to maintain an accurate record of the cost of sourcing throughout the month. At the close of the month, the internal control process outlined in Figure 4-1 enables Global Sourcing to adjust the cost of sourcing based on inputs from the Division and vendors and produce an accurate financial report on sourcing costs for the month. And, Global Procurement begins the following month with a correct starting point for the new order that was placed during the prior month.

"Looks good," Jim Wilde says. "You're in control there, right?"

"Yes and no," Linda Fuller replies. "As you and I both know, sometimes the officially stated policy is not adhered to." Smiles all around. "However," she continued. "We are realists. My team has prepared a process flow that represents how things actually happen from time to time here at DexCo." She refers Wilde to Figure 4-2.

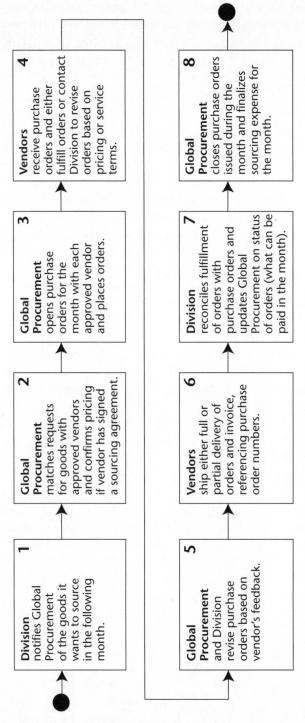

1 Division
notifies Global Procurement of the goods it wants to source in the following month.

2 Global Procurement
matches requests for goods with approved vendors and confirms pricing if vendor has signed a sourcing agreement.

3 Global Procurement
opens purchase orders for the month with each approved vendor and places orders.

4 Vendors
receive purchase orders and either fulfill orders or contact Division to revise orders based on pricing or service terms.

5 Global Procurement
and Division revise purchase orders based on vendor's feedback.

6 Vendors
ship either full or partial delivery of orders and invoice, referencing purchase order numbers.

7 Division
reconciles fulfillment of orders with purchase orders and updates Global Procurement on status of orders (what can be paid in the month).

8 Global Procurement
closes purchase orders issued during the month and finalizes sourcing expense for the month.

Figure 4-1 DexCo's official process for sourcing goods from approved vendors

Table 4-2 **Example of Single Purchase Order Process in Official Control of Sourcing**

PROCESS STEP	DAY OF THE MONTH	ACTIVITY	FINANCIAL REPORTING DATA
1	2	Division notifies Global Procurement (GP) that it needs 100,000 circuit boards.	
2	3	GP sources 1000 circuit boards from an approved vendor at a pre-negotiated rate of $10 each.	$1,000,000 procurement planned and placed in monthly financial forecast
3	4	GP opens a PO for the circuit boards and place order with vendor.	$1,000,000 PO opened with vendor
4	7	Vendor begins to fulfill order. Division increases order to 120,000 circuit boards and notifies GP of change.	
5	8	GP revises PO to reflect change.	PO changed to $1,200,000
6	28	Vendor ships all 120,000 circuit boards to DexCo.	
7	29	Division acknowledges shipment, endorses $1,200,000 invoice, and orders 25,000 more circuit boards.	GP authorizes payment of $1,200,000 to complete the order
8	30	GP closes the PO for the month. GP opens a second PO for $250,000 for the following month for the new order of 25,000 circuit boards.	DexCo recognizes $1,200,000 in expense for the circuit boards for the month—an accurate number

As Figure 4-2 shows, in many cases the Division places the order with its own preferred supplier first, and then notifies Global Procurement of the order. Global Procurement then opens a purchase order to match what has already transpired. Although this is not the stated policy of DexCo, it is reality. The company simply moves too quickly for Global Procurement to keep up. Assuming open communication is taking place in real time, though, even this system can result in effective controls. However, on occasion, the extant process can get out of control, a scenario outlined in Table 4-3.

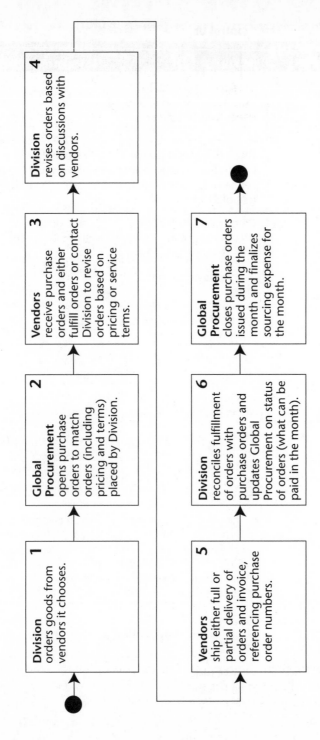

1 Division
orders goods from vendors it chooses.

2 Global Procurement
opens purchase orders to match orders (including pricing and terms) placed by Division.

3 Vendors
receive purchase orders and either fulfill orders or contact Division to revise orders based on pricing or service terms.

4 Division
revises orders based on discussions with vendors.

5 Vendors
ship either full or partial delivery of orders and invoice, referencing purchase order numbers.

6 Division
reconciles fulfillment of orders with purchase orders and updates Global Procurement on status of orders (what can be paid in the month).

7 Global Procurement
closes purchase orders issued during the month and finalizes sourcing expense for the month.

Figure 4-2 A more accurate representation of DexCo's procurement and purchase order process

Table 4-3 Possible Lapses in Control Under Current System

PROCESS STEP	DAY OF THE MONTH	ACTIVITY	FINANCIAL REPORTING DATA
1	1	Division orders 100,000 circuit boards from Vendor A at a price of $10 each.	
2	15	Global Procurement inquires about Division's purchasing activities and discovers that the division has placed a $1,000,000 order. GP opens a PO.	$1,000,000 PO opened for Vendor A.
3	20	Vendor A receives purchase order for 100,000 circuit boards.	
4	22	Vendor A notifies Division that it cannot fulfill 50 percentof the order because of a problem at its factory. Division does not communicate this to GP. Division places a rush order for 50,000 circuit boards with Vendor B at a price of $15 each, but does not notify GP of the second order.	Purchase order for Vendor A still remains at $1,000,000 even though the order is now for $500,000.
5	28	Vendor A ships 50,000 circuit boards and invoices for $500,000. For Vendor A, the order is complete even though the PO still calls for an additional $500,000 in billing. Vendor B ships 50,000 circuit boards, and shipment is accepted by Division. Yet, GP still does not know of order from Vendor B. Even if it did, Vendor B is not an approved Vendor, so GP would not be able to issue a PO.	Vendor A purchase order shows $500,000 still open pending delivery of additional goods.
6	30	GP asks Division to reconcile open POs with invoices. Division notifies GP that it has received $500,000 of the $1,000,000 order from Vendor A.	

(continued)

Table 4-3   *(continued)*

PROCESS STEP	DAY OF THE MONTH	ACTIVITY	FINANCIAL REPORTING DATA
7	30	GP closes the POs for the month, but is lacking accurate information.	GP reports cost of goods for the month of $500,000, a misstatement of expense that will inflate earnings by $750,000.
	Next Month	Vendor B submits invoice for $750,000 for prior month's shipment, for which there is no PO.	

Under the scenario outlined in Table 4-3, DexCo runs the risk of understating its expenses in the month by $750,000. This will result in an overstatement of its earnings, a mistake that will have to be corrected—assuming it is caught in time—in the following month. Given that DexCo has three divisions, dozens of suppliers and global operations, the implications even for this simple type of example could be quite grave. With this type of process, the company is, in fact, lacking sufficient internal controls that would permit management to attest to the their effectiveness as mandated by the Sarbanes Oxley Act. The auditor may note this and record a material weakness in the control, a situation that will require remediation.

Then, there is the issue of approving suppliers, which can teach us a little about how internal controls tend to be linked. In this example, the COSO framework adopted by DexCo calls for Global Procurement to work only with approved suppliers. Yet, as we have seen, the divisions of the company frequently tap into sources of supply that are not approved. Going further, what if we look at the issue of who has the authority to approve new suppliers. COSO guidelines would suggest that the individual with that authority be segregated in terms of roles and responsibility from the people who approve POs and invoices and authorize check payments. Otherwise, DexCo faces the risk that an unscrupulous person could single-handedly create a new approved vendor, issue a PO to that vendor, and cut a check as well. The vendor could easily be his brother-in-law, and they could split the proceeds. If this same person also has the ability to validate shipment and receipt of merchandise, then DexCo could be robbed blind quite easily.

Internal controls, explains Linda Fuller, are most effective when they match business processes in day-to-day operations. As outlined in Figure 4-3, the business process of sourcing goods involves three concurrent flows of activities. The Global Procurement department, Division, and the vendor must operate together to ensure that the internal controls can work. If there is a breakdown in communication or coordination between the processes, then DexCo is at a greater risk of a financial misstatement due to a breakdown in controls. And that, Fuller adds, is largely a matter of information technology.

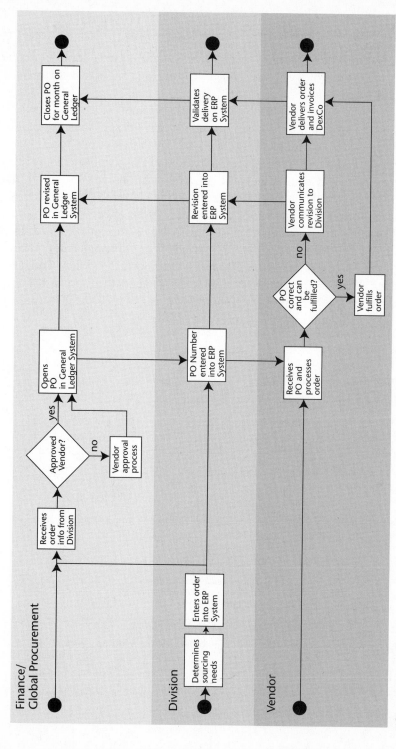

Figure 4-3 Business process flow for Global Procurement, Division, and the vendor in the case of an individual PO

Internal Controls and Information Technology

At this point, Jim Wilde begins to get a three-Tylenol kind of look on his face. "I thought we were going to talk about accounting," he says. "Information technology is a separate subject, right?"

"Well," Linda replies. "They are quite deeply related. Although a lot of our internal controls are manual, they frequently touch up against computer systems. We keep our books on computer systems. In this example, we report our financial results out of our general ledger system at the corporate level, but we operate on a day-to-day basis, in terms of vendor relationships and order placement, through each division's Enterprise Resource Planning (ERP) system."

Without looking at him, she hands the white board marker to Sebastian Harris, who diagrams an approximation of Figure 4-4 on the white board. IT has two main roles in internal controls. At one level, IT solutions can coordinate the dissemination of organizational knowledge about the policy and procedural aspects of internal control. This is accomplished through technologies such as intranets and content management systems, which publish rules and control processes in real time to all relevant parties.

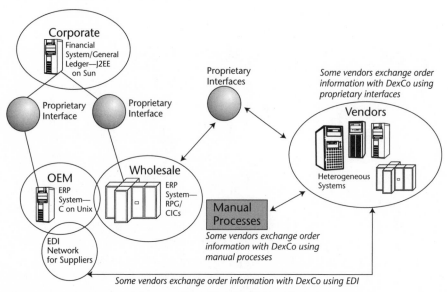

Figure 4-4   System overview and logical architecture of sourcing process

More important, IT can play a critical role in defining and enforcing internal controls, providing auditability and real-time (or at least within the period) visibility into processes occurring in multiple business units and their respective systems. IT's role in control definition and enforcement works at two levels simultaneously. At the level of the individual system, the integrity and soundness of a specific control procedure depends on the quality of its implementation as an information technology process. In our example, a well-designed and implemented internal control would prohibit errors or malfeasance regarding purchase orders within the system that created it. If a user is able to access purchase order records and change them without proper authorization, or without leaving a proper audit log of the activity, then the effectiveness of the internal control has been badly compromised.

Furthermore, IT includes the critical link in internal controls that exist between separate systems. Because DexCo's controls over sourcing are dependent on interoperation between separate business units (Global Procurement [GP], Division, and Vendor) and their respective IT systems, then the effectiveness of those controls depends on the quality of those systemic interoperations. DexCo's internal controls over sourcing rely on a connection between the Divisional ERP systems, which generate the request for sourcing of goods, and the general ledger system, which generates the actual purchase orders and maintains the lists of approved vendors. As you can see in Figure 4-4, each Division connects its ERP with the corporate general ledger through a proprietary interface.

A brief IT digression is in order: A proprietary interface is a customized software program that allows two separate computer systems to exchange data and operational instructions. In the example of DexCo, the proprietary interface is necessary for the Division's ERP system to automatically update the purchase order detail in the general ledger system. When it is functioning, the proprietary interface receives a PO change instruction from the ERP system and communicates it to the general ledger system, which inputs it automatically. The entire process is transparent to system users at both ends.

Assuming a properly functioning interface between ERP and general ledger systems, you can see that IT can provide real teeth to internal controls. With good IT-enforced controls in place, it becomes difficult, or even impossible, for an individual to commit fraud without engaging in broad collusion. In other words, if a PO is locked once it is issued, and only an approved user of the general ledger system can modify it, or override an automated change made from the ERP system, then it will be quite challenging for a single person on either side to change the PO without it being noticed by someone internally or by an auditor.

If the proprietary interface did not exist, or if it were broken, then the Division staff would have to communicate manually, a situation that occurs frequently. If the systems are not integrated, and people must manually update each other on the status of orders, and then input changes in order status into their respective systems according to published procedures, then the internal controls are in far greater risk of falling apart.

DexCo's systemic communication with suppliers is far more sketchy. The suppliers comprise a heterogeneous group of systems—mainframes, mini-computers, Windows servers, Linux, and so on. For some suppliers, DexCo maintains an Electronic Data Interchange (EDI) system, and with a few large, steady suppliers, the company has actually invested in proprietary interfaces for constant coordination of orders and invoices. Both EDI and proprietary interfaces make it possible for DexCo's computer systems to communicate directly with the systems of its suppliers. However, for many suppliers, including the ever-changing group of new and unapproved sources of goods, DexCo must rely on manual communications to stay up to date.

The result of this mixed set of systems and their various connections is an unpredictable state of internal control for sourcing. If the IT aspects of sourcing form a tight control, such as when the fully integrated systems of Vendor, Division, and Global Procurement lock out all but correct purchase orders issued to approved vendors, then the internal controls work effectively with relatively little potential for human error.

Control Points

In virtually all internal controls, there will be places where the control procedure that is designed to realize a control objective will be supported by a specific set of functions in an underlying IT system. I refer to these connections as control points. A control point may not necessarily be an actual IT system or application. Rather, a control point is a combination of application design, internal control procedures, IT system functions, and system logic. Together, these factors support the proper definition and enforcement of an internal control.

In the example of sourcing of goods at DexCo, the business processes involved in DexCo's internal controls match up with the IT systems that support those processes in several places. These are the control points in the internal controls for sourcing. DexCo's control points for sourcing of goods are shown in Figure 4-5. The IT systems, including the general ledger and ERP applications, enable DexCo to carry out its internal controls. As with most companies, a good portion of the actual internal controls exist as software functions.

The interfaces that connect the systems with each other form the critical bonds that enable internal controls to stay in place across divisional and corporate boundaries. In the case of sourcing, as shown in Figure 4-5, it is the ability of the Vendor systems to update the Division's ERP, which updates the general ledger—all in automated processes—that enables full internal controls to be in effect. Of course, it is possible for people to manage the updating process, but with the kind of transaction volume and unpredictability of DexCo's sourcing operations, it is unlikely that people would be able to keep the controls in effect adequately without proper systemic support.

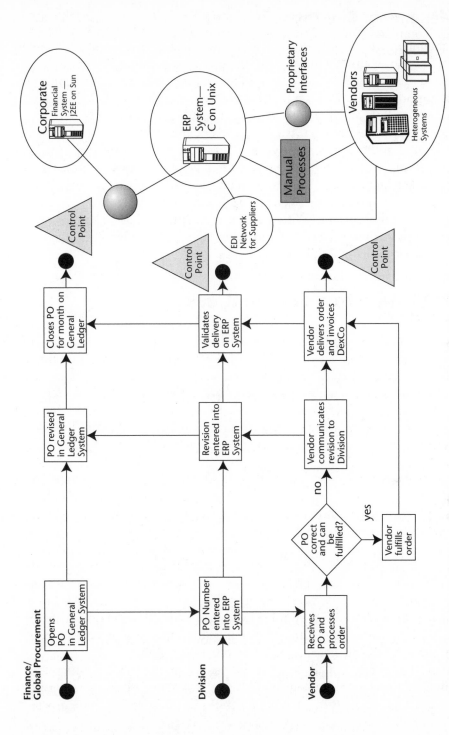

Figure 4-5 Control points formed by links between the internal controls built into the business process and the supporting information technology systems

Interdependent Controls

And, remember, we are only dealing with one narrow set of controls. As we noted previously, controls tend to be interdependent. Going back to the issue of approval of new vendors and segregation of duties, we see that IT again can play an important role. Though it currently does not do this, DexCo is contemplating installing an enterprise identity management system that will provide a role for each system user. The user's role will identify whether or not he or she has the authority to approve a vendor, authorize a purchase order, approve a shipment, or authorize payment to a vendor. With a well-designed identity management system integrated with the ERP and general ledger systems, DexCo can monitor the vendor approval and segregation of duties aspects of its internal controls. Without such a system, DexCo is reliant on published procedures that must be monitored using subjective tests such as surveys and inspection of manual records.

The FAST Track to a Control Breakdown

DexCo, like most large companies, is at least partly dependent on its IT systems for the definition and enforcement of the business processes that make up its internal controls under Sarbanes Oxley. Where the company has only manual internal controls, it may want the ability to achieve control automation through the use of IT. There is absolutely nothing wrong with this. We live in an age of computers, and most of our business records, as well as our business processes, are maintained through the use of sophisticated computer software. So, what's the problem?

The problem is that computers and the software that runs on them, and especially the interfaces that connect systems, are notoriously difficult to change with any speed or accuracy. If you have ever worked on a major IT initiative, whether it is installing an enterprise system, upgrading software, or changing interfaces between systems, then you probably understand how potentially long and costly the process can be. Of course, there are some superb IT organizations and consultants who can speed things up, and some systems are designed to change more easily than others. However, as you may know, many of the obstacles to simple IT change have nothing to do with technology at all. Hurdles for IT projects come in the form of budget problems, political turf battles, and snags in business process design.

A major IT initiative usually goes in phases, beginning with requirements gathering, followed by a technology audit, and a project plan. These early project elements must usually go through several iterations with stakeholders, a process that can take months. Then, there is the actual implementation of the technology, followed by beta testing, quality control, revisions, and deployment. In the best-case scenario, this is a one-year process, although it can take much longer.

At the risk of oversimplifying, the major bugaboo that slows down IT projects is the prevalence of *hard coding*, or the necessity for expert software developers to write specialized programming code in specific programming languages to enable changes to take place in the systemic environment. For example, if you have a mainframe computer involved in your IT operations, any change in the application functioning of that mainframe will require budget and time for software developers experienced at CICS, RPG, or COBOL programming. Modifications to software code on the mainframe require methodical processes and testing for accuracy and bugs.

In addition, any major (and most minor) IT projects that involve changes to enterprise systems necessarily get you quickly into issues related to network functioning, message transport protocols (HTTP, JMS), identity management, operating system and programming language compatibility, data loading, data integrity, audit logging, accuracy, security, and on and on.

Then, if you're involved in connecting more than one system together in a distributed computing environment, where multiple computers and software applications must operate in concert to accomplish business process tasks—as is the case with DexCo in its interactions between ERP and general ledger systems—there is going to be a hard coding exercise on both sides of the situation.

Most difficult of all is the challenge of replacing a major enterprise system. This is the ultimate hard coding tour de force. Typically, with time and budget pressure all along the way, developers with complementary disciplines must work together to ensure smooth functioning and accurate processing of data as the company migrates from one platform to another. It is a demanding, error-prone process.

The net effect of hard coding and its related problems with network, infrastructure, operating systems, quality control, de-bugging, and testing, as well as shifting project requirements and political influences, is that IT initiatives usually take a long time to realize. Although there is nothing inherently wrong with taking a long time to accomplish IT changes, the change cycle is often a lot slower than the needs of operations and strategy would dictate. As I have noted earlier, the pace of change in the business world continues to accelerate. A major company may have the need to shift its operational mode every couple of quarters. In contrast, the average large-scale IT change initiative might take two or three times longer to complete. Figure 4-6 illustrates the differential between the time periods involved in an IT change initiative and changes in business process at a large company.

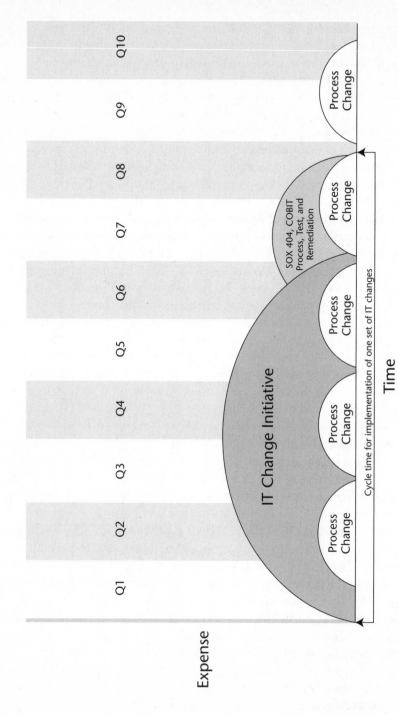

Figure 4-6 The difference in the time span and expense level for periodic changes in business process versus the time and expense for IT change initiatives and resulting SOX 404 certification processes

As Figure 4-6 shows, over the course of a year or two, a company may attempt to make several changes in its business processes to achieve various operational and strategic objectives. During this time, the company may be able to accomplish perhaps one major IT change initiative. My standard disclaimer holds—this is a generic example and of course, every company is different—but the general effect should be recognizable to anyone who's ever been close to a major system migration or functional requirements implementation on a set of enterprise systems.

What can happen, in fact, is an unfortunate devolution to a kind of perpetual state of unfinished IT initiatives. As priorities change, executives come and go, and the business climate changes, requirements for IT projects change. Some initiatives never get finished, while others get rushed. The results can vary from resentment among the ranks of those whose IT projects go unfulfilled to short-term, expedient adoption of inappropriate technological solutions to accomplish a task that eventually just causes conflict and more trouble at a later date.

From the perspective of internal controls and Sarbanes Oxley, the differential between IT change and business process change cycle times is especially worrisome. Bear in mind that the eight quarters required to implement a major set of IT changes will result in the perfect adoption of a set of IT requirements that are two years old. (Remember SOX certifications are done annually.) Figure 4-6 alludes to COBIT (the IT side of COSO) and other Sarbanes Oxley IT processes. I will delve much more deeply into this in the next chapter, but at this point just recognize that SOX adds more time to the completion of any IT project.

This may seem obvious, but think about what that means. If you are the CFO of a large company, you will be certain that, as of 2007, the IT systems you need to support the controls you needed in 2005 will actually be working . . . Yikes! And that's assuming that everyone holds his or her other changes off and keeps everything pretty much static in terms of IT and business process changes.

In DexCo's case, the company's new FAST program, which has been ambitiously designed to provide improved operational functionality and reduced IT maintenance cost, is going to cause a lot of difficulty for the company's Sarbanes Oxley efforts. The reason? The IT change process simply cannot keep up with the business process changes necessary to implement the internal controls.

Broken Control Points

Changes in IT have the potential to break the control points between IT and business process that ensure the proper functioning of internal controls. If you recall from Chapter 1, DexCo is in the middle of an ambitious IT upgrade called FAST, which stands for Future Activity and Transaction System. As Figure 4-7 shows in DexCo's case, the advent of the FAST system, which replaces existing IT systems with a new Enterprise Application Integration (EAI) framework Identity, breaks the existing control points necessary for the company's Sarbanes Oxley 404 compliance.

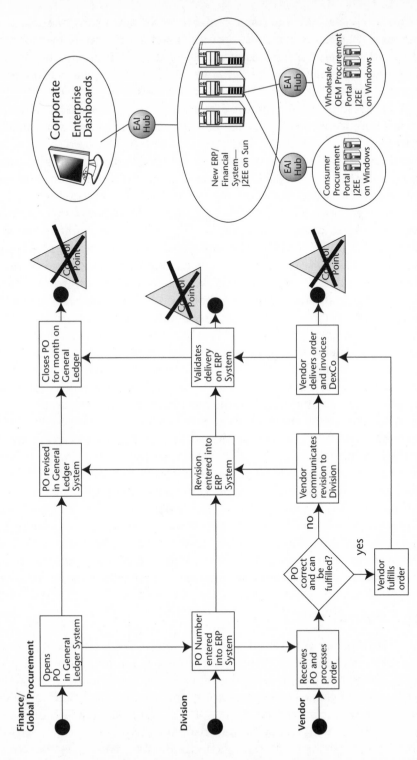

Figure 4-7 Breakdown in controls results from changes in IT systems that support the internal controls built into the business process.

Keeping narrowly focused on the internal controls that ensure that sourcing of goods can meet the test of an auditor and SOX 404 attestation, let's look at the control problems that arise when the company disrupts its existing IT systems to implement FAST. First, you have the problem of adapting the internal control processes to the new systems. For example, if you want to be sure that a purchase order is not modified by Division staff without the knowledge of the Global Procurement staff, then you have to make sure that the new ERP and financial systems implemented under the FAST program are configured to meet these control specifications. Alternatively, if there is a modification to the PO, the SOX 404 internal controls would dictate that the modification be visible within the accounting period to both the Division and GP staffs, and that the data contained in the PO modification has integrity—that is, no unauthorized person has changed it.

Linda Fuller says, "The big problem with FAS is the faulty assumption that it can be implemented with proper functionality in anything like the time period required for DexCo to keep on top of its SOX 404 internal controls. The reality is that FAST will take at least a year to set up, and that is a very optimistic estimate." She continues, expressing a concern that during the transition period, DexCo's management team will not be able to attest to the strength of its internal controls as required under SOX 404. The management team, at that point, has two choices: It can lie and state that it is in compliance or it can risk having its auditors expose a material weakness in internal controls, which will then have to be remediated. Either way, the company is exposed to risk to its stock price and reputation in the financial markets. And, even if DexCo can complete the entire IT implementation, internal control process coordination, and COBIT cycles, the company is still only complying with an out-of-date set of control objectives.

Sebastian Harris sighs irritably and says, "If we had done COBIT like I wanted to, we would have fewer of these problems. However, someone didn't want to give me the budget." He glares at Linda.

"Can someone clue me in as to what COBIT is?" Jim Wilde asks.

"COBIT," Sebastian responds, "is a set of IT guidelines that help companies be more compliant. It's a process that mandates that the systems be secured and functioning within the bounds of COBIT standards. This means, among many other considerations, that the developers of the ERP Financial System, and its various EAI interfaces with other DexCo systems, the vendor portal, and so on, have access to the systems through a development environment. COBIT requires that software developers not have access to a system once it has been launched and put into production servicing real accounting transactions. If this standard is not adhered to, COBIT contends, then the company is not maintaining control over its IT systems that would ensure accurate financial results. The risk is that an unscrupulous software developer, or someone pretending to be a software developer, could hack a production system and configure it to put money into accounts without the knowledge of those who enforce the internal controls. Or, at the very least, non-compliance with COBIT generates a level of uncertainty about the integrity of IT systems that is worrisome."

Dale Steyer comments, "I think I'm getting a sense of where we are at with all of this, and I am kind of unhappy about what I see. If you accept the argument that IT changes and SOX internal controls compliance processes are slow, and you agree that business in the twenty-first century requires companies to be agile but business agility requires fast action, then you will probably start to see the major bind that a lot of companies are finding themselves in today. With change needed in a two-quarter cycle, and IT change and attendant SOX issues requiring at least six quarters, how can a company stay on top of its business and remain compliant? How can DexCo get out in front of rapidly moving markets, shifting supply chains, and merger and acquisition activity and still certify its financial statements under Sarbanes Oxley?"

"That's what I've been trying to explain to you," Linda says. "This is a potentially huge mess. My people have been working their tails off on this and now they're going to have to do it again."

"My people, too," Sebastian adds. "This is a monster that's eating my department alive. And I have to tell you, being forced to work hand in glove with accounting just makes things worse."

"Those in glass houses shouldn't throw stones," Linda says tartly.

"Alright," Dale says. "I get it. We need to look at COBIT in depth, and all the other ramifications of SOX in our business. But let's get one thing clear right now. If we're going to do this, let's do it, and let's be professional and courteous to one another. We're going to get nowhere if you two can't agree to work together." Linda and Sebastian exchange a look. "Do we have a deal?" Dale asks. Everyone nods. Good. The remainder of this book will describe how the DexCo management team explore answers to the vexing questions posed by the simultaneous demands of SOX, COBIT, internal controls, business agility, and operational management.

Summary

The DexCo management team goes off site for a retreat to discuss the Sarbanes Oxley matter. At this retreat, CEO Jim Wilde and COO Dale Steyer hear an analysis of DexCo's business that takes into account internal controls, business process, and IT. The three subjects run together, the CFO and CIO explain, because the IT systems are used to run business processes that are the subject of internal controls.

Using an example of a simple order for circuit boards, the team learns how the internal control for ensuring accurate in-period expense reporting relies on proper use of the ERP and financial IT systems. A set of internal control problems emerge from the analysis, which have a bearing on DexCo's ability to be compliant under SOX.

At one level, differences between the official, stated internal controls and business process for purchasing and the actual process used informally by DexCo's staff could result in the company certifying financial statements that are not accurate. Furthermore, the plan to change virtually everything about DexCo's business, as set out by the new CEO, will wreak havoc on already overburdened IT and accounting departments. And, even if they had the resources to enact all the changes, the pace of IT work is simply too slow for it to keep pace with the rapidly cycling business moves anticipated by Jim Wilde. It appears that DexCo will be permanently out of control or out of compliance. The choice seems to be agility or compliance, although the team wants both agility and compliance. The team resolves to look deeply into the matter and try to arrive at a solution.

CHAPTER 5

Commit to COBIT?

Dale Steyer throws a log into the cast iron stove that heats the barn on Jim Wilde's ranch. He has summoned Sebastian Harris and Linda Fuller to a meeting in the barn as a way to get them to focus on SOX without the formality of an official meeting and the tension that it might engender. He also wants to get them away from Jim Wilde for a little while so they can speak more freely without feeling as if they have to perform for the boss. Besides, Jim is not available for the meeting anyway. He's busy taking his prized bull to a nearby ranch to breed him with his neighbor's cows.

Dale removes a scrap of paper from his pocket and says, "Okay, I want to play a game. It's called, 'Name that Company.'" He reads, "'Blank company assessed its internal control system as of December 31, 1999, 1998, and 1997, relative to current standards of control criteria. Based upon this assessment, management believes that its system of internal control was adequate during the periods to provide reasonable assurance as to the reliability of financial statements and the protection of assets against unauthorized acquisition, use, or disposition.' Can you name the company that wrote those words in its 2000 annual report?"

Linda and Sebastian are not sure what to say. "It could be anyone," Linda offers.

"Yes," Dale says. "But in this case, it was Enron. Funny, don't you think? It seems almost a cheap shot to look back at Enron's bland assurances that it had assessed its internal control system. Yet, look at what happened. Are we going to suffer the same fate?"

"Not if I can help it," Sebastian says. "That's why I'm pushing COBIT."

"Yes," Linda says. "And I'm the one who's feeling pushed."

"Alright, let's stay on track," Dale says. "We ended our last meeting with a desire to learn more about COBIT. Sebastian, this is your opportunity to tell us what it's all about."

"Thank you," Sebastian says and proceeds to explain his views on IT and SOX. He begins by stating that SOX was enacted to put some teeth into internal controls and corporate governance. The Public Company Accounting Oversight Board (PCAOB), which is responsible for establishing regulations for auditors of public companies, is charged with, among other duties, providing practical details for the enforcement of the Sarbanes Oxley Act.

In 2004, the PCAOB issued a set of rules that were intended to provide some clarity to the specific challenges faced in complying with the Sarbanes Oxley Act and auditing for that compliance. Not surprisingly, one of the most critical aspects of maintaining compliance that the PCAOB identified was the role of information technology in internal controls. As PCAOB #2, as the document is known, comments:

> ". . . information technology general controls over program development, program changes, computer operations, and access to programs and data help ensure that specific controls over the processing of transactions are operating effectively." (PCAOB Standards AS2—as of 2/15/05—paragraph 50)

Yet, as we know, information technology and compliance are often at odds. The cartoon in Figure 5-1 is a great illustration of this point. It's a tug-of-war, with IT on one side and compliance on the other. Yet, with the water full of alligators, we can see that everyone stands to lose if the effort to keep IT and compliance in sync falls apart.

Figure 5-1 IT vs. Compliance—a tug-of-war that nobody wins

This Is a High Stakes Game

"The stakes are high," Sebastian says. "In case you think I'm making this up, let me share with you some data from KPMG's Sarbanes Oxley 404 benchmark study." He shows them Table 5-1, which breaks down the percentage of internal control deficiencies, significant deficiencies, and material weaknesses by category.

Table 5-1   IT Controls as a Percentage of Material Weaknesses, Significant Deficiencies, and Deficiencies (KMPG Benchmark Study)

ESTIMATED PERCENTAGE OF DEFICIENCIES:
*   IT Controls (34%)
*   Revenue (13%)
*   Procure to pay (10%)
*   Fixed assets (10%)

ESTIMATED PERCENTAGE OF SIGNIFICANT DEFICIENCIES:
*   IT Controls (23%)
*   Financial Reporting and Close (14%)
*   Procure to pay (13%)
*   Revenue (12%)

ESTIMATED PERCENTAGE OF MATERIAL WEAKNESSES:
*   IT Controls (27%)
*   Revenue (18%)
*   Taxes (11%)
*   Financial Reporting and Close (10%)

As you can see, IT tops the charts in each case. "If you still don't think this is a big deal," Sebastian adds, "let me tell you what's going on with Goodyear. In 2003, the world's largest tire company determined that it needed to restate its earnings going back to 1998. The adjustments included a decrease in income before taxes of $89.2 million due to problems with account reconciliations, $1.4 million in out-of-period adjustments, and $30.2 million in incorrectly valued state and federal tax valuations. (*CFO Magazine*, November 21, 2003) Goodyear reported that the SEC would be looking into the restatement on an informal basis. In December, 2003, the company reported additional accounting problems and further restatements and indicated that it would delay filing its amended 2002 annual report."

For a multibillion dollar company, this restatement may not seem so major, but the perceptions of problems and challenges to credibility that it caused were quite marked. In February 2004, the SEC upgraded its informal inquiry into Goodyear's restatement to a full-fledged investigation. Between January 20, 2004, and February 23, 2004, the time period in which the company released its official 8K report that detailed the restatement information and informed shareholders that the SEC was going to investigate the causes of the restatement, Goodyear lost $323,840,000 in value, or 18 percent of its market capitalization. (During the same period of time, the Dow Industrials went down 1.8 percent.) Of course, there are many causes of such swings in value. In Goodyear's case, the company was losing money, but it is quite likely that the release of the 8K report was a contributor to the loss in shareholder confidence.

PricewaterhouseCoopers, Goodyear's auditors, reported material weaknesses in internal controls. The culprit? The company's ERP system. As *CFO Magazine* reported, "The restatement was aimed at recording adjustments mainly caused by a 1999 enterprise resource planning (ERP) system implementation and errors in intercompany billing systems." (*CFO Magazine*, August 17, 2005)

"So," Sebastian concludes, "next time an IT executive tells you that it's going to take more time and money than originally planned to implement the ERP system, instead of rolling your eyes and cursing all IT people everywhere, you might think of Goodyear's troubles and consider giving the ERP project the time and space it needs to nail down the business logic and comply with the COBIT control framework." Linda rolls her eyes.

Strong Medicine: COBIT

Sebastian goes on to explain that the Sarbanes Oxley community looks to the IT Governance Institute's Control Objectives for Information and Related Technology (COBIT) as an answer for situations such as Goodyear's, where IT problems can endanger effective internal controls. Let's take a more in-depth look at COBIT and how it can help a company maintain strong internal controls backed up by well-designed, auditable IT systems.

COBIT is an approach to the challenge of making sure that IT can provide the systemic rigor needed for strong internal controls. If you are involved in Sarbanes Oxley compliance, and you are anywhere near IT, I suspect you are going to be hearing a great deal about COBIT, if you have not already. For this reason, I want to go into detail on what COBIT is all about, what it can do for you, and the ways it might affect your ability to get things done in your business.

For starters, let's clarify an important point about COBIT right up front. Although COBIT is the most common and widely accepted set of IT control guidelines, it is not the only such standard. For example, the International Standards Organization (ISO), which facilitates the well-known ISO 9001 credentialing of businesses, also has what is known as the ISO/IEC 17799 Code of Practice for Information Security Management. Nor is COBIT officially validated by the PCAOB or any other government body. COBIT is the unofficial winner of the COSO IT sweepstakes. The reason I mention this is because there is already a fair amount of confusion about how to attain best practices for making IT comply with SOX, and there are people and organizations out there that will tell you that you have to use COBIT, because it is the only way to comply with SOX. Not so.

What is COBIT? COBIT is a standard for IT Governance, which is defined by ITGI and ISACA as the structure that links IT processes, IT resources, and IT information to company strategies and objectives. IT governance integrates and institutionalizes best practices for planning and organizing. COBIT is an IT governance tool.

COBIT is also consistent with COSO. The Sarbanes Oxley Act requires that a public company define a control framework and specifically recommends COSO as that framework for general accounting controls. COBIT is the unofficial control framework for the IT systems that support the COSO controls.

COBIT: Where IT Enables Controls

The premise of COBIT, indeed the premise of this entire book, is that IT is the foundation of controls that enable reliable financial reporting. COBIT advocates five main areas where IT plays this role:

- **Information management and data classification:** There is a saying in management that goes, "You can't manage what you cannot measure." The accountant might say, "You cannot control what you cannot measure." Computers, software, and IT in general are the measuring tools that we use to keep track of the dollars in our businesses. Accounting, ERP, and other software, and the systems that run them, contain the vital data about your company's finances. To provide assurance that an IT system is enforcing internal controls, the system managers must be able to demonstrate that it manages and classifies data in accordance with those specified controls. Although this may seem obvious to you, this concept is not always clear to managers. The $11 billion fraud at WorldCom was essentially a matter of poorly controlled data classification. Expenses were booked as investments, but the systems involved either lacked the controls to catch this malfeasance, or they lacked the control to detect an improper management override, which is a prime lever of fraud.

- **User management:** To have any semblance of control in the IT that supports your financial reporting, you need to know who is using specific systems, at what time, and for what purpose. And, you must be sure that users of systems are authorized to do so, and can be authenticated as the actual people they claim to be. Depending on the level of sensitivity, greater or lesser levels of user management may be required. In a highly sensitive transaction, such as wiring funds from an investment house to a private bank account, the investment house may have numerous controls in place to avert a situation where a single system user might steal, or accidentally lose, a client's money. Typically, more than one system user must each verify and authorize the transaction independently. The system must log the actions of each user for later review in an audit, if that is necessary. To make all of this happen, the system must have a robust user management mechanism, or be linked to a company-wide user management system. In most cases, user management systems, also known as Identity Management or Access Management applications, have the capacity to assign roles to individual users. As a user, your access rights and functional privileges are dictated by the role you are assigned in the user management system. If you are paying attention, you might notice that there needs to be someone managing the user management system. If that person's actions are not controlled, then the whole control system may be impaired.

- **Real-time reporting:** As you have seen in the DexCo case, reporting of transactions within each accounting period is part of the entire internal controls process as outlined in COSO. Now, if you are one of those people who believes that there is no such thing as real-time processing in IT, then I will grant you that computer system operations tend to be unpredictable and indeed somewhat slower than real time. Yes, software processes, especially those occurring between more than one system in a distributed environment are prone to pauses, latency, batching of data in transfers, and buffering. Yet, in terms of internal controls, a well-configured system will usually be able to deliver information in a suitable time frame for financial reporting

- **Transaction thresholds and tolerance levels:** IT systems that enable COSO controls should be able to monitor transactions and alert system managers if a situation occurs that requires investigation. For example, if the DexCo web site booked an individual consumer's order for $50 million worth of monitors, then a well-configured accounting system should be able to flag the transaction as suspicious. Some people refer to this process as an Exception Alert. The causes of the large dollar figure might be a user input error, a computational error, or a fraud. Whatever it is, the internal controls should catch it so the financial reports are not compromised. Yet, like so many other aspects of IT controls, the system managers themselves must be under a control framework of their own, or else there is the potential for them to override the exception alert and either ignore it or hide it from auditors.

- **Data processing integrity and validation:** Goodyear showed how relatively small problems in the calculation of local taxes and asset valuation in an ERP system can cause big problems for the company. You may find this hard to believe, but computer software is highly error-prone if it is not configured correctly. Although the actual processors and logic structure of a program may be the work of legions of Caltech geniuses, the specific, customized setup of an accounting software package is often a team effort involving numerous people who may or may not be under good controls. Without a proper control framework, deployment process, and testing regimen, it is possible for an accounting or ERP system to be set up with errors or fraudulent intent built into the programming functionality. To use a simple example, DexCo has a table of local sales tax rates to charge on its web site. If this table is set up correctly, and updated regularly as required, then the web site's e-commerce engine will always calculate the correct sales tax. If it is set up wrong, or not updated, then DexCo faces a risk in its COSO control objective of collecting and paying the correct sales tax on its web site transactions. Although the actual amount of money involved might be small, as we saw with Goodyear, even a small financial error or restatement can trigger trouble with the SEC and private litigators. To be in control, DexCo needs to establish and enforce a rigorous data integrity and validation process in all its software deployments. This is the essence of COBIT.

Components of COBIT

COBIT is a framework that puts into action the tenets of IT governance outlined previously. COBIT can be a little confusing, however, because it consists of several overlapping sets of guidelines. If you listen with the untrained ear to a COBIT practitioner, you will hear that COBIT has 300 generic control statements, 34 Processes, 34 Management Guidelines, 6 Maturity Model stages, and 318 Critical Success Factors. So, if you can do seventh-grade math, you might conclude that COBIT has 6.6 million potential configurations for your IT governance setup. Not quite.

The best way to understand COBIT is to start with the framework's four primary domains for IT Governance: Planning and Organization (PO), Acquisition and Implementation (AI), Delivery and Support (DS), Monitoring (M). Figure 5-2 provides an overview of the COBIT domains and the processes that fall under each domain.

Each domain comprises several processes. For example, the Planning and Organization Domain consists of 11 processes, including Define a Strategic IT Plan, Assess Risks, and others. Each process has a number, preceded by a prefix that indicates the domain to which it belongs. Thus, PO 10 is Planning and Organization #10 or Manage Projects. In some COBIT literature, you will see references to PO10 or M3—that is what the authors are talking about.

COBIT

DOMAIN **PO** Planning & Organization	DOMAIN **AI** Acquisition & Implementation	DOMAIN **DS** Delivery & Support	DOMAIN **M** Monitoring
PO 1 - Define a Strategic IT Plan Critical Success Factors Key Goal Indicators Key Performance Indicators Maturity Models	**AI 1** - Identify Automated Solutions Critical Success Factors Key Goal Indicators Key Performance Indicators Maturity Models	**DS 1** - Define and Manage Service Levels Critical Success Factors Key Goal Indicators Key Performance Indicators Maturity Models	**M 1** - Monitor the Processes Critical Success Factors Key Goal Indicators Key Performance Indicators Maturity Models
PO 2 - Define the Information Architecture Critical Success Factors Key Goal Indicators Key Performance Indicators Maturity Models	**AI 2** - Acqure and Maintain Application Software Critical Success Factors Key Goal Indicators Key Performance Indicators Maturity Models	**DS 2** - Manage Third-Party Services Critical Success Factors Key Goal Indicators Key Performance Indicators Maturity Models	**M 2** - Assess Internal Control Adequacy Critical Success Factors Key Goal Indicators Key Performance Indicators Maturity Models
PO 3 - Determine the Technological Direction Critical Success Factors Key Goal Indicators Key Performance Indicators Maturity Models	**AI 3** - Acquire and Maintain Technology Infrastructure Critical Success Factors Key Goal Indicators Key Performance Indicators Maturity Models	**DS 3** - Manage Performance and Capacity Critical Success Factors Key Goal Indicators Key Performance Indicators Maturity Models	**M 3** - Obtain Independent Assurance Critical Success Factors Key Goal Indicators Key Performance Indicators Maturity Models
PO 4 - Define the IT Organization and Relationships Critical Success Factors Key Goal Indicators Key Performance Indicators Maturity Models	**AI 4** - Develop and Maintain Procedures Critical Success Factors Key Goal Indicators Key Performance Indicators Maturity Models	**DS 4** - Ensure Continuous Service Critical Success Factors Key Goal Indicators Key Performance Indicators Maturity Models	**M 4** - Provide for Independent Audit Critical Success Factors Key Goal Indicators Key Performance Indicators Maturity Models
PO 5 - Manage the IT Investment Critical Success Factors Key Goal Indicators Key Performance Indicators Maturity Models	**AI 5** - Install and Accredit Systems Critical Success Factors Key Goal Indicators Key Performance Indicators Maturity Models	**DS 5** - Ensure System Security Critical Success Factors Key Goal Indicators Key Performance Indicators Maturity Models	
PO 6 - Communicate Management Aims/Direction Critical Success Factors Key Goal Indicators Key Performance Indicators Maturity Models	**AI 6** - Manage Changes Critical Success Factors Key Goal Indicators Key Performance Indicators Maturity Models	**DS 6** - Identify and Allocate Costs Critical Success Factors Key Goal Indicators Key Performance Indicators Maturity Models	
PO 7 - Manage Human Resources Critical Success Factors Key Goal Indicators Key Performance Indicators Maturity Models		**DS 7** - Educate and Train Users Critical Success Factors Key Goal Indicators Key Performance Indicators Maturity Models	
PO 8 - Ensure Compliance w/ External Requirements Critical Success Factors Key Goal Indicators Key Performance Indicators Maturity Models		**DS 8** - Assist and Advise Customers Critical Success Factors Key Goal Indicators Key Performance Indicators Maturity Models	
PO 9 - Assess Risks Critical Success Factors Key Goal Indicators Key Performance Indicators Maturity Models		**DS 9** - Manage the Configuration Critical Success Factors Key Goal Indicators Key Performance Indicators Maturity Models	
PO 10 - Manage Projects Critical Success Factors Key Goal Indicators Key Performance Indicators Maturity Models		**DS 10** - Manage Problems and Incidents Critical Success Factors Key Goal Indicators Key Performance Indicators Maturity Models	
PO 11 - Manage Quality Critical Success Factors Key Goal Indicators Key Performance Indicators Maturity Models		**DS 11** - Manage Data Critical Success Factors Key Goal Indicators Key Performance Indicators Maturity Models	
		DS 12 - Manage Facilities Critical Success Factors Key Goal Indicators Key Performance Indicators Maturity Models	
		DS 13 - Manage Operations Critical Success Factors Key Goal Indicators Key Performance Indicators Maturity Models	

Figure 5-2   Overview of the 4 COBIT Domains and 34 processes

Each COBIT process, in turn, is composed of a distinct set of control statements, critical success factors, key performance indicators, key goal indicators, and maturity models. Collectively these are known as the Management Guidelines for each process. From my travels in the land of SOX and IT, I perceive that there is some confusion about all of these various guidelines, success factors, performance indicators, and maturity models. My intent with Figure 5-2 is to show how they are related. Each process has its own dedicated set of related Management Guidelines, and so on. Overall, the official documents that set out the details of these processes are more than 300 pages long.

COBIT is a framework of suggested guidelines, not a required checklist of activity. For this reason, each company that applies COBIT to its IT operations typically selects the most relevant processes and subsidiary key performance indicators and control measures for each of those processes. Indeed, you could go stark raving mad if you had to apply each of the processes and its related components to all your systems. ISACA conducted a survey of its members and identified the 15 most commonly used COBIT processes. Table 5-2 shows the following top COBIT processes the survey reported.

Table 5-2   Most Commonly Used COBIT Control Objectives (ITGI and ISACA Survey)

COBIT CONTROL OBJECTIVE	DESCRIPTION
PO 1	Define a strategic IT plan
PO 3	Determine the technological direction
PO 5	Manage the IT investment
PO 9	Assess risks
PO 10	Manage projects
AI 1	Identify solutions
AI 2	Acquire and maintain applications software
AI 5	Install and accredit systems
AI 6	Manage changes
DS 1	Define service levels
DS 4	Ensure continuous service
DS 5	Ensure system security
DS 10	Manage problems and incidents
DS 11	Manage data
M 1	Monitor the processes

COBIT and Sarbanes Oxley

ISACA and ITGI don't assume that the IT department of a public company will have an intuitive sense of how to apply COBIT to achieve COSO control objectives. For this reason, there are several ways to map COBIT to COSO. Table 5-3 shows how the Institute of Internal Auditors maps the two control frameworks. (IT Audit Vol 7, October 1, 2004)

In an interesting contrast to the IIA COSO/COBIT mapping shown in Table 5-1, Table 5-4 shows the most commonly used COBIT controls for the creation of internal controls for Sarbanes Oxley Compliance according to the ISACA and ITGI survey of its members.

Table 5-3   The IIA's Mapping of COSO to COBIT

COSO INTERNAL CONTROL COMPONENTS	COBIT DOMAINS (WITH SAMPLE CONTROL OBJECTIVES RELEVANT TO SARBANES OXLEY)
Control Environment	Planning and Organization (PO)
	PO 4.2: Organizational placement of the IT function
	PO 6.1: Positive information control environment
	PO 6.2: Management's responsibility for policies
Risk Assessment	Planning and Organization (PO)
	PO 9.0: Assess risks
Control Activities	Acquisition and Implementation (AI)
	AI 1.4: Third-party service requirements
	AI 6.0–6.8: Manage changes
	Delivery and Support (DS)
	DS 5.0–5.21: Ensure System Security
	DS 11.0–11.30: Manage Data
Information and Communication	Planning and Organization (PO)
	PO 6.0–6.11: Communicate management aims and direction
Monitoring	Monitoring (M)
	M 2.0–2.4: Assess internal Control

Table 5-4   Most Commonly Used COBIT Control Objectives for Sarbanes Oxley Controls

COBIT CONTROL OBJECTIVE HEADING	DESCRIPTION OF SPECIFIC CONTROL OBJECTIVE IN USE
AI 6	Manage changes
DS 4	Manage third-party services
DS 5	Ensure system security
DS 10	Manage problems and incidents
DS 11	Manage data
M 1	Monitor the processes

It is worth noting that the IIA's mapping of COSO to COBIT includes four Planning and Organization (PO) COBIT control objectives, while the list drawn from actual IT users, shown in Table 5-4, has none. For example, do you see PO 9, Manage Risk, contained in the preceding list? PO 9 does make it onto the top 15 COBIT control objectives in general use. This hints to me that a lot of day-to-day operational IT people are not involved in risk assessment, at least not on a level of including it in their COBIT programs. (Or perhaps, they are not consulted.) This is a mistake, in my opinion. Another possible conclusion to be drawn from the discrepancy between these two charts is that IT people may not be consulted about some important factors in their role in the controls process, such as Organization Placement of the IT Function.

COBIT in Depth: The DS 11 Process

I will explore just one process, DS 11, in detail to show you how COBIT would work at DexCo or any other organization. Note that DS 11 appears on all of the previous lists—COBIT to COSO mapping, top COBIT processes in use, and most common COBIT processes used with Sarbanes Oxley. Managing the integrity of data is a core concept that links COBIT with COSO. Indeed, accurate business data is a prerequisite for accurate financial reporting. While it may be possible to have problems in financial reporting even with good underlying data, it is inevitable that reporting trouble will result if the supporting data is compromised or suspicious. To illustrate what COBIT involves, let's take an in-depth look at DS 11 and see what it might take to make a company comply with COBIT.

Control Statements

The IT Governance Institute gives Delivery and Support process 11 (DS 11) the name Manage Data. The Control Objective associated with the DS 11 process is defined as "Control over the IT process Manage Data with the business goal of ensuring that data remains complete, accurate and valid during its input, update, and storage." The ITGI document continues with its basic definition of DS 11 by stating: ". . . [DS 11] ensures delivery of information to the business that addresses the required *Information Criteria* and is measured by *Key Goal Indicators*" (IT Governance Institute COBIT Control Objectives).

The Information Criteria are defined as follows: effectiveness, efficiency, confidentiality, *integrity*, availability, compliance, *reliability*. The two italicized criteria are considered Primary by the ITGI for effective implementation of the DS 11 process. Thus, to make your systems compliant with COBIT DS 11, you need to develop ways to ensure that the data in your system has integrity and is reliably available. Making sure that your data has integrity involves designing your system in a way that avoids permitting it to accept faulty data or allow modification of data once it has been entered into the system.

For example, if DexCo's financial system stores Visa card numbers, then DS 11 would require the company to build a card validation function into the system. If someone entered a 10-digit Visa card number, the system should reject the data input because Visa card numbers are supposed to have 16 digits. The system should also check to make sure that the expiration data is later than the current date, and so on. In terms of modification, the system should provide a way to lock the database so that no user except an authorized administrator could possibly go in and change someone's credit card number, rendering it unusable. If the system lacks these functions, then it is at risk for acquiring and passing along bad data. The old phrase, "garbage in, garbage out," refers to data integrity.

Because COBIT is a complete framework, it doesn't just tell you to ensure that your data has integrity. Making that statement and not providing any specifics for backing it up or measuring the effectiveness of the data integrity efforts would be worthless. To provide you with the tools to ensure the integrity of your data, the DS 11 process also lays out a number of ways to measure the effectiveness of your DS 11 efforts. These are known as the DS 11 Critical Success Factors, Key Goal Indicators, Key Performance Indicators, and Maturity Models.

Key Goal Indicators

The DS 11 Key Goal Indicators, contained in Table 5-5, are a set of guidelines for measuring the success of a DS 11 implementation. They answer the basic question, "How can you tell if you are doing DS 11 right?" If you are doing DS 11 correctly, you observe, for example, "a measured reduction in the data preparation process and tasks," or "a measured decrease in corrective activities and exposure to data corruption."

Table 5-5 DS 11 Key Goal Indicators Provide Guidelines for Measuring the Effectiveness of a DS 11 Implementation

DS 11 KEY GOAL INDICATORS
A measured reduction in the data preparation process and tasks
A measured improvement in the quality, timeline, and availability of data
A measured increase in customer satisfaction and reliance upon data
A measured decrease in corrective activities and exposure to data corruption
Reduced number of data defects, such as redundancy, duplication, and inconsistency
No legal or regulatory data compliance conflicts

What do these Key Goal Indicators actually mean, though? Although we might have an intuitive sense of what "a measured decrease in corrective activities and exposure to data corruption" might look like, COBIT is telling us that DS 11 requires a specific measurement of corrective activities and exposure to data corruption. That is, IT management must measure corrective activities and exposure to corruption. The specifics of that measurement process are left open, but DS 11 makes clear that there must be some kind of tracking system in place that keeps tabs on the number of times a month that system users must correct data entries, or the percentage of data entries that must be corrected, and so on. The DS 11 Key Performance Indicators expand on this measurement process.

Key Performance Indicators

DS 11's Key Performance Indicators give COBIT users some specific measurements to enact to gain compliance with the DS 11 Control Objective.

Table 5-6 lists the DS 11 Key Performance Indicators. They provide a high level of specificity for measuring data integrity and reliability, the two primary Information Criteria indicated for the DS 11 process. While the Key Goal Indicators might suggest that you set a goal for your systems to create a measured improvement in the quality of data, the Key Performance Indicators give you the actual way to set up the metrics for such a measure improvement.

Table 5-6   DS 11 Key Performance Indicators

DS 11 KEY PERFORMANCE INDICATORS
Percent of data input errors
Percent of updates reprocessed
Percent of automated data integrity checks incorporated into the applications
Percent of errors prevented at the point of entry
Number of automated data integrity checks run independently of the applications
Time interval between error occurrence, detection, and correction
Reduced data output problems
Reduced time for recovery of archived data

If DexCo were to attempt DS 11, it might set up a chart such as the one shown in Table 5-7, which puts Key Performance Indicators to work in the realization of a Key Goal Indicators. Table 5-7 is the IT equivalent of New York Mayor Ed Koch, who used to ask voters, "How'm I doin'?" Table 5-7 is a scorecard by which DexCo can measure the results of its attempt to implement DS 11. Going line by line, management can look at the specific results of each measurement process. In some cases, the company is doing well. In others, work is required to keep the numbers trending in the right direction.

Table 5-7   Measurement Results for DS 11 Key Goal Indicators

KEY GOAL INDICATOR	Q1 RESULT	Q2 RESULT	DELTA
Percent of data input errors	5.00%	4.00%	20.00%
Percent of updates reprocessed	2.00%	3.00%	−50.00%
Percent of automated data integrity checks incorporated into the applications	10.00%	15.00%	−50.00%
Percent of errors prevented at the point of entry	3.00%	4.00%	−33.33%
Number of automated data integrity checks run independently of the applications	5.00	7.00	40.00%
Time interval between error occurrence, detection, and correction	1.00	2.00	100.00%
Reduced data output problems	0.05	0.04	20.00%
Reduced time for recovery of archived data	0.05	0.04	20.00%

The example shown in Table 5-7 is purely hypothetical. DexCo has not actually measured itself. If they were to go ahead, however, it would be necessary to think carefully about the measurement process and criteria involved. Unfortunately, people often take advantage of situations where they can give themselves a high score on a test if they have too much control over the data used for the evaluation. Ideally, the measurements should be automated and objective, rather than manually gathered and based on subjective criteria.

Looking at the Key Goal Indicators and Key Performance Indicators side by side, however, you can see that there is some overlap between the two sets of guidelines. This is by design. The creators of the COBIT framework understand that one cannot do absolutely everything that is called for in COBIT. Instead, the ITGI has outlined a number of comparable approaches with the idea that perhaps one or more will speak to the needs of your business.

For example, DexCo's systems might have a built-in function that creates a report of time intervals between error occurrence and detection, which is one of the Key Performance Indicators. The system you use at your business might not have that capability, but it might be able to report on the percent of errors detected at the point of entry.

Critical Success Factors

COBIT also spells out a set of Critical Success Factors for DS 11, which are shown in Table 5-8. Together with the Key Goal Indicators and Key Performance Indicators, the Critical Success Factors lay down a series of steps that an IT organization must take to manage its data to ensure integrity of that data. These three sets of guides, if followed, give the IT organization a clear path to follow in data management. Taken together, they essentially say, "Here are the specific processes that your data management practice should comprise; here are the specific goals you should try to attain; and, here are the specific ways that you can should measure your results."

Table 5-8   DS 11 Critical Success Factors

DS 11 CRITICAL SUCCESS FACTORS
Data entry requirements are clearly stated, enforced, and supported by automated techniques at all levels, including database and file interfaces.
The responsibilities for data ownership and integrity requirements are clearly stated and accepted throughout the organization.
Data accuracy and standards are clearly communicated and incorporated into the training and personnel development processes.
Data entry standards and correction are enforced at the point of entry.
Data input, processing, and output integrity standards are formalized and enforced.

Table 5-8 *(continued)*

DS 11 CRITICAL SUCCESS FACTORS
Data is held in suspense until corrected.
Effective detection methods are used to enforce data accuracy and integrity standards.
Effective translation of data across platforms is implemented without loss of integrity or reliability to meet changing business demands.
There is a decreased reliance on manual data input and rekeying processes.
Efficient and flexible solutions promote effective use of data.
Data is archived and protected and is readily available when needed for recovery.

If you read Table 5-8 and gulped, thinking, "My IT organization follows maybe two out of those 11 Critical Success Factors," you are probably far from alone. Reading the Critical Success Factors reminds me a little of paging through the Boy Scout Handbook in the early 1970s and learning that I needed to be respectful to adults at all times, never let the phone ring more than twice before answering it politely, calling my teacher "sir," and so on. In what universe was that supposed to be happening? In an ideal universe, of course, the cosmically perfect place where all companies strive to attain the Critical Success Factors of COBIT.

Yet, there is a profound power to these Critical Success Factors. They tell us how far we are from hitting the high mark of compliance. Within each of the 11 factors is an implicit risk of not complying. For example, take "Data entry standards and correction are enforced at the point of entry." What does that mean? At DexCo, there are dozens of customer service representatives who process incoming orders at call centers. Each of these CSRs has the ability and responsibility for inputting customer order entry data into DexCo's systems. Each time a CSR types in a customer's name or credit card number and hits enter, he or she has just made an entry into the database. If DexCo wants to follow COBIT DS 11, how does it ensure that its CSRs follow the data entry standards? Should DexCo try to build data validation into the entry process and data entry interfaces, which might make interface modification and upgrading more costly, or should the company attempt to train its employees in correct data entry standards and hope that the lessons stick? Given that some of DexCo's CSRs actually work for third-party vendors, the question becomes even more complicated.

However the question is answered, what is clear is that DS 11 provides a workable set of tools that would help DexCo evaluate whether or not it was complying with DS 11 and if not, how to measure its success or failure in that effort.

Maturity Models

The final Management Guideline provided by the ITGI for implementing COBIT processes is the ranking of readiness known as the Maturity Model. Each of the 34 COBIT processes has its own uniquely defined six-point Maturity Model that is designed to inform IT management about how they are doing with respect to the completeness of the process's implementation. The Maturity Model is different from the Key Goal Criteria. Although the Key Goal Criteria measure the performance of a COBIT process such as DS 11, the Maturity Model is a scorecard for the state of the process itself. Table 5-9 shows the Maturity Model for DS 11.

Table 5-9   DS 11 Critical Success Factors

SCORE	TITLE	DESCRIPTION
0	Non-Existent	Data is not recognized as a corporate resource and asset. There is no assigned data ownership or individual accountability for data integrity and reliability. Data quality and security is poor or non-existent.
1	Initial/Ad Hoc	The organization recognizes a need for accurate data. Some methods are developed at the individual level to prevent and detect data input, processing, and output errors. The process of error identification and correction is dependent upon manual activities of individuals, and rules and requirements are not passed on as staff movement and turnover occur. Management assumes that data is accurate because a computer is involved in the process. Data integrity and security are not management requirements and, if security exists, it is administered by the information services function.
2	Repeatable but intuitive	The awareness of the need for data accuracy and maintaining integrity is prevalent throughout the organization. Data ownership begins to occur, but at a department or group level. The rules and requirements are documented by key individuals and are not consistent across the organization and platforms. Data is in the custody of the information services function and the rules and definitions are driven by the IT requirements. Data security and integrity are primarily the information services function's responsibilities, with minor departmental involvement.

Table 5-9   *(continued)*

SCORE	TITLE	DESCRIPTION
3	Defined process	The need for data integrity within and across the organization is understood and accepted. Data input, processing and output standards have been formalized and are enforced. The process of error identification and correction is automated. Data ownership is assigned, and integrity and security are controlled by the responsible party. Automated techniques are utilized to prevent and detect errors and inconsistencies. Data definitions, rules and requirements are clearly documented by a database administration function. Data becomes consistent across platforms and throughout the organization. The information services function takes on a custodian role, while data integrity controls shifts to the data owner. Management relies on reports and analyses for decision and future planning.
4	Managed and Measurable	Data is defined as a corporate resource and asset, as management demands more decision support and profitability reporting. The responsibility for data quality is clearly defined, assigned, and communicated within the organization. Standardized methods are documented, maintained, and used to control data quality. Rules are enforced and data is consistent across platforms and business units. Data quality is measured and customer satisfaction with information is monitored. Management reporting takes on a strategic value in assessing customers, trends, and product evaluations. Integrity of data becomes a significant factor, with data security recognized as a control requirement. A formal, organization-wide data administration function has been established, with the resources and authority to enforce data standardization.
5	Optimized	Data management is a mature, integrated, and cross-functional process that has a clearly defined and well-understood goal of delivering quality information to the user, with clearly defined integrity, availability and reliability criteria. The organization actively manages data, information and knowledge as corporate resources and assets, with the objective of maximizing business value. The corporate culture stresses the importance of high-quality data that needs to be protected and treated as a key component of intellectual capital. The ownership of data is a strategic responsibility with all requirements, rules, regulations, and considerations clearly documented, maintained, and communicated.

The Maturity Model provides IT managers and business managers who rely on the IT department (also described by ITGI as *information services*) with a way to assess how well they are doing in complying with the COBIT standards. For anyone who has ever attended an IT conference, some of the descriptions contained in the Maturity Model smack of idealism—"The corporate culture stresses the importance of high quality data . . ."—and that can be a little bit groan-inducing. However, the Maturity Model does set out a clear guide to evaluating how well you are doing with COBIT and ways in which you can set your sights higher to achieve better quality IT Operations.

Implications of DS 11's Maturity Scale

Sebastian pauses for a breath. Linda and Dale are looking at him in a state of shock. This is a lot more complex than they could ever have dreamed. Sebastian smiles, "If you're feeling a little overwhelmed by all the intense detail and strict requirements for DS 11—and remember, it's just one of 34 COBIT processes—you are probably not alone. In fact, you may just be human. Remember, COBIT is a standard that consists of many suggested objectives, success factors, and measurement criteria. No one in their right mind would imagine that an IT manager would attempt to do all of COBIT."

"In my experience," Sebastian continues, "most companies hover around a stage two or three maturity level for data management and most other IT functions. It is quite rare to see a system, and its attendant users, administrators, and business unit owners reach a level of five in maturity. As is often the case with this kind of thing, the organizations that can attain that level of maturity are the ones with the most static business models, such as banks."

Luckily for all of us, the PCAOB has suggested that public companies attempt to reach a level five maturity only for selected COBIT processes that apply to highly critical financial reporting functions. This makes sense. It would be truly insane to try to attempt to reach a level five on all IT operations at the same time. There would be little time or money to accomplish much else at the business in that scenario. In the next chapter, I will explore in more detail the actual workaday implementation of COBIT and what it can mean for a company.

Data integrity and retention is a very serious issue, however, even without Sarbanes Oxley or COSO. Morgan Stanley, the respected Wall Street firm, recently lost a $604 million lawsuit brought by Ronald Perelman. Here is *Forbes Magazine*'s comment on why the case did not go their way:

Morgan Stanley lost its case with Perelman after angering the Florida state court judge presiding in the case, who punished it for dawdling in turning over documents. What happened is Morgan Stanley counsel first said it had found everything, then turned around and said there was more. It later found still more computer tapes of e-mails.

The company blamed faulty technology for leading to the failure to find and turn over all the requested documents as quickly as possible. But the judge ruled that the pattern meant it was "inescapable" that Morgan Stanley "sought to thwart discovery." (Forbes Magazine 5.17.05)

"Oops!" Sebastian says, slapping his forehead playfully. "Next time we're in a budget argument about the high cost of data archiving, I'm going to say, 'Well, I'm sure we can get a system for less than 600 million bucks.'"

Dale laughs. Linda doesn't. She looks like she wants a martini, even though it's still early in the morning. "Okay," Dale says. "I get it. But we need to look at this from the perspective of where we are now. What can we reasonably do about COBIT? We can't do it all, certainly not now."

Summary

This chapter introduces the subject of COBIT, which is a framework for helping IT organizations get in compliance with Sarbanes Oxley. COBIT, which stands for Control Objectives for Information and Related Technology, was created by the IT Governance Institute. With COBIT, an IT organization is supposed to evaluate itself and its systems according to a set of criteria, including a maturity model, a scale that measures the level of implementation of control-oriented practices and policies. COBIT also specifies key performance indicators, key goal indicators, and key success factors for IT systems and areas of work.

COBIT's measurement criteria help an IT organization assess how effectively its systems are keeping up with internal controls. In addition, COBIT provides a defined path for improving the level of the IT organization's adherence to controls. COBIT maps to COSO in several areas. For example, COSO's Control Environment maps to COBIT's Planning and Organization guidelines. The former relates to a company's overall control environment (tone at the top) while the latter deals specifically with how the IT organization is set up to support internal controls.

COBIT is quite extensive and complex, but it is not meant to be applied in its totality. Rather, an IT organization is supposed to select the most relevant COBIT components, such as data security or monitoring, and work through a process of assessing its systems according to the key performance indicators specified for each component. Sebastian Harris would like to undertake an exhaustive COBIT effort, while Dale Steyer wants to understand how DexCo can do a limited COBIT process and improve its IT controls without expending too much time and money.

COBIT for Mere Mortals

At the end of Chapter 5, Dale Steyer, Linda Fuller, and Sebastian Harris were trying to figure out if they could get involved with COBIT but not make it the object of an obsessive quest that would distract them from reality. Perhaps you finished the last chapter feeling as if your organization would never be able to attain the level of IT performance necessary to comply with COBIT, and therefore COSO as well. Take heart. You are far from alone. This chapter will look at how you can work through the COBIT processes as a mere mortal—that is, as a person in a real organization with real budgets, politics, and requirements.

The following discussion, introduced by Dale Steyer, is based on the work of Dr. Don Sanders, a COBIT consultant. Dale has taken it upon himself to investigate a way to begin to do COBIT but remain practical and focused on immediate business concerns.

The 80/20 Heat Map

Don Sanders is a COBIT consultant and author of *The COBIT SOX Solution*. He has worked with many large companies. Don's background, which combines considerable experience with continuous improvement as well as COBIT and IT, gives him a unique perspective on the interplay between business and technology drivers of compliance.

Don says, "I think the problem with COBIT starts when people see the 34 management guidelines. They ask, do I need all 34 to be at a level 5 maturity on all of them? That's a lot of wasted time and effort. I recommend the use of the 80-20 principle—Nail down 20 percent of your most critical controls and you've got 80 percent of your overall control of key processes. Focus on the 20 percent that's going to give you 80 percent return, and then move on to the others."

In addition to being sound, pragmatic advice, Don's approach also reflects the view of the PCAOB. The PCAOB recommends that public companies evaluate their requirements for internal controls and focus the bulk of their compliance efforts on those controls that most materially affect financial reporting. Don refers to this process as "building a heat map"—creating a matrix of the controls that are the hottest in terms of potential impact on financial reporting. Then put your COBIT efforts into those controls.

As Don says, "You go through the heat map and you identify your areas of high risk. In compliance terms, you have two audiences—the CIO and the CFO. CFOs are worried about money and the significant cost of compliance. CIOs are wondering how they can get their normal work done plus ensure compliance. So you approach the CFO and say, 'How do we save money?' To the CIO, you ask, 'How can we save time?' You ask both, 'How can you get the best results?' The answer is let's do our 80/20 process. Let's actually identify those things where the highest opportunity for fraudulent practices or material errors occur in terms of IT, and then, let's go to COBIT practices and say, all right, what are some of the practices that we can now implement that will prevent this from occurring?"

COBIT Implementation

How do you create an 80/20 heat map? It's a subjective process, but as Don notes, it helps to work with those who understand the situation best. "My concept is that nobody knows the system better than the people who work in the system," Don says. "You don't want to come in and say, 'All right. Here's a one-size-fits-all system.' You want to come in and say, 'All right. Here are guidelines, and this is what a control is, and this is what a test is for your control' because a lot of times, what I find is that programmers, who are very creative and focused on elegant solutions, don't want to do tests; they don't want to do controls; they just want to write code, so controls are not a concept that they're either familiar or happy with."

Finding the Hot Areas for COBIT

Finding the controls that are most critical to fraud and error is more art than science, at least partly a matter of "knowing it when you see it." If you look at a set of internal controls, one way to evaluate whether it should be on your 20 percent of controls that deserve attention is to ask yourself what the material impact of a breakdown in that control would be for the company's financial reports. That is, after all, the core goal of COSO, COBIT, and SOX. (Quick accounting digression—when we talk about a financial result or control being *material*, we mean that it is large enough to make a real difference in the company's bottom line. For DexCo, a $10 error or discrepancy in a transaction would not be material. A $10,000 error might be material if it were part of a pattern of control problems, and a $1,000,000 error or discrepancy would certainly be material.) What is going to happen to financial statements and SEC filings if this or that control is absolutely ineffective? If it seems that a materially significant difference would occur in the financials, then that control needs attention.

To build a heat map for DexCo and try to find the key controls that need attention for COBIT, we can begin by listing the control areas and rank their materiality. The scorecard shown in Table 6-1 arrives at a heat score for each major transaction area—in this case, the inbound side of the business, or revenue. DexCo would also need to do a scorecard for outbound transactions or purchasing.

Table 6-1 is coarse grained. It looks at only big chunks of the financial reporting process. That is by design. The intent of the exercise is to identify the transaction areas that are most material and thus most deserving of our attention under the concept of the 80/20 heat map. This scorecard is not an official PCAOB document. I developed it in order to combine two aspects of materiality for COBIT. My goal is to show which transaction areas have the greatest potential to cause problems in control based on a set of factors, including the size of the transaction area in relation to the overall business, but also the vulnerability of the underlying IT systems to control problems.

Table 6-1 Coarse-Grained Scorecard for Evaluating Which Transaction Areas at DexCo Are Material to Financial Reporting and Also Vulnerable to Systemic Control Problems

TRANSACTION AREA	PERCENTAGE OF REVENUE	PERCENTAGE OF REVENUE TRANSACTIONS	NUMBER OF IT SUB-SYSTEMS	AGE OF SYSTEM (YEARS)	NUMBER OF SYSTEM USERS	SCORE ("HEAT")
(Product of All Factors)						
Retail point of sale	7%	20%	3	10	1000	**420**
Retail web site	6%	30%	3	3	100	16
OEM sales	20%	20%	3	7	50	42
Wholesale sales	68%	30%	3	10	50	306

You might wonder why I recommend measuring the number of system users, the number of subsystems involved, and the age of the system. I recommend using these factors as measurement tools because I have found that the risk of control problems rises with the number of users on the system, the interdependence of multiple subsystems, and the age of the system. The more people are using a system, the greater the risk that some or all of them will be poorly trained. This is an intuitive fact of business life, although I am sure many companies might claim otherwise. Similarly, the more systems that need to be cobbled together in a distributed computing environment, the greater the risk for control breakdowns. And, the older the system, the more likely it is that the system will have been updated without proper retraining or truly thorough control testing.

Thus, even though retail point of sale (POS) is only 7 percent of DexCo's revenue, the large number of system users, the age of the system, and the number of actual transactions give it a lot of COBIT heat. (Note that 20 percent of DexCo's transactions are retail POS, but only 7 percent of its revenue in dollars). Retail POS at DexCo is a situation where a large number of people are using an out-of-date system for a large proportion of the company's revenue transactions. The potential for a material error or fraud is probably bigger than it might be for OEM sales, even though OEM sales are a bigger slice of the revenue pie. With OEM sales, fewer users are operating a newer system. Of course, this may not mean that OEM sales are free from problems. What this means is that we should probably pay more attention to the COBIT issues with retail POS because it appears to carry a higher risk of problems, and thus deserves more heat on our heat map. We're going to take a deep dive into COBIT implementation for DexCo's POS revenue transactions.

Deep Dive—Maturity of COBIT in a Hot Area

Now that we have established a potentially hot area to work in with COBIT—the retail POS revenue transactions—let's take a look at how that area rates in terms of COBIT maturity. We will rate the maturity models for each of the relevant COBIT processes that map to the COSO framework's control activities. Table 6-2 shows the rating of the maturity models and notes the gaps between the current maturity of the COBIT process and the desired maturity, which we will define as a level 4. Level 5 would be optimal but we are dealing with such mere mortals as ourselves here and level 5 is just a little too much for most of us at this time. Don Sanders remarks that it is often difficult to cost justify level 5 maturity.

Table 6-2 Rating of COBIT Maturity Model for Each of the Four Key COBIT Processes As They Relate to DexCo's Retail POS Revenue Transactions

COBIT PROCESS	AI 1	AI 6	DS 5	DS 11
Definition and control statements	Identify automated solutions. Control over IT process. Identify automated solutions with the business goal of ensuring an effective and efficient approach to satisfy the user requirements.	Manage changes. Control the IT process. Manage changes with the business goal of minimizing the likelihood of disruption, unauthorized alterations, and errors.	Ensure systems security. Control the IT process. Ensure systems security with the business goal of safeguarding information against unauthorized use, disclosure or modification, damage, or loss.	Manage data. Control the IT process. Manage data with the business goal of ensuring that data remains complete, accurate, and valid during its input, update, and storage.
Rating of DexCo's maturity for this COBIT process	Repeatable but intuitive. There is no formally defined acquisition methodology, but requirements tend to be defined in a similar way across the business practices within IT. Solutions are identified informally based on the internal experience of the IT function. The success of each project depends on the expertise of a few key IT individuals and the quality of documentation and decision making varies considerably.	Defined process. There is a defined formal change management process in place, including categorization, prioritization, emergency procedures, change authorization, and release management, but compliance is not enforced. The defined process is not always seen as suitable or practical and as a result, workarounds take place and processes are bypassed. Errors are likely to occur and unauthorized changes will occasionally occur. The analysis of the impact of IT changes on business operations is becoming formalized, to support planned rollouts of new applications and technologies.	Initial/Ad hoc. The organization recognizes the need for IT security, but security awareness depends on the individual. IT security is addressed on a reactive basis and not measured. IT security breaches invoke finger-pointing responses if detected, because responsibilities are unclear. Responses to IT security breaches are unpredictable.	Initial/Ad hoc. The organization recognizes a need for accurate data. Some methods are developed at the individual level to prevent and detect data input, processing, and output errors. The process of error identification and correction is dependent upon manual activities of individuals, and rules and requirements are not passed on as staff movement and turnover occur. Management assumes that data is accurate because a computer is involved in the process. Data integrity and security are not management requirements and, if security exists, it is administered by the information services function.

(continued)

Table 6-2 *(continued)*

COBIT PROCESS	AI 1	AI 6	DS 5	DS 11
Relevant key goal indicator(s)	■ Percent of implemented solutions formally approved by business owners and by IT. ■ Number of backlog or non-addressed solutions.	■ Number of emergency fixes. ■ Reduced number of disruptions because of poorly managed change.	■ Alignment of access rights with organizational responsibilities. ■ Immediate reporting on critical incidents.	■ A measured decrease in corrective activities and exposure to data corruption. ■ Reduced number of data data defects, such as redundancy, duplication, and inconsistency.
Relevant critical success factor(s)	■ There is a transparent, fast, and efficient process for planning, initiation, and approval of solutions. ■ A structured requirements analysis process is implemented.	■ Change policies are clear and known and they are rigorously and systemically implemented. ■ There is a segregation of duties between development and production.	A centralized user management process and system provides the means to identify and assign authorizations in a standard and efficient manner.	■ Data entry requirements are clearly stated, enforced and supported by automated techniques at all levels, including database and file interfaces. ■ Data accuracy and standards are clearly communicated and incorporated into the training and personnel development processes.
Relevant key performance indicator(s)	■ Time lag between requirements definition and identification of a solution. ■ Number of projects involving users in requirements definition and solution selection.	■ Number of deviations from the standard configuration. ■ Time lag between the availability of the fix and its implementation. ■ Number of software release and distribution methods per platform.	■ Number of systems with active monitoring capabilities. ■ Time lag between detection, reporting, and acting on security incidents. ■ Reduced number of security related calls, change requests, and fixes.	■ Percent of data input errors. ■ Percent of automated data integrity checks incorporated into the applications.

COBIT PROCESS	AI 1	AI 6	DS 5	DS 11
Level 4 maturity definition (goal)	Managed and measurable. The organization has established an acquisition and implementation methodology, which has evolved to the point where it is unusual for it not to be applied. Documentation is of good quality and each stage is properly approved. Requirements are well articulated and in accordance with pre-defined structures. The methodology forces proper consideration of solution alternatives and analysis of costs and benefits enabling informed choices to be made. The methodology is clear, defined, generally understood, and measurable. Therefore, exceptions can be easily determined and corrected by management. Solutions respond efficiently to user requirements and there is awareness that forward-looking solutions can improve business processes and the competitive solution.	Managed and measurable. The change management process is well developed and consistently followed for all changes and management is confident that there are no exceptions. The process is efficient and effective, but relies on considerable manual procedures and controls to ensure that quality is achieved. All changes are subject to thorough planning and impact assessment to minimize the likelihood of post-production problems. An approval process for changes is in place. Change management documentation is current and correct, with changes formally tracked. Configuration documentation is generally accurate. IT change management planning and implementation is becoming more integrated with changes in business process, to ensure that training, organizational changes, and business continuity issues are addressed. There is increased coordination between IT change management and business process re-design.	Managed and measurable. Responsibilities for IT security are clearly assigned, managed, and enforced. IT security risk and impact analysis is consistently performed. Security policies and practices are completed with specific security base-lines. Security awareness briefings have become mandatory. User identification, authentication, and authorization are being standardized. Security certification of staff is being established. Intrusion testing is a standard and formalized process leading to improvements. Cost/benefit analysis, supporting the implementation of security measures, is increasingly being utilized. IT security processes are coordinated with the overall organization security function. IT security reporting is linked to business objectives.	Managed and measurable. Data is defined as a corporate resource and asset, as management demands more decision support and profitability reporting. The responsibility for data quality is clearly defined, assigned, and communicated within the organization. Standardized methods are documented, maintained, and used to control data quality, rules are enforced and data is consistent across platforms and business units. Data quality is measured and customer satisfaction with information is monitored. Management reporting takes on a strategic value in assessing customers, trends, and product evaluations. Integrity of data becomes a significant factor, with data security recognized as a control requirement. A formal, organization-wide data administration function has been established, with the resources and authority to enforce data standardization.

Just to be clear, the kind of rating and breakdown of COBIT criteria shown in Table 6-2 would normally be the result a review process conducted by COBIT specialists, in all likelihood from outside DexCo. (Another option is to have employees who are independent of the process conduct a COBIT analysis. For example, the business applications group might review the maturity model of the infrastructure and operations group.) Once this raw information is available, the consultants will then conduct a gap analysis, which identifies gaps between the existing level of COBIT compliance and the desired level that DexCo wishes to attain.

In the case of DexCo's retail POS revenue transactions, we can see several significant gaps. Table 6-3 provides a high-level breakdown of the gaps that DexCo needs to address if it wants to increase its maturity model scores for each of the four main COBIT processes involved in Sarbanes Oxley compliance. For example, applying COBIT Process AI 1, which covers DexCo's ability to identify and implement automated solutions for retail POS (theoretically superior to manual solutions), reveals that the company does not have a consistent methodology for evaluating or installing these kinds of solutions. For example, bar code scanning and UPC coding are automated solutions to manual data entry at the cash register. Although DexCo does have barcode scanning at every one of its stores, the software that each store uses may vary either by version or make. The company does not have a uniform product coding standard, a problem exacerbated by its tendency to buy large amounts of closeout items that have been coded elsewhere with identification numbers that are useless for DexCo's systems. As manufacturers begin to tag merchandise with Radio Frequency Identity cards (RFID), DexCo is struggling to catch up with its POS terminal software. However, as Table 6-3 shows, the company lacks a rigorous process to adopt RFID consistently. This lack of consistency can cause a potential internal control weakness.

Looking at Table 6-3, you can see that DexCo is trying to do the right thing but is falling short in most areas. Change management is its best process. The company's software engineers recognized the need for a proper change management methodology, but politics, budget constraints, and staff turnover have prevented a fully mature change management approach from coming to life. Security is a major weak point, one I will explore in the next section. Data integrity, covered in Chapter 5, is also a COBIT Process that DexCo could do much to improve.

Perhaps you may have noticed a strange irony to many of the COBIT management guidelines, namely that a lot of the key goal indicators, key performance indicators, and critical success factors rely on measurement of systemic performance. With much of COBIT, you can determine how well you are doing only if you can analyze reliable, consistently produced measurement data about your system performance. However, if your COBIT processes are immature, then you will have few such data. It's a Catch 22—how can you know how you are doing if you can't measure it. Yet, maybe that's the point. If you don't know, then you must be immature.

Table 6-3   High-Level Gap Analysis for COBIT Processes Involved in DexCo's Retail POS Revenue Transactions

COBIT PROCESS	AI 1	AI 6	DS 5	DS 11
Definition	Identify automated solutions.	Manage changes.	Ensure systems security.	Manage data.
Significant gaps	■ Lack of consistently applied methodology for evaluating and implementing automated solutions. ■ Lack of consistent requirements gathering and approval processes for automated solutions.	■ Process is defined but not followed consistently or uniformly. ■ Documentation of process is not thorough or uniform. ■ Inconsistent segregation of duties between development and production installations of POS software.	■ Lack of unified identity management system or methodology. ■ Security roles not clearly defined or understood. ■ Inconsistent system monitoring and reporting of security problems.	■ Inconsistent data validation process. ■ Inadequate training of personnel for data entry. ■ Lack of reporting on data integrity.

Deeper Dive—COBIT Issues for a Specific Function

If we were really conducting a COBIT review and implementation, we would have to go through every one of the relevant management guidelines associated with the COBIT processes that map to COSO. However, because I am not trying to provide you with an exhaustive how-to manual on COBIT, I am just going to look in depth at one COBIT process for one specific system function. The idea is to show you the power of COBIT to bring systems under control and comply with COSO. Let's look, then, at security as it relates to the software programs that run the cash register, or point-of-sales (POS) terminals at the DexCo retail stores.

First, however, I want to articulate a working definition of security in the corporate computing context. Having done IT work with many business people, I have come to the conclusion that there is a widespread misunderstanding of what we mean when we talk about IT security. For some, IT security refers only to intrusion detection and antivirus issues. While these are both important areas of security, they represent just two facets of a much broader subject. IT security encompasses a range of work areas, which break down into two categories: security policy and privacy.

Security policy is a set of procedures, rules, software applications, and system hardware configurations that are required to realize the stated policy objectives of the organization. Security policy generally refers to the issue of who can use a system, at what times, and for what purpose. Similarly, security policy should dictate who has physical or virtual access to system controls for purposes of modification of system functionality or configuration. The larger the organization, the more complex and compelling the security policy issues can be. In a small company, security policy is generally a matter of common sense. The IT guy has the only key to the server room. Everyone has a personal log-in name and password and you're done. At a large bank, in contrast, you might have 10,000 employees in 200 offices with selective access to 5 dozen financially critical systems. Figuring out who should be using what system for what purpose is a major ongoing challenge.

Privacy, the other category of IT security, covers all matters relating to the ability of an organization to conduct its business without its private systems being compromised. Privacy covers such issues as encryption of records and messages while in transit, intrusion detection, virus control, and so on. Privacy and security policy overlap in the area of user identity. Indeed, most hacking or violation of security policy for the purpose of breaching a company's privacy, is done by illegal acquisition of legitimate user identifications. Security policy and privacy overlap as well. For example, a company might have a policy that calls for encryption of messages.

With this fuller definition of IT security in mind, let's look at DexCo's retail POS terminals. For a variety of reasons, DexCo has not maintained a uniform set of POS terminals in its stores. Some run on Windows 2000, others on Windows NT, and a few still on DOS. Two POS software packages run amidst this multiplicity of operating systems. Both POS software packages are customized versions of off-the-shelf POS applications. One of the vendors that created one of DexCo's POS software packages is out of business. That package has been supported by a group of software developers at DexCo's headquarters.

COBIT process DS 5 (ensure systems security) contains the critical success factor that calls for, "A centralized user management process and system provides the means to identify and assign authorizations in a standard and efficient manner." Let's understand what this means. Then, let's look at why would this be necessary to ensure security for DexCo and its POS terminals?

A system can be secure only if there is effective control over who is using it and who has the authorization to change it. If there are unknown or unauthorized system users who can access the POS terminals, which have money in them after all, then DexCo cannot possibly have effective internal controls.

In practical terms, DexCo's retail outlets are lacking in the most basic security policy enforcement. Employees are hired and fired frequently, a typical turnover pattern for a low-paying retail staffing situation. Even store managers come and go with regularity. The average store manager has been on the job with DexCo for less than a year. Most DexCo retail employees at a specific store use just one common user name and password to log onto the POS terminal. Thus, in a store with a staff of ten, all share the same user credentials. The company has no way to track who was using the POS terminal at any specific time. In addition, the company has no way to know if an employee who has been terminated is still accessing the system. Imagine a scenario where an employee is terminated for theft, but then re-enters the store, perhaps with the help of a friend who still works there, and empties the register drawer. The ex-employee can also use the shared user credentials to override the manager's end-of-day cash report and blind DexCo to the robbery.

In most cases, that common user name and password is also the administrator password, so the user can modify the system configuration and even upload new code in some cases. DexCo does not really know if the software that it thinks is installed at a store is actually the valid software that is supposed to be there. Of course, there is a regional IT manager that tends to the IT needs of each store periodically. However, there is no way that the IT manager is going to be able to monitor every single configuration or software component on every POS terminal in his territory.

And, this odd but unfortunately common scenario at DexCo does not exist for the lack of a well-written user manual for the security of the POS systems. Each store in fact has, in its manager's office, an unopened and yellowing binder that contains dozens of pages of clear instructions on how the store manager is required to assign each store employee a basic user-level password while retaining the administrative password for himself or herself. The passwords are stored at a central system at DexCo headquarters, where an administrator is supposed to oversee their status. However, that administrator quit years ago and his successor was never told to oversee the retail POS passwords. The manual states that any employee who is terminated must have his or her user credentials voided out by the store manager at the time of termination, and so on. The manual says that the POS system may not be upgraded by anyone except an authorized employee or contractor of DexCo, acting on instructions for headquarters.

DexCo has ample security policy definition. What it lacks is security policy enforcement (security policy definition and security policy enforcement are terms that often appear in IT security literature). For this reason, DexCo's POS terminals merit a COBIT DS 5 maturity model score of 1—the system is partly there in theory but not at all in practice.

Deep Dive—Circle Back to COSO

If you are enjoying this lengthy digression into COBIT (if so, I recommend that you seek professional help), you may still be wondering where it all connects back to Sarbanes Oxley. You've gone deeply into IT issues with COBIT, but let's circle back and do some finer grained mapping of COBIT to COSO, the heart of the Sarbanes Oxley 404 internal controls process, and see how it all fits together.

Table 6-4 compares the COSO risk/objective/control pairings that you learned about in Chapter 4 with the COBIT processes most relevant for COSO. Each COSO control is supported by a specific COBIT process, or set of processes. If a COBIT process lacks maturity, then the effectiveness of the COSO control will almost certainly suffer. This is virtually guaranteed if the controls are meant to govern a distributed, computer-based set of operations, such as DexCo's far-flung retail operations with its disaggregated POS terminals.

COBIT processes also work in combination to support or undermine a COSO control pairing. The stronger the COBIT implementation, the stronger the overall COSO framework, although the reverse is also true. Here's what I mean: For example, although I have identified DS 11 as a relevant COBIT process for the COSO controls governing sales commissions, records accuracy, and correct period cutoffs, the other three COBIT processes we discussed can also have an impact on the COSO controls. If DexCo establishes and enforces rigorous data management controls and reaches a high level of DS 11 maturity, those efforts could be rendered meaningless if the company does not also provide robust system security (DS 5) and change management (AI 6).

If it is possible for an unauthorized user to access DexCo's POS systems and modify records after the fact, then the DS 11 process will be badly compromised. Or, at the very least, it will become highly subject to audit and detection of improper activity, an endless game of catch-up that will cast suspicion on the very data that is seeks to protect. Ideally, DexCo will have good security to ensure that its DS 11 data integrity can be unquestioned.

Similarly, if DexCo does not have thorough and consistent change management processes, then whatever efforts it makes to provide good data integrity under DS 11 will be short lived and subject to suspicion. An example from home ownership can illustrate this point. If you remodel your house, you will invariably disconnect your burglar alarm. When you are finished remodeling, you may neglect to reconnect the alarm, or you may be suspicious that it was not reconnected correctly. If your burglar alarm goes off every night for a week after it is reconnected, you may assume that there is something wrong with the wiring after the construction work. The fact that a burglar has tried to break in seven nights in a row will probably not enter your mind. This is how it is with IT systems. If a software upgrade is not subject to strict change management process, it may result in data irregularities that cause trouble for the maintenance of a good data integrity standard.

Table 6-4   COSO Objective/Risk/Control Pairings for the Sales Process As They Relate to COBIT

OBJECTIVES	RISKS	CONTROLS	RELEVANT COBIT PROCESS
Initiate Safeguard sales documents and related accounting files.	Inadequate physical security over sales documents.	Sales department is independent of credit and billing and access to accounts receivable records is restricted.	DS 5, ensure systems security, needs to provide user identity management to ensure segregation of roles.
All sales revenues are accurately booked in the proper period.	Improper cut-off of sales records at the end of the period.	There are proper cut-off procedures at the end of the month for all sales orders.	DS 11, manage data, must validate correct period cut-offs in sales revenue data entries.
Document Support Completely and accurately record all authorized sales.	Documents may be missing or lost, or information may be untimely or incorrect.	▪ Sales orders are pre-numbered. ▪ Sequence of sales order records is checked periodically. ▪ All unused forms are controlled. ▪ Records are main tained for all voided forms.	DS 11, manage data, must provide auditable record tracking.
Summarize Ensure that only valid sales orders are processed.	Customer order information may be inaccurate or incomplete.	Sales commissions are calculated from sales ledgers to encourage commissioned sales representatives to effectively monitor recorded sales.	DS 11, manage data, must provide auditable record tracking.
Report Operating results are compared to management standards and budgets.	Lack of pre-established standards or inaccurate information to compare actual to budgeted results.	Management periodically compares actual sales to budgeted sales and investigates significant variances	AI 1, identify automated solutions, enable real-time automated monitoring of sales through automated systems.

Source: IPC primer Karl Nagel & Co.

COBIT and People

However technical the discussion of COBIT and COSO can be, you should never forget that it is largely a human process. No, you're probably thinking. It's all about IT—isn't that what this book says? Yes and no. What is a computer if not a machine built and configured by people to achieve human objectives? (When we get to the Terminator stage, we'll rewrite the book.) For this reason, COBIT involves interpersonal process. We are going to dip our toes in this idea now as it relates to the specifics of COBIT, but we shall return to it several more times in depth throughout the rest of the book.

Getting COBIT to work means enabling people with different backgrounds, agendas, and business languages to communicate and cooperate. Accountants have to connect with software developers to make COBIT a success. Don Sanders says, "Let's take a Fortune 500 company. I would advise the CEO to say, 'Mr. CFO, Mr. CIO: Cooperate and break down your silos, and you're going to work together to make sure that we're fine in terms of SOX compliance' You may have seen it where finance and accounting and IT just don't talk. I think it's very hard for an IT manager to do what needs to be done without the cooperation of the CFO and accounting. I would say, 'All right, let's sit down together, and let's plan.'"

Arranging a meeting is just a start, however, because the mental universes of the CFO's and CIO's respective staffs are often just too far apart to come together naturally. Effective COBIT requires living translation of issues between diverse groups of people. Now, of course, I'm dealing in generalities here—there are surely many IT people who have a deep understanding of accounting and controls and surely just as many accountants and auditors with above average command of computing and software issues. In my experience, however, there is a great potential for misunderstanding between these two groups.

One of the main challenges in implementing COBIT is the inherent contrast between IT and COSO. IT problems tend to be highly direct and practical while COSO controls tend to be somewhat generalized and non-specific. Similarly, many IT people tend to think in terms of functional systemic requirements, practical problem solving, and project-oriented workflow. If there is a need to change functional requirements, then most IT departments will initiate a change project and a team will work for a limited period of time on implementing whatever specific set of requirements has been delineated for them or by them. Typically, controls are just one aspect of requirements. When the project is finished, or the problem resolved, the team disbands and goes on to the next project.

In contrast, accounting is a more permanent process. Accounting is eternal, essentially, as the balance sheet presents an unending series of snapshots of a company's assets and liabilities. Financial reporting is a ceaseless procession of income and cash flow statements. Inventories are forever extant and always changing.

As a result, finding precise, workable matches between COSO controls and COBIT management guidelines—matches that can be understood by people of such varying backgrounds—can be a challenge. Table 6-5 lays out the different approaches that might be taken by accountants versus IT people on a specific set of COSO controls and related COBIT processes.

In the control situation shown in Table 6-5, accounting and IT people are probably on the same page, but speaking different languages. For the accountant, the systems involved in booking sales orders must provide a reasonable level of assurance that orders are correctly booked. To the IT person, the system must do exactly what the requirements ask or it is not functioning correctly. The accountant may go through a testing process that determines that a control exists, when in fact the control may be weaker than it appears. The IT person, in turn, may verify that certain software functions exist without gaining a complete understanding of how the functional requirements of a system map to the control framework. Overall, there may be a great interest in documentation to identify the existence of controls or the lack thereof. As any seasoned IT person will tell you, however, documentation often lags far behind the most recent system installation, if it exists at all.

Table 6-5 COSO Objective/Risk/Control Pairings for the Sales Process, COBIT Processes, and Accounting versus IT Approach to the Control

OBJECTIVES	RISKS	CONTROLS	RELEVANT COBIT PROCESS	ACCOUNTING APPROACH TO THE CONTROLS	IT APPROACH TO THE CONTROLS
Ensure that only valid sales orders are processed.	Customer order information may be inaccurate or incomplete.	Sales commissions are calculated from sales ledgers to encourage commissioned sales representatives to monitor recorded sales effectively.	DS 11, manage data, must provide auditable record tracking.	■ Ask the IT people a list of questions about the systems' ability to provide auditable record tracking. ■ Perform testing of the controls using audit standards. ■ Examine system documentation.	■ Build data validation into transaction processing that ensures that orders are complete and that sales commissions are correctly calculated.

Don Sanders tries to address the potential communication pitfalls in COBIT up front. "In a consulting situation," he says, "I always bring somebody that speaks 1s and 0s at a deeper level than I do. When IT managers and IT folks start talking, they get into a very specialized language, and I think that when you're talking controls, it's important to remember that this is not just simply something that's IT-specific. This is generalized across the company, so you need to be able to speak COBIT, controls, as well as IT."

Paying the Tab for COBIT

Don Sanders recommends finishing a COBIT engagement by delivering a documented process with identified controls and tests for the IT staff to run to make sure they care keeping on top of the COSO controls that pertain to them. In addition, he leaves them with time-series charts that help the IT staff monitor how they are doing with the COBIT and COSO controls over predefined periods of time. If everyone is focused on following through, then COBIT can be a strong component of the company's COSO internal controls framework and ongoing Sarbanes Oxley compliance program.

"My goal," explains Sanders, "is to enable the company to be proactive in dealing with an auditor. The CIO needs to be able to say, 'Look, here's how we identified the risks and here's how we address and mitigated those risks—and here is what we will be doing in the future to further minimize risks. Now, ask your questions!"

However, by its very nature COBIT tends toward being fragile and vulnerable to a number of threats in the business environment. For example, COBIT rewards long-term employee loyalty in IT organizations. If an IT staff is dedicated to COBIT, and they stay on the job for a long time, then COBIT will likely be a strong, long-lived foundation for controls. If the IT organization has high turnover, or even a high internal transfer rate amongst divisions and project teams, then COBIT efforts may lag.

Certain types of outsourcing can be damaging to COBIT. Shipping half the IT function off to Bangalore might sound great to the CFO, but it could be murder on internal controls. A few thorough change cycles on any set of systems will eradicate COBIT-based controls if the IT team is not given the time, responsibility, money, and training to keep them maintained.

Even without the budget cutter's axe, however, COBIT has at least one nearly fatal built-in flaw, and that is the actual cost and complexity of doing it. Steady measurement of system performance is a core factor of COBIT. The maturity models, critical success factors, objectives, and criteria all depend on the ability of the organization to measure the functioning of a set of systems and compare current measurements to historical records. What many non-IT people fail to understand is that the ability to measure system performance is itself a system requirement. And, as with any system requirement, the measurement function must be planned, developed, tested, documented, and paid for.

It's fine for an auditor to ask that the IT department build a measurement function into its systems that tracks "time lag between detection, reporting, and acting on security incidents" to pick one of the hundreds critical success factors. To implement this requirement in reality is quite complex and burdensome. Imagine the following: A software engineer must develop an automated function that transmits an alert of a security problem to a central "security incident monitoring" application (which also must be developed or purchased, installed, tested, controlled, and monitored by a living salary earning human being).

Every time the software engineer makes a modification to the application, he or she must then modify, test, and debug whatever connection has been created to the security monitoring application. As more systems are joined together, the situation becomes more complex, time consuming and costly to maintain. Eventually, the software engineer may begin to ignore this security monitoring system, or sacrifice it to the gods of budget cutting. Only a company with a very solid commitment to COBIT will have the stamina to maintain strong COBIT on an ongoing basis. And if you understand COBIT, there's no other kind. COBIT on a periodic basis is going to be a disaster. Add in some personnel changes, outsourcing, and vendor problems and COBIT could have an easy obit.

DexCo's Next Steps on COBIT

After going over this practical approach to COBIT, Dale, Linda, and Sebastian agree that they need to make COBIT part of their plan for Sarbanes Oxley compliance. They feel that the heat map and careful planning will enable them to incorporate COBIT into their overall compliance process without distracting them from other compliance issues that also deserve serious attention. As Don says, they want to be able to address risks and auditor questions proactively. More on this later in the book.

Summary

It is possible to implement COBIT without getting bogged down in esoteric and excessive detail that does not bear on workaday internal controls. Based on the work of Dr. Don Sanders, a COBIT consultant, the DexCo team reviews an approach to COBIT that stresses evaluating where in the internal control landscape COBIT would have the most traction for real effect. Dubbed the *heat map*, this approach calls for applying COBIT selectively and only in those areas where IT is deeply enmeshed in realizing the effectiveness of internal controls.

The heat map process calls for DexCo to score its IT systems and measure how susceptible they might be to control problems using factors such as number of system users, age of system, and number of subsystems involved. The greater the number of each of these respective aspects of the system, the greater the likelihood that there will be a control failure. For this reason, the high-scoring systems deserve more COBIT attention than a low-scoring system.

After the candidates for COBIT have been identified in this way, the IT organization can then focus on those COBIT management guidelines that will make the greatest impact on ensuring that the IT system in question will support specific internal controls that need to be documented under SOX 404. The net result is a situation where the IT organization can apply the methods and metrics of COBIT in a practical, results-oriented way that will have a positive impact on the company's SOX efforts.

CHAPTER 7

The Pain of SOX

"I have a problem," Jim Wilde says as everyone takes his or her seat in the main ranch house. "I've got a plan that I cannot execute without risking DexCo's compliance. I feel the pressure of the marketplace, but for once in my life, I am a little uncertain about what to do. I know I have to run fast, but all of a sudden, I feel like I'm wearing cement shoes."

Linda and Sebastian are both about to launch into their personal version of what's wrong and how it's the other's fault, but Dale silences them with a wave of his hand. "I think," Dale says, "that we are ready to make a firm assessment of just what our problem is. Once defined, we can then start looking at a solution."

This chapter explores in further detail just what this predicament means. I will look at DexCo's dilemma as it tries to be agile but also achieve COSO control objectives, mitigate risks, and establish control procedures. At the same time, I will look at the company's IT issues that relate to Sarbanes Oxley compliance.

COSO, COBIT, and Controls versus the Wilde Plan

The key objective of the Wilde plan is to make DexCo a leader and generate strong earnings growth over a sustained period of time. To make this happen, Wilde has several separate initiatives he plans to implement. He is hoping to enter into a variety of partnerships and alliances with other firms, including manufacturers, retailers, and airlines. Specifically, he believes there is great potential for DexCo in the wireless sector.

Wilde is intent on re-engineering the DexCo organization, including centralizing the management of the three divisions. He wants to have one set of corporate departments (Sales, Marketing, Logistics and Operations, IT) supporting three strategic business units (SBUs), rather than have a light-weight corporate office oversee the activities of three relatively autonomous divisions. And he wants to create big incentives for executive performance in each SBU. He would like to outsource non-core functions. Finally, Wilde is interested in doing mergers and acquisitions (M&A). He may want to acquire businesses and turn them into new SBUs. In turn, he may spin off various business units.

As I've discussed previously, changes in business operations can reduce the effectiveness of a company's internal controls. Let's take a look at some of the major aspects of the Wilde plan and see their impact on internal controls and Sarbanes Oxley compliance at DexCo.

Jim wants to make changes to the product line. That alone should not have much of an effect on the company's Sarbanes Oxley compliance efforts. However, in Wilde's case, he envisions a radical change in the way the company works with its partners to produce products. Instead of sourcing product or manufacturing it, he wants to enter into rapid cycling co-ventures with wireless manufacturers and carriers. This vision is problematic from the perspective of internal controls.

Flex-acturing

Jim's vision for DexCo's wireless co-venturing strategy assumes that the company is going to source a proprietary component of a new wireless device from a manufacturer in China. Then, DexCo will partner with a manufacturer in the United States that will assemble the wireless devices together with its own technologies and then deliver the finished devices to DexCo for retail and wholesale distribution. Jim Wilde loves this approach to product development and manufacturing. With this approach, which he calls "flex-acturing," DexCo can rapidly release an ever-changing set of unique products in the market without having to invest in R&D nor carrying the expense and liability of owning a manufacturing facility. Though flex-acturing is just one of Jim's ideas, we will use it throughout the rest of the book as an example of how agility and internal controls can be at odds.

What about internal controls, though? From a basic COSO perspective, flex-acturing causes a number of troubles. Remember that COSO has five core control components: control environment, risk assessment, control procedures, information and communication, and monitoring. For each component, there is a reason to be worried about Wilde's flex-acturing idea.

The control environment suffers in co-venturing situations. By definition, alliances involve more than one entity. One entity has limited control over another, even when there are strict guidelines in place. The scandal at Card Systems, the credit card processing company that violated its agreement with banks by retaining unencrypted cardholder data, is a great example of the kind of difficulty a company can get into with internal controls when it relies on partners for compliance.

Risk assessment reveals a number of problems for flex-acturing. The joint nature of the process exposes DexCo to increased inventory and technology risks. By committing to a product line that relies on the ability of a manufacturer in China to deliver consistently also exposes DexCo trade and currency risks as well.

Control procedures will need attention if they are to be maintained during the rapid realignment of partners and vendors contemplated in flex-acturing. There is nothing inherently wrong with flex-acturing in terms of control procedures. However, the rapid cycling nature of the process puts pressure on DexCo's Finance and IT organizations to keep the control procedures current.

Indeed, it is with the COSO control components of information, communication, and monitoring where flex-acturing may cause the most trouble for Sarbanes Oxley. Jim Wilde puts his emphasis on the *flex* aspects of his idea. In his mind, he sees spending six months with one manufacturing partner, and six with another, and then on to the next. That's great, except as we have seen, it could take six months just to connect with the information systems of the manufacturing partner, and that's a very generous estimate. It could take a year to connect, test, and be satisfied that internal controls are in effect. That's six months too late. Jim will already be on to his next flex-acturing partner, *sans* controls, and the previous partnership will also lack controls or monitoring.

Distribution

Jim Wilde's plans for centralizing distribution and logistics at DexCo present similar threats to internal controls. While combining the logistics operations may be a sound business decision, it will lack proper internal controls for a period of time while the systemic aspects of the consolidation can be realized.

At one level, the consolidation of logistics operations will create a potential vacuum in the management ranks of these operating areas. For whatever period of time the logistics operation remains a headless horseman—during which a new team gets fully acquainted with the logistics of three previously autonomous groups—business will continue to be conducted by whatever skeleton crew remains. That crew will continue to use whatever rump IT systems and accounting controls are required, or perceived to be required. Depending on the quality of the transition management effort, the transition period will likely result in some accounting irregularities or worse.

Factoring in the time it would take to transition the IT systems that support the three current distribution systems, DexCo might face a year or more of loose controls in its nascent consolidated logistics operation. Challenges abound in this kind of situation. If DexCo opts to keep its existing IT infrastructure and application architecture in place, it may simplify its logistics consolidation somewhat—at the very least, there will be no system migration tacked onto an already complex operational change—but the company will lose the momentum and IT cost benefits it counts on gaining with the deployment of FAST. If you recall, FAST (Future Applications and Systems for Transactions) is DexCo's proposed new IT architecture.

If Jim Wilde wants to outsource selected areas of logistics, or at a minimum have the option to outsource logistics as needed, then he will further compromise his internal controls for logistics. With inadequately integrated relationships with outsourced distribution vendors, DexCo could find itself staring down the barrel of serious inventory management issues, chargebacks, reporting period irregularities, loss, or theft, all without proper internal controls to manage or monitor those risks.

Marketing

Wilde plans to combine all of DexCo's Marketing groups into one central department. This is probably a very good idea from a management perspective. The redundancy of the three marketing teams was costly for the company. At a basic level, too, Marketing seems an easy fix in terms of internal controls. Marketing is a cost center that is budgeted and journalized into the expense side of the income statement. There's no inventory or technology risk and little currency risk. Not a lot of room for serious internal control problems, right? The answer depends on how the controls are implemented and how sound the oversight is over the marketing expenditures.

Marketing, however, reveals some unusual control issues that are not present in other areas. Marketing expenditures tend to be subjective and difficult to predict or categorize. Although a marketing budget may be locked—a department can spend only so much per month, and so on—the actual detail of what was spent spend may be quite fluid. When you deal with marketing, you see many unpredictable charges for creative work, rushed production, and change orders. It's a complex situation to control, and one that is exacerbated by the informal nature of many vendor relationships in marketing.

It's time to let you in on one of DexCo's dirty little secrets. The head of DexCo's wholesale marketing team is a crook. (With the abundance of crooks in the world, I hope you don't think that I'm picking on marketing executives by singling this one out). One of the wholesale division's advertising agencies arranges to pay a bribe to this executive each quarter. The agency pays the bribe in the following way: Each quarter, one or two outdoor advertising campaigns is deliberately over budgeted. The advertising agency then deliberately overpays the company that prints the billboards for DexCo. The printer then delivers a gift to the marketing executive that is difficult to trace. In the last year, this executive has received a new car for his son, a vacation in Hawaii, an envelope full of gift cards to major stores, and jewelry. In total this year, he has received over a hundred thousand dollars in kickbacks from his advertising agency, paid for by DexCo's marketing dollars that he is stealing.

This may not sound like a lot of money, but recent events have shown that fraud in marketing can be a liability for public companies. In the last few years in New York, for example, a number of employees of prominent companies, their ad agencies, and printing suppliers have gone to jail for this kind of crime. How does that affect DexCo? Jim Wilde's problem, which he doesn't even know about, is that he might inadvertently put this fox in charge of the complete marketing henhouse. If he promotes this corrupt executive, he will be handing the entire marketing budget of the company over to a thief.

Catching fraud of this kind can be very tricky, but rigorous internal controls that mandate and enforce multiple bids, approved vendors, as well as careful auditing of project billing records can uncover even a dedicated crook. What is virtually certain, though, is that DexCo's controls for marketing spending are way too loose to catch the problem. Combining the three departments will only make it worse.

Organizational Changes

The Wilde plan to get rid of the formerly autonomous operating divisions and turn them into SBUs is again a sound business idea with bad potential consequences for internal controls. Major realignments of management and organization structure can have an impact on the COSO guideline that covers the control environment component. Control environment translates into the "tone at the top" for DexCo. By essentially stripping each of his division general managers of a portion of their responsibilities, Wilde is also decapitating some of the most salient aspects of the company's control environment.

As we saw with COBIT, the intangible issue of who's in charge can be absolutely critical to achieving sound Sarbanes Oxley 404 compliance. Almost every single COBIT management guideline and maturity model criteria can be rendered useless by the phrase, "What if nobody cares about it enough to make sure it gets done?"

Who will pick up the mastery of the control environment? To the extent that they can cope, the CFO and CIO's staffs will take over the responsibility for the systemic backbone of DexCo's internal controls. That's okay in theory, but each of those groups has a lot of other tasks to pay attention to in the massive Wilde transformation. Attention to internal controls may lag as more pressing issues of organizational integration and transformation take precedence.

In addition, the company is in the middle of migrating to the FAST architecture. FAST, which is only partially complete, will need a great deal of focus and commitment to be seen through a successful launch. However, not only are the project's sponsors in flux, the actual functional requirements for FAST will likely change drastically as the Wilde plan is implemented.

The IT situation at DexCo, then, during the Wilde plan implementation, offers management a range of bad choices: Continue with costly bandaid changes to existing IT systems as the Wilde plan unfolds (which will beget more expensive IT inflexibility and system migrations later on). Revamp FAST requirements, which means losing a year and operating essentially without controls for that period; or do nothing—pledging to install FAST when the organizational changes settle down—and try to pretend that DexCo doesn't have an internal controls problem.

The absolute knock-out punch for DexCo's overall IT compliance effort, however, is Wilde's interest in outsourcing the IT function off shore. While I am not opposed to this trend in general, I will point out that an undisciplined or purely cost-motivated decision to shift IT out of the core business entity can be disastrous for the IT component of internal controls.

The Lose-Lose-Lose Proposition

Although I acknowledge that this may sound a bit histrionic, I have come to believe that Sarbanes Oxley presents many companies with a lose-lose-lose proposition. (There are not two, but three ways to lose out with poor compliance, so I have thrown in one more "lose" to the standard lose-lose proposition.)

- If you comply, you may harm your ability to be agile and stay competitive.
- If you don't comply, you could go out of business.
- If you make an empty effort at compliance, you may pass through the process but merely bury company-killing problems (and spend a lot doing so).

Let's look at some of today's common approaches to SOX. See if you can place your company in one of these categories.

For many companies, Sarbanes Oxley 404 compliance is mostly a matter of calling a consulting firm, paying them to do SOX and signing off on the certifications. A company's accounting staff will probably be involved in gathering documents and information for the consultants, but there may be little actual deep analysis of serious control issues or IT.

In a phone-it-in situation, a company pays lip service to compliance and hopes that it has no major internal control problems. Chances are, it probably doesn't have any material weaknesses. Yet, it will never know. Certainly, a company that phones it in will derive little business value from the process and not much more in the way of effective compliance. Furthermore, a phone-it-in company will ultimately overspend on compliance year after year, because they will not have incorporated compliance into their basic business management and IT processes.

Think Globally but Act Recklessly

A relative of the phone-it-in school, the think-globally-but-act-recklessly approach to SOX compliance is favored by companies managed by executives with gambling personalities. In this kind of situation, a company will continue to pursue an agile, aggressive business plan but pay little attention to compliance. The managers of such a company will probably do a perfunctory SOX compliance (after all, they have to), but ignore or disguise warnings that controls are not working. Alternatively, managers of this type of firm might knowingly sign off on controls certifications that are erroneous. A company of this kind is a potential time bomb for compliance penalties.

Comply and Die

As I have noted throughout the book so far, there are no gold medals for SOX compliance. This is a great shame, because all you get for your hard work is a lack of SEC investigations and related penalties. Getting back to the analogy I used in the introduction, it's sort of like saying that your reward for being a good driver is that you never get killed. It's a major reward, but a hard one to use to motivate much activity in people.

The worst part of SOX, however, is that if you're really doing 404 correctly, and trying to push up your COBIT maturity levels, you will be compliant, but in all likelihood you will also have locked your company into a fixed operating and strategic mode that could kill your business. Comply and die. Not a very palatable choice for most CEOs.

And the irony of the situation is that you can be compliant and still get in trouble. For example, Card Systems had complied—at least on paper—with security rules imposed by its banking clients. Card Systems would probably have passed a SOX audit. But, its day-to-day practices were highly problematic.

The Remediation Doom Loop

If you've been around accounting and IT for a while, you might be observing that the situation at DexCo is far from unique or new. The difference today is that the Sarbanes Oxley Act requires that a company assess and sign off on its internal controls. Then, an outside auditor will also examine those internal controls in depth and report on any deficiencies or material weaknesses.

If the auditor finds a material weakness in DexCo's internal controls, then the company will be compelled to remediate, or fix, the weakness. This process, known as SOX 404 Remediation, is a necessary step in a company regaining its health from the perspective of the SEC. In a 404 remediation, DexCo would have to demonstrate to its auditors that it has corrected the problem in internal controls that caused the material weakness.

SOX 404 Remediation is not optional unless you can establish that other internal controls compensate for the deficiencies identified. Failure to conduct it to the satisfaction of the auditor can result in many damaging repercussions for a public company. Because 404 Remediation is so serious, a company that is undergoing the process is not likely to be pursuing many aggressive organizational or strategic transformations at the same time. Audit firms generally need sometime to see that a remediation has taken effect. This could take several months. A remediating firm is essentially frozen. It has to work through the remediation process so that its auditors will be satisfied that the weakness in internal controls has been fixed. Only then can the company move forward with needed changes to its business processes, strategies, and systems. 404 Remediation can be a drain on resources, a costly waste of time, and a dampener of change.

Non-Compliance Penalties

Non-compliance with Sarbanes Oxley is a serious matter. A public company that either failed to certify its financial statements per the SOX requirements, or failed to remediate a material weakness, would face significant SEC sanctions. It might even be delisted from the exchanges and cease to be a public company.

In addition, the Sarbanes Oxley law provides potential criminal prosecution for executives who knowingly sign off on fraudulent financial statements. It's too early to tell if the criminal prosecution aspect of SOX is going to mean much in reality. The whole going-to-jail threat is a bit overblown. Some serious crooks are going to do time, but in general, the jail issue seems to be more of a political grandstanding scare tactic than an actual SEC enforcement policy. However, there is now a level of personal liability in compliance that did not exist before.

Goodyear, which drew an SEC investigation after restating its earnings for a five-year period due to a faulty installation of an ERP system, faces liabilities on both the corporate and personal levels. In August of 2005, two years after the SEC announced its initial investigation into Goodyear's restatement, the SEC filed what are known as Wells Notices—which state the agencies intention to recommend a civil or administrative enforcement action—against Goodyear as well as two of its former top financial executives. For those people, compliance is a highly personal issue.

Another great "I'm not making this up" example of a compliance disaster brought on by ill-conceived agility plans is the case of Interpublic Group. Interpublic, the multibillion dollar number three advertising agency holding company in the world, announced in October of 2005 that it was restating its financial results for the previous five years—for the third year in a row. In the most recent announcement, the company stated that its income over the previous five years was more than $500,000,000 less than reported. As you may know, this kind of restatement activity can be murder on a company's stock price and reputation.

Major factors in the restatement include improper accounting for revenue and acquisitions, employee malfeasance (the company faces allegations of bribery, theft, and other individual improprieties), and bookkeeping errors. The SEC investigation is underway. Whether or not the company will face prosecution for violation of the Sarbanes Oxley act is not known, although it is certainly possible given the circumstances.

According to the *New York Times*, "Interpublic . . . has grappled with substantial weaknesses in internal controls that led to several changes in chief executives and chief financial officers since the problems were first disclosed in 2002." The *New York Times* reported that Interpublic's problems stemmed from an overly aggressive acquisition strategy. The strategy, ". . . brought hundreds of agencies with disparate financial systems under the Interpublic umbrella [and] overwhelmed its ability to manage its affairs . . ." Sound familiar?

Jim's Big Question

The CEO says, "I have a pretty good idea of what is really going at DexCo and how Sarbanes Oxley compliance could put a major crimp in my strategic plans." Although he doesn't say it out loud, he has also gained some sense of the fraud occurring under his nose—he's been around enough to see the signs—and now, he's worried that he won't be able to do what he wants to do without risking SEC problems or worse.

"Isn't there something we can do to get compliant but still be agile?" he asks the room full of advisors and executives. "I don't want to phone in compliance or be reckless. We have to comply. Yet, I don't want to abandon my plan. I want it all. Somebody tell me I can do it all."

After a prolonged silence in the room, a voice finally speaks up. It's his CIO, who says, "There is a way to do this. It's not easy, or cheap, but it can be done."

Summary

At this juncture, it looks as if DexCo's CEO, Jim Wilde is not going to be able to execute his plan to transform the company without seriously jeopardizing his compliance with Sarbanes Oxley and all that it represents in terms of sound business practices.

His vision for flexible manufacturing of rapidly developed and marketed products—a process he dubs *flex-acturing*—will push the company into internal control problems with inventory management and transaction period reporting. His plans for streamlining the company's distribution and logistics operations face similar problems. Notably, during whatever transition period ensues, the distribution operation will be a headless horseman, unmanaged and prone to internal control deficiencies. Marketing, an area where Wilde plans to consolidate and save, is a complex internal control challenge because of the subjective nature of the marketing procurement process. In addition, DexCo's marketing departments are hiding a fraudulent operation. The company risks widening the fraud if it cannot use internal controls to detect and prevent the illegal activity. Finally, Wilde's plans to change the organizational structure of the company may exacerbate some of the critical but highly subjective tone-at-the-top control objectives.

What can Wilde do? At this point, it seems as if he is facing a lose-lose-lose proposition: He can ignore compliance and phone in a perfunctory SOX 404 effort. He could ignore compliance and do whatever he pleases, signing off on the SOX certifications without really looking into the work that underlies them. Both of these courses expose him to the risks of an internal control breakdown and resulting SEC troubles. Or, he could comply rigorously and force his company to freeze itself into a compliant zombie that is too tightly controlled to be agile. If the internal controls fail and he gets caught by his auditor, he could be pushed into a SOX 404 remediation doom loop where he constantly tries to get the controls in order but has to freeze a lot of agility choices in the process.

Penalties for non-compliance can be quite severe, including SEC fines, personal liability, and even de-listing of a company from the exchanges. Wilde is perplexed and alarmed. However, his CIO believes that he has a way to make the company both agile and compliant. This I will explore in Chapter 8.

Thinking Outside the SOX

Part I was a little bit dire, I admit. You might conclude that your situation is hopeless, that you are doomed to a losing proposition where your company will never attain the compliance or the agility it needs to compete. However, I know you can do it. How do I know? Because, when I was a kid, my parents took me to see *PDQ Bach*.

PDQ Bach is an ingenious spoof of classical music that was the brainchild of Professor Peter Schikele, a composer who had started his career as a professional bassoonist. The bassoon is allegedly one of the most difficult instruments to learn. As Professor Schikele put it, at age three he was offered a choice: learn bassoon or join the French Foreign Legion. He chose bassoon, and the world has since been illuminated by his great gifts in music and comedy. It was by mastering bassoon that Shikele developed the artistic rigor to become a composer and share with us his creation – PDQ Bach—a "forgotten" brother of the more famous Bach who left us with such masterpieces as "The Hindenberg Concerto" and "The Royal Firewater Music."

Like aspiring bassoonists, compliance-minded accountants, IT people, and business managers face a monumental challenge. The French Foreign Legion looks awfully seductive from our perspective. Yet, we know we can surmount the challenges ahead and find our way to the win-win of agile compliance with SOX.

This part explores ways that a company can approach compliance with a practical, results-oriented win-win philosophy. You are going to look again at DexCo. Instead of viewing every aspect of the company as a disaster waiting to happen (or already happening), you will see the potential that CEO Jim Wilde has to realize his vision for the company and stay compliant. You are going to think outside the SOX.

As the sun comes up over Little Big Horn, Linda, Sebastian, and Dale see the gravestones of Custer's soldiers in the faint morning light. Dale had rousted Linda and Sebastian from their rooms in the middle of the night and driven with them for hours to get here. Still half asleep, they marvel at the tragic beauty of the place.

"So," Dale barks. "You probably want to know why the heck we came all the way over here." Well, yeah, the other two reply. "I'll tell you. You're standing on one of the most famous battlefields in history. This is where Custer made his last stand against a Sioux army that outnumbered him three to one. He ordered his men to shoot their horses so they couldn't retreat. He chose to die rather than surrender. It was the worst defeat for the U.S. Army ever, and it was also the beginning of the end for the Sioux."

Linda and Sebastian regard their new boss skeptically. "You didn't see a Starbucks on the way in here, did you?" Sebastian asks.

"Ha ha," Dale replies. "You two have a choice," Dale continues. "You can battle it out and we'll all get nowhere. Be like Custer. Dying for a principle but being dead just the same. Or, we can work together and learn to listen to one another." Linda and Sebastian are silent. "What's it going to be?"

"Okay," Linda says. "I'd rather try to make it work than keep butting heads and complaining about it."

"Me too," Sebastian says.

"Let's shake on it," Dale says. This, they do. "Now, let's find a Starbucks."

Back at the Ranch

Back at the ranch, Sebastian asks Jim Wilde, "What if we could be agile but also compliant?"

"Stop twisting my arm," Wilde replies. "Tell us how we do it and I'm on board."

"Honestly, Jim," Sebastian says, "I don't know exactly how yet, but I know it can be done." Wilde looks puzzled and a little irritated. Is this guy trying to make fun of me, he wonders? A voice from across the room interrupts his thoughts.

"If we upgrade the enterprise application integration component of our proposed FAST architecture to include a business process modeling tool from the same vendor," says Ramesh Subramanian, one of Harris's deputies, "then we can absolutely address the app server containers and Enterprise Java Beans to the rules engine. It's all business process modeling. We'll be compliant in no time."

"Why don't you IT folks talk about it and get back to me," Wilde says, his eyes not actually rolling, although they might as well have been. The rules engine. Yeah, that's going to work.

"I appreciate your eagerness to get started, Ramesh," Sebastian says, "But I believe we have to approach this subject differently from the way we have in the past if we are going to have a prayer of figuring out Sarbanes Oxley. We have to sit down and talk—business units, finance, and IT—all together and come up with a plan of action that is going to meet all of our respective goals in this."

Linda Fuller nods in agreement. "I like this idea," she says. "Why don't we get started right now." Ramesh needs no further encouragement. He leaps up and starts diagramming the FAST system architecture on the board. Everyone watches him as he maps out the company's major computers, software packages, and networks. He is about to start talking when Sebastian cuts him off again.

"Don't erase that board," he says. "That architecture is definitely part of this discussion. However, before we can start thinking about a solution, I think we need to work up a good definition of the problem itself, and also what our solution might actually look like. This is virgin territory, as far as I know. How does an agile compliant company function?"

Defining Agile Compliance

"Alright," Sebastian says. "I want you to imagine that I have a big old magic wand in my hand like Harry Potter." Everyone chuckles. "I'm a magician and

I can wave a magic wand over DexCo and make it exactly the way we want it to be." Someone in the back of the room says, "Make all the employees better looking."

"There's a limit to my magical powers," Sebastian says. "Especially in your case." More laughs. "Now, let's try to picture the company the way it should be, not the way it is." At first no one says a word. Jim Wilde disrupts the group awkwardness by saying, "I want to make my moves whenever I want."

"You want agility," says Sebastian.

"Right. I want to do what I want when I want with whomever I want—create products, make alliances, break 'em, buy companies, sell divisions, promote people, change the org chart, at the touch of a button."

"That's impossible," says Ramesh.

"Nothing's impossible with this magic wand," Sebastian says. "We are merely developing a wish list."

"I want timely, accurate financial reports from every operating unit," says Linda Fuller. "I want real-time reporting, and I want to know that we're going to pass our fiscal and Sarbanes Oxley audits without ruining my life."

"I want to know where every piece of inventory is in my business unit, what it costs, and how much I can sell it for and when," says the wholesale General Manager.

"I want to be able to deliver more IT services on the same budget," adds Sebastian. "I want to cut my integration budget and shorten my cycle times for rolling out new solutions. I want to be a value-add to the company, not a pesky cost center that everyone grumbles about." He starts writing some of the wishes onto the board.

"I want to know if my suppliers are running late, or if they're billing me right for work that they're doing," says the General Manager of the OEM division. "I want real-time access to information on payables, purchase orders, and delivery status. I hate double ordering. And I want to be able to juggle suppliers at will."

"I want instant credit checks for all new customers," says the wholesale General Manager.

"A 360-degree view of all of our businesses," Wilde adds. "What's going on with every customer at every minute—no matter how many times I change the shape of the company. I wanna be a darned control freak."

"And whatever we do," Fuller says. "We need to be out ahead of the Sarbanes Oxley Section 404 internal controls guidelines. All of our business processes need to be reflective of COSO."

"Our IT divisions have to have critical processes on a continuous improvement cycle to a level four COBIT maturity," Ramesh says. Sebastian is struggling to keep up writing down all of the comments.

"And dashboards," Wilde yelps. "I want a real-time dashboard of the whole company. I want to see every dollar we make or spend, every sales quota, projection, share price change, showing up in my gun sights every minute of the day. I want on-demand diagnostics and data mining that changes when I change the business."

"And security," says Linda Fuller. "Nothing we do can compromise security—that's a given for Sarbanes Oxley as well as just plain common sense. We can't risk any kind of intrusion or impropriety."

Sebastian puts the marker down and lets out a sigh. "This is gotta be a heck of a magic wand, don't you think?"

"We can do it if we leverage our EAI vendor," Ramesh says, but Sebastian cuts him off again.

"Maybe, maybe not," he says. "Let's put the IT specifics in neutral for a little while longer. All we've really done here is lay out what we're wishing for, which is a great first step. Now, we need to get a better understanding of how each wish relates to accounting and IT—and of course, compliance."

Sebastian steps back to show what he had written on the board. His chart resembles Table 8-1. "This is our general wish list," he says. "We can't take any steps to improve our situation until we know what we want, right?" Nods all around.

Table 8-1   DexCo's General Wish List for Business Agility, Compliance, and IT Efficiency

BUSINESS AGILITY	ACCOUNTING/ CONTROL	IT
Make moves at will	Accurate, timely financial reports	Deliver more IT services within same budget
Create products in rapid cycles, including flex-acturing	Real-time reporting	Not have IT be a bottleneck—shorten IT project cycle times
Buy/sell companies	Real-time inventory, PO, and payable status	Improve COBIT maturity in key areas
Change org chart	Pass SOX audit and fiscal audit without incurring excessive annual fees from consultants	
Make/break alliances	Business processes need to incorporate COSO where relevant	
Instant credit checks		
360-degree view of customer and business		

"Now," Sebastion continues. "Let's go another step forward and map each business goal with a specific set of control and IT requirements. This way, we can begin to build a specific objective for realizing our wish list." He shows them Table 8-2.

Table 8-2 Matching Agile Compliance Wish List with Relevant Control and IT Requirements

BUSINESS GOAL	CONTROL REQUIREMENT	IT REQUIREMENT
Make moves at will	Moves should not adversely affect internal control framework, or if they do, the remediation should be fast and inexpensive.	IT needs to be able to enable rapid business moves or delivery remediation to resulting control problems within a meaningful time period. IT cannot be a drag on agility.
Create products in rapid cycles, including flex-acturing	Internal control framework needs to accommodate rapid changes in partnerships structure, which can affect inventory, vendors, POs, and payables.	Accounting and ERP systems needs to be flexible enough to accommodate changes in controls brought about by rapid changes in partnering and product creation.
Buy/sell companies	Merge operations without negative impact on controls.	Merge operations but achieve rapid integration of core systems and IT-based internal controls.
Change org chart	Enable fast, effective assignment of responsibilities that ensure continuous enforcement of internal controls related to organization—for example, segregation of roles.	Give IT enough flexibility to assign administrative privileges, set system change management authority, and provide clear separation of roles—all within a rapid timeframe and cost-effective budget.
Make/break alliances	Ensure internal controls framework can identify and enforce internal controls in sync with changing business alliances. Must be able to make or break alliances with rapid and cost-effective modification of internal controls.	Ensure that systems can be rapidly and cost effectively configured to enable internal controls for new alliances or discontinue old alliances.

(continued)

Table 8-2   *(continued)*

BUSINESS GOAL	CONTROL REQUIREMENT	IT REQUIREMENT
Instant credit checks	Establish clear business processes and rules for credit checks on incoming orders and new accounts.	Ensure that systems can meet internal controls requirement—based on business processes and rules—for instant credit checks.
Accurate, timely financial reports	Ensure that internal controls framework provides clear roles and responsibilities, processes, and business rules, for generation of financial reports—and also be changed as needed without diminishing the capability.	Ensure that systems can meet internal controls framework requirements for accurate, timely financial reports—and also be changed as needed without diminishing the capability: Control points between relevant systems need to be flexible enough to change.
Real-time reporting	Provide flexible internal controls framework that can enable real-time reporting, continuing to do so even when the shape of the organization or its requirements change.	Provide flexible systems capability that can enable real-time reporting, continuing to do so even when the shape of the organization or its requirements change: Control points between relevant systems need to be flexible enough to change.
Real-time inventory, PO, and payable status	Ensure that internal controls framework provides clear roles and responsibilities, processes, and business rules, for generation of financial reports—and can also be changed as needed without diminishing the capability.	Integration of systems that support inventory and payables (ERP and financial) need to maintain flexible control points. Control points must be able to change rapidly and cost effectively.

"There's a lot here," Sebastian says. "What I want you to see is that every business agility goal carries with it an associated set of internal controls requirements and IT requirements. If we can't help the internal controls and IT keep up with the agility decisions, they will eventually get left behind, or get left out altogether. Do we want that?" A loud chorus of "No" echoes through the room. "Good," he says. "Just checking."

"Let's simplify it a little, so we can come up with some solid ground rules for agile compliance. What words do we keep seeing in this process?"

"Rapid" says someone in the room.

"Right. Anything else?"

"Yes, cost effective," another voice chimes in.

"Rapid and cost effective," Sebastian repeats. "Very good. You are right. Agility is about making decisions and putting them into action quickly. For a company to be agile and compliant, it needs to be able to move its control framework and supporting IT systems just as quickly—but it can't break the bank every time. Okay, then, I think we have arrived at a critical rule for agile compliance—solutions must be fast and cheap, or rapid and cost-effective."

"But," Linda Fuller states, "You still need to have IT integrated into a business objective framework for any of this to work. Improving IT in isolation doesn't really get you much. It's like tuning up your car just so you can rev the engine in the parking lot. IT improvements need to match business objectives (like agility) or else they are unnecessary investments."

"Very true, Linda," Sebastian says. "We'll talk a lot more about that in a little while." The two exchange a small high-five as he continues. "But first, let's map out exactly what our problem is."

Sebastian draws a diagram resembling Figure 8-1 on the white board. "As we discussed," he says. "IT and controls tend to lag business agility moves by a substantial margin of time. By the time you've planned, developed, tested, implemented, and documented the changes brought about by a decision motivated by agility, you may have to get ready to do it all over again. And, we're assuming that the changes were done correctly. If they were done wrong, then the company will be busy remediating a change from two years ago as it holds off on making new changes—that's so long as it cares about being compliant."

"What has to happen for this IT change management and control framework changes to get more in line with business agility?" he asks.

"For one thing," Jim Wilde says, "I'm looking at your diagram and I see that the IT and internal controls requirements don't start to change until we're way into the agility move. Why can't they start sooner?"

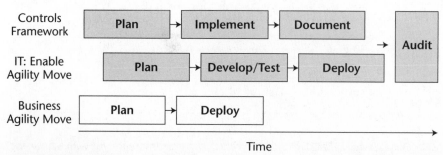

Figure 8-1 Traditional time differential between business agility move and related controls and IT requirements

"Great point," Sebastian says. "That's one big problem right away. Sometimes, it just takes too long to get everyone up to speed on what changes are taking place. It's like giving the business managers a big head start in the race and then making fun of IT and the accounting people for being slow. That's not fair."

Sebastian starts to redraw the diagram, this time with the starting points of the IT and internal controls change processes beginning closer to the business agility move. "What else has to happen?"

"It all has to synchronize," Linda says. "You have to be able to make your IT and controls changes at about the same speed as you make your business moves."

"Like this," Sebastian says, completing Figure 8-2. "You're more or less in sync. One other thing, though . . ."

"Certification and audit," says one of the internal auditors. "You need to be sure that you did your IT and controls right the first time or you won't be able to keep pace with the next set of agility changes coming down the pike."

"Right," Sebastian says, adding an audit box at the end of the process.

"What about cost?" Linda asks. "You need to factor in the expense of doing this. Anything is possible if you have enough money, and we don't."

"And," Ramesh interjects. "That makes me wonder about delivering more IT service within the same budget, or not making IT a bottleneck, or improving COBIT maturity. You forgot about those."

"Yes and no," Sebastian answers. "All of these issues are interrelated. If you can deliver more IT services for the same budget, you're making a big step towards rapid and cost-effective IT—assuming you're enabling compliance along the way. If you're enabling rapid and cost-effective IT solutions, then you're making IT less of a bottleneck and more of a value-added service. Commitment to COBIT keeps you focused on compliance."

"I still don't think this is possible," Ramesh says. "The mainframe guys don't work that fast, and we still don't have a good integration module for CICS. Plus, our documentation writer is freelance and we have to wait for her schedule to be free and then we never have enough budget for everything we want . . ."

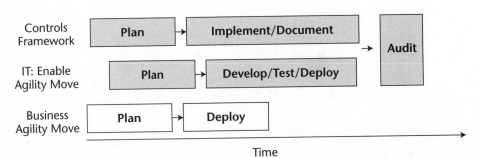

Figure 8-2 A cycle where IT and internal controls changes are more in sync with a business agility move

"Let's hold off on the specifics for another minute," Sebastian counters. "This is the point of the exercise: I want everyone to see what it would take for the company to be agile and compliant. This is about putting a vision together. Getting everyone to share the vision is a crucial first step in the whole process. However, you're right that making it happen certainly won't be easy."

Compliance as a Driver of Positive Change

"Okay," Sebastian says. "Let's check in and see where we all are. Who wants to be agile?" Everyone's hand goes up. "Who wants to be compliant?" Again, everyone raises their hand. "Who wants to be agile and compliant at the same time?" All hands, again. "Who wants to quadruple the budgets for IT and internal audit?" No hands go up, including Sebastian's. "Didn't think so. See, even I don't want to do that. So, what's our goal? Agile compliance but cost effective. Yes?" Nods all around. "We all agree that compliance and agility are worthwhile goals, assuming we can do it for a reasonable cost. We also agree that we should not be agile without being compliant, and we should not be compliant if it kills our agility. Yes?

"I also believe that we have to view compliance as a catalyst for positive change, not a nuisance. Otherwise, compliance will always drag down profits or kill agility." He draws a target on the board that looks like Figure 8-3. "This is our goal—the high-profit bull's-eye. The wind of compliance problems or lack of agility can throw off even our best shot."

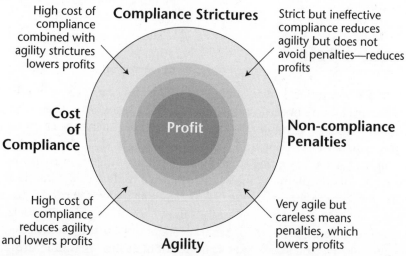

Figure 8-3 With high profit as the target, compliance and agility must be in balance to attain a bull's-eye. Combinations of high compliance costs, compliance strictures, lack of agility, and non-compliance penalties can reduce profits.

"Think of it like a diet," he continues. "Let's say your doctor tells you to go on a diet because you need to lose 20 pounds. You're overweight and you want to exercise, too, but you're too tired all the time. Before your diet, you eat junk food and excess sugar. Then, you start eating in a healthy way. You count your calories, cut down on fat and sugar, and only eat nutritious food. What happens? You start to lose weight. Your health improves because you're not loading up on junk. And, you have the ability to exercise because your body has the energy it needs. Overall, it's a good thing for you."

"We can go on a SOX diet," Sebastian says. "SOX can serve the same purpose for our overall business agility needs as the diet does for the unhealthy person. By taking a dieter's discipline and applying it to compliance, we can use compliance as a way to keep us healthy in a business sense."

"I think I get it," says Jim Wilde. "You're saying that if we can keep our focus on staying compliant, our overall business could run better because our controls would be tighter and our reporting would be faster, and so on. And, we could be agile without having to worry about compliance. I'd be free to do what I want when I want it, which is what I started out saying at the beginning of this whole discussion."

"Right," Linda says. "SOX is good for you. Or at least, it can be."

"I don't know," says Jim. "I hate to be negative about this," but I've never seen anything like this work in the past. Regulations just get in the way."

"You know," Linda says. "I think you're mistaken. Perhaps in your own experience what you're saying is true, but in the overall context of American business, there are several good examples of businesses improving as the result of regulation."

"Try me," says Jim.

It's Happened Before

"I can think of two examples," says Linda. "Whether they are precisely relevant to what we are talking about can be debated, but I think you'll see what I'm getting at. Remember when the government started requiring the car companies to limit exhaust emissions and keep gas mileage high? At first, the industry was aghast. This was going to be the end of the domestic auto industry, and so on. Lots of complaining, lobbying, attempts to deflect the intent of the law. Then, you know what happened? Japanese car makers started introducing fuel-efficient cars with lower emissions than a lot of American models, and American auto makers began to lose market share. As a result, they had to compete. To compete, Detroit started to use more sophisticated manufacturing techniques including six-sigma quality control, numerically controlled manufacturing, robotics, just in time, and more. It was like they went on their own kind of diet—a low bad-manufacturing-practices diet—and the quality of their cars improved. Not only did this help sales, it also helped the bottom line. Better manufacturing meant lower warranty exposure and less customer service work. Fewer defects in manufacturing led to higher customer satisfaction and repeat purchases. In some very important ways, the environmental rules, combined with foreign competition, lit a serious fire under their behinds. They benefited from adversity and regulation."

"I'll give you another one," she says. "Years ago, workers started agitating for more rights and entitlements. In some cases, it was actual unionization. In other situations, it was state and federal laws mandating certain policies like paid maternity leave. Overall, business was very hostile to this notion. Paying people more, or granting them more benefits, went against the low-cost grain of most American companies. Yet, if you look at what's happened since the 1990s, I think you'll see that American businesses have benefited greatly from creating more hospitable workplaces. A lot of companies began to discover that they could retain their best people longer if they committed to benefits and diversity. For companies that actually lived up to the ideal that people were their greatest asset, the revolution in benefits and entitlements gave them a great way to attract and keep the best people—and succeed in total as businesses. They went on a low-bad-hiring-practices diet and kept off the weight of low employee retention and low staff skill levels off permanently.

"The whole point," she says, "is to try to see the potential for growth in the regulatory environment. Not all regulations are good, and some of what we are talking about is going to be a major hassle. Certainly, some of it will be costly, at least in the short term. But, are we ready to take a serious look at it?"

Everyone in the room looked at her with expressions of willingness and interest. They were hooked, ready to listen, ready to talk and learn. "Okay, then," Jim Wilde says. "I'm going to make a decision here. I want to be compliant, but I am not going to sacrifice my plans to be agile. I am putting Dale here in charge of the company's overall SOX efforts. I want Dale to work closely with Linda's and Sebastian's teams and figure out how we are going to make this work. Dale nods in agreement. This is the kind of challenge he enjoys. He asks Linda and Sebastian to prepare in-depth material for a subsequent meeting.

Sebastian says, "Okay, then, let's get started. Linda and I are going to take you on a very, very deep dive into how DexCo can be compliant and agile. Fasten your seat belts. This is going to be intense."

Summary

After spending the first section of the book laying out just how thoroughly compliance issues can stall much-needed corporate agility, we now turn to the big question that is on Jim Wilde's mind: Can DexCo—or your company—be both agile and compliant? Although the answer is yes, the approaches to attaining such a state are challenging. Jumping right into technological solutions without considering business process, for example, is certain to fail.

At DexCo, CIO Sebastian Harris undertakes an exercise with the executive team. Wielding an imaginary magic wand, he asks the team to come up with their dream scenario for agility and compliance. His goal, he states, is to arrive at a wish list for agile compliance. After all, he says, we cannot truly start working on a goal until we know what it is.

The team has various goals, including being able to switch suppliers at will, change the organization chart, make alliances, and so on, without affecting compliance. The underlying finding in this process is a realization that compliance must be able to shift in tempo with the changes that the agility requires.

The CIO and CFO then illustrate how each objective on the wish list consists of both an IT and accounting control requirement. Thus, the team needs to view the attainment of each wish list item as a two-track process that includes IT and accounting.

The challenge that emerges right away, as we have seen in a slightly different form before, is that the cycle time for realizing a change to the accounting controls framework and the IT systems is far longer than that required for making the basic agility move. By the time accounting and IT catches up, management is probably going to be on to its next move.

The ultimate, generic goal of agile compliance, therefore, is to develop an integrated set of accounting and IT change processes that work rapidly enough to match the cycle time of agility changes.

This is not easy, but it can be done. Beyond that, the CIO and CFO tell the group, compliance can even be a driver of improvement in the business overall. Like an overweight person who finds, through dieting, that exercise is easier to do, a company with compliance problems can become more agile if its compliance efforts become speedier.

The Technology of Agile Compliance

Jim Wilde asked Linda Fuller's and Sebastian Harris's teams to review what they had discussed at his ranch and present detailed findings and a recommended plan of action. COO Dale Steyer scheduled a second retreat for a week hence. He would moderate the two teams while Jim Wilde was off on Wall Street for an analyst road show. Given their long relationship, as well as Steyer's history of military command, Wilde felt that he was the best choice to supervise such an important discussion. Steyer was to report back to him upon his return. This next meeting, which was to be held at the decidedly less glamorous setting of the local Ramada Inn, was intended to be a detailed working session with a firm goal of achieving consensus on pragmatic next steps to attaining the objective of agile compliance for DexCo.

Living Up to Potential

In recounting the Ramada Inn session and the various follow-up discussions that occurred at DexCo, I am reminded of a great quote by Professor James Cash, who taught me about information systems and controls at Harvard Business School. Cash, who is six foot six, had played college basketball. He had thought he was headed for a career in the NBA until his coach called him in to the office and told him, "Jim, you have great potential . . . ." Cash advised us to be wary whenever someone expressed a belief that we had "potential." Cash explained that the coach followed the comment on his potential by adding, "But, you're too short, too slow, can't shoot, and can't play defense." Cash realized at that moment that he had better get serious about computer science because the NBA wasn't going to be working out for him after all.

So it is with DexCo. Everyone at the company, including the accounting and IT teams, has the potential to make the company agile and compliant. Their challenge is to rise to the occasion and live up to that potential. Dale Steyer seizes the initiative in this regard at the start of the Ramada Inn session and sets two ground rules for making the process work: "One, we are going to listen to each other here. Two, we are not allowed to make any negative comments about what we hear from each other in the first round of discussion. After we have discussed an idea, we can then introduce challenges or negative aspects of it. If we don't take this approach, we're going to get bogged down in negativity and defensiveness. We'll get nowhere."

The Four Questions

"In addition," Steyer says. "We need to structure the discussion so we don't get off course. Although our goal here today is to achieve a better understanding of the technology aspects of our compliance situation, we need to root our discussion in the overall business context. At DexCo, IT serves the needs of the business organization. The two cannot do much that is meaningful without the other. So, we have here two basic groups, Accounting/Finance and IT. And, we have two essential questions about agility and compliance that we must address. First, is a given business process compliant to start with? That is, if we're going to talk about flex-acturing, is it compliant in its current state? Second, after we have satisfied ourselves that it is—or satisfied ourselves that we can fix whatever's wrong with it compliance-wise—then we can look at whether or not we can be agile without breaking the compliance. Got it? Two groups, two issues. Four questions." He writes them on the whiteboard:

Is it under control?

1. Does the business process have effective internal controls from an accounting perspective, as is?

2. Does the business process have effective internal controls from an IT perspective, as is?

Will it flex?

3. Can the process be flexible in terms of internal controls from an accounting perspective?

4. Can the process be flexible in terms of internal controls from an IT perspective?

"Here's another way of looking at it," Dale says as he draws an xyz axis chart on the whiteboard that resembles Figure 9-1. He explains that any business process or partnership scenario that they examine needs to be rated on all three axes—IT compliance with COSO control objectives, internal controls compliance from an accounting perspective, and ability to change and be agile. The optimum state is represented by the upper-right corner and point closest to the front, the theoretical third dimension of the graph represented by the asterisk. "We want be out here," he says. "Chances are very good that we are nowhere near that point now, but I want to place the goal in front of our faces to remind us what we're trying to accomplish."

"I'm impressed," says Linda Fuller. "You're a quick study."

"Oh, that I am," Steyer says, and shoots her a wink. "When I see the value of an idea, I'm all over it."

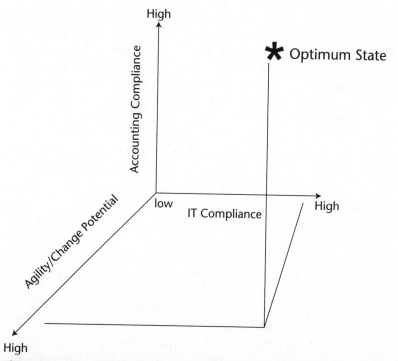

Figure 9-1   The optimum state for a business process requires that it have a baseline state of compliance but also the potential to be agile, from both the accounting and IT perspectives

Mapping Business Process and IT Architecture

Having set the ground rules and objectives for the meeting, Steyer yields the floor to Linda Fuller's accounting team. By prior agreement, they will be discussing flex-acturing as the working example of a challenging and complex business process that needs compliance attention. Working with members of the wholesale procurement organization, they lay out the basic business processes envisioned for flex-acturing.

Contractual Relationships

First, Linda draws a diagram that maps the main contractual relationships between the parties involved in flex-acturing. Figure 9-2 shows that DexCo has to enter into contracts with three separate entities, one of which is a group of companies, to conduct flex-acturing. There is the provider of the proprietary part—in this case a specialized cell phone chip—with which DexCo has a contract that calls for intellectual property licensing and manufacturing orders. Notably, DexCo has to agree to a 30-day cutoff if it decides to cease the production orders. This means that should DexCo cancel production of the item it is selling, but does not give the parts supplier 30-days notice, DexCo could get stuck paying for chips produced in that time period even though they will never be used. The contract calls for a standing order of 10,000 chips per month for 12 months. The contract can be renewed for another 12 months with 30 days notice at the end of the year. DexCo can request more chips or fewer, as long as it gives the supplier 30-days notice. If DexCo wants to order fewer chips, but does not give the supplier proper notice, then DexCo must pay for the full monthly order. Keep this in mind, as it will have an impact on inventory write-down issues.

DexCo also holds contracts with suppliers of other, non-proprietary parts used in the custom cell phone product envisioned for flex-acturing. These contracts are standard and allow DexCo broad powers to cancel or modify orders with little notice. In addition, they allow DexCo to return unused parts for full credit within 30 days of delivery.

Finally, DexCo contracts with an electronics assembly supplier. This company is contracted to receive the parts from the various suppliers and produce finished cell phones. The contract calls for a substantial set-up fee to establish the production line, and then a minimum monthly guarantee of production. The supplier is able to add a second shift with a week's notice, but the second shift must be used for a minimum of two weeks, because of union rules at the plant. DexCo anticipates running two shifts for the month of September as it ramps up the pre-Christmas orders to retailers. The contract lasts for 12 months, with a penalty of one month's minimum fees if DexCo cancels before 12 months are over. DexCo can renew the contract for another 12 months with 30-days notice.

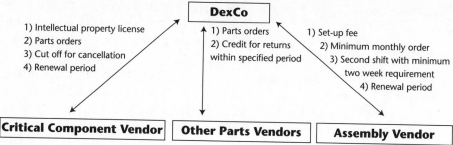

Figure 9-2 Contractual relationships required for flex-acturing

Process Flow

Linda asks, "Got it?" A few people chuckle. This one example shows how complex supply chain management can be. "We're not even started yet," she says, and proceeds to draw an activity flow chart resembling Figure 9-3 on the board. Flex-acturing requires the orchestration of business processes amongst different divisions of DexCo as well as the contracted vendors.

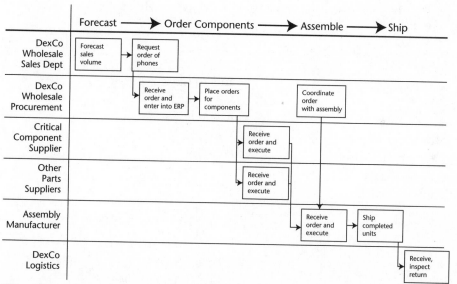

Figure 9-3 Flex-acturing's Business Process Flow amongst multiple departments and DexCo vendors

The process flow begins with DexCo's sales department developing a forecast for the number of units it will require. The forecast drives the demand for manufacturing. The sales department hands the forecast off to the procurement department, which arranges for the manufacture of the components and their assembly into finished pieces for sale. The component manufacturers deliver their goods to the assembly manufacturer, who completes the product assembly and delivers to DexCo's logistics division. The logistics division inspects the finished goods and returns any defective pieces for credit.

IT Architecture

Linda hands the markers to Sebastian, who now begins to draw the IT architecture that supports flex-acturing's process flow. As I mentioned in Chapter 1, DexCo relies on a centralized financial general ledger system at the corporate level. An interface connects the financial system to the ERP system used by the wholesale and original equipment manufacturer (OEM) divisions. It is this enterprise resource planning (ERP) system that is most critical to controlling the flex-acturing process. DexCo's sales teams will prepare their forecasts for the products made by flex-acturing using the wholesale division's customer resource management (CRM) systems. Currently, this is a manual process, although it has the potential to be integrated system-to-system, as shown in Figure 9-4.

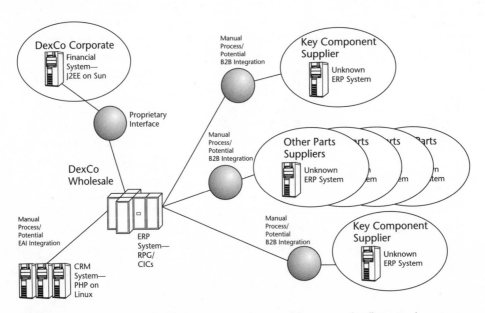

Figure 9-4   Logical architecture of systems that would support the flex-acturing process

When DexCo places purchase orders, manages invoices and payables, and handles returns and credits with each of its flex-acturing suppliers, it has a choice. It can rely on a manual process, or it can integrate its systems with those of the supplier. Unlike the main OEM suppliers, who are on an EDI system with DexCo, the flex-acturing suppliers have no set integration. This could be a good or bad thing, depending on the control factors involved.

Is Flex-Acturing Under Control?

Now that Linda and Sebastian have outlined the business processes and IT architecture involved in flex-acturing, it's time to look at the first of the four questions posed by Dale Steyer: Does flex-acturing have adequate internal controls from both an accounting and systemic perspective?

Using the COSO framework and relevant COBIT guidelines, Linda and Sebastian proceed to outline several high-priority control objectives, together with their attendant risks and control procedures. In addition, the two note DexCo's existing internal controls for these objective-risk-procedure pairings, as well as the current IT factors that affect each one.

As shown in Table 9-1, several of the risks are mitigated adequately by DexCo's internal controls and IT systems. For example, the ERP can track approved suppliers, which supports the internal control that requires use of approved suppliers only. Other controls are less robust. The users of the ERP system can override the system in many cases, a factor that gives them the potential to rewrite purchase orders and inventory reports after the fact. The culprit is a poorly managed user access rights feature. The problem is not actually technological in nature. If the company managed its staff better, then the designated policies would be followed more rigorously.

Overall, flex-acturing is partially in control and has the potential to be more in control if the company had the management discipline to enforce all of its internal control policies. On paper, especially adding in requirements to improve system security, flex-acturing probably has sufficient internal controls to pass a Sarbanes Oxley 404 audit.

As my grandmother used to say, however, "Where's the rub?" Could DexCo really have such good internal controls? DexCo personnel often follow their own particular approach to business process, and bend the internal controls and IT systems to meet those practices. This kind of loose management can have the greatest negative impact on effective internal controls.

Table 9-1 Control Objectives, Risks, and Control Procedures for Flex-acturing, with Internal Controls and IT Factors Also Considered

CONTROL OBJECTIVE	RISK	CONTROL PROCEDURE	DEXCO'S INTERNAL CONTROLS	IT/COBIT CONTROL FACTORS
Only pre-approved suppliers can be used to meet price, service level, and quality specifications.	Suppliers or their products may be incapable of meeting DexCo's needs.	Establish an approved supplier list and set up periodic review of prices, quality parameters, and service levels.	Controls call for use of approved suppliers only.	ERP system can track approved suppliers. ■ COBIT AI 1 in effect, automated system
All sourcing costs are booked into the correct accounting period.	Improper cutoff of purchase records at the end of the period.	Establish proper cut-off procedures at the end of the month for all purchase orders.	Controls call for cutoff of purchase orders at end of period.	ERP system users can override period ending, mitigating effectiveness of the control. ■ COBIT DS 11 issue, data quality ■ COBIT DS 5, issue security
Completely and accurately record all authorized transfers from inventory.	Documents may be missing or lost, or information may be untimely or incorrect.	All inventory handling, transfer, and movement documents are pre-numbered.	Controls mandate pre-numbered forms. Such forms exist on paper and electronically.	ERP system has auto-generated pre-numbered forms. Users can also input serial numbers of paper forms. Distinct numbering schemes exist in ERP system. ■ COBIT DS 11 in effect, data quality
		Inventory document sequence is periodically checked.	Controls call for quarterly internal audit of inventory documents.	ERP system has module for reporting results of quarterly internal audit and flagging exceptions to controls.
		All unused forms are controlled.	Controls call for collection and filing of unused forms and electronic records.	Covered in ERP inventory document report ■ COBIT AI 1 in effect, automated system
		Records are maintained for voided forms.	Controls call for collection and filing of voided forms and electronic records.	Covered in ERP inventory document report. ■ COBIT AI 1 in effect, automated system

CONTROL OBJECTIVE	RISK	CONTROL PROCEDURE	DEXCO'S INTERNAL CONTROLS	IT/COBIT CONTROL FACTORS
Ensure that customer, inventory, and sales order information is accurately updated to reflect released and delivered goods.	Inventory information may be incomplete, inaccurate, or lost.	Inventory records are maintained based on shipping records, and are periodically counted, costed, and compared to inventory control accounts.	Controls call for monthly counting and costing of inventory records and comparison to inventory control accounts.	ERP system enables counting, costing, and comparison of inventory documents. However, system users can override. ■ COBIT DS 11 issue, data quality
Ensure completeness and accuracy of inventory records.	Unauthorized input for non-existent shipments or handling.	Inventory control accounts are reconciled against the general ledger.	Controls call for monthly reconciliation of general ledger accounts.	ERP system generates inventory detail report that is used to reconcile the general ledger accounts. However, system users can override. ■ COBIT DS 11 issue, data quality System user management is not adequately implemented to guarantee this control. ■ COBIT DS 5 issue, security
Process inventory handling records only for authorized transactions.	Inadequate segregation of custodial, supervisory and record-keeping functions.	Reconciliations are made by persons independent of shipping; all reconciling items are appropriate and approved, and reconciliations are reviewed by management.	Controls call for internal audit staff to review inventory records and report to management.	System log-in has capacity to enforce segregation of roles, but system user management is not adequately implemented to guarantee this control. ■ COBIT DS 5 issue, security

Source of Control Objective Descriptions: Karl Nagel

A deeper look, too, will reveal an even more problematic issue in flex-acturing's basic compliance with sound internal controls. The control objective of "ensure completeness and accuracy of inventory records" is a potential land mine for DexCo when one includes the ramifications of the various contractual relationships in play with flex-acturing. What would happen if DexCo were to increase its production orders based on increased sales forecasts—an action that would trigger increased output from the parts suppliers and possibly require the second shift at the assembly plant—but then revise the estimates down after a customer's credit failed to prove adequate for the order? The company could find itself paying for excess production of goods that it had not forecasted for sale. If such a chain of events were to occur close to the end of a product's life cycle (and remember, flex-acturing is all about changing product lines every six to nine months) then DexCo might have to write down its excess inventory of useless goods. Depending on the quality of the manual processes that connect the ERP, CRM, and vendor systems, DexCo might have to adjust its inventory accounts after the close of the reporting period.

Will It Flex?

As they stand now, according to Linda and Sebastian, the internal controls and supporting IT systems cannot be flexible enough to enable flex-acturing. Although the accounting aspects of the internal controls exist on paper, and paper controls can be endlessly redone and always be perfect, the reality is that the whole system is overly rigid. In this example, the discussions of accounting internal controls and IT controls are tightly integrated. The accounting controls are inflexible because of the innate inflexibility of the IT components of those controls. Business management issues further impair the ability for DexCo's IT systems to be flexible enough to enable agility for flex-acturing. The net result is an overall lack of flexibility.

One basic problem is the reliance on manual processes to integrate the systems involved, and thus enforce the controls. As shown in Figure 9-4, there are manual processes at each key intersection between systems. The sales forecasts in the CRM system are entered into the ERP system manually. The connections between DexCo's ERP and its vendors' ERP systems are also manual. Only the connection between DexCo's ERP and its financial system is automated, and that is the one area that has the best potential internal controls.

Why is a manual system inimical to flexibility? In some ways, it ought not be—manual systems are in theory the most flexible of all. Yet, in reality they are generally too slow and too dependent on individual people to be able to change and still enforce internal controls. If you have ever worked in management, then you can probably relate to the frustration of trying to get people to perform a task in a consistent and specific way. You might also be familiar with the difficulty you can have following up and seeing if a manual process has been executed correctly.

Manual processes do not change easily; nor do they provide good scalability. For these reasons, DexCo would need to establish some level of automated integration between its CRM system and ERP system, as well as between its ERP system and that of its key suppliers, to enable any real flexibility in the flex-acturing process. Yet, integrating the existing systems might cause difficulty for compliance. Let's examine why.

One problem in remediating the kind of control deficiencies under discussion here is the lack of flexibility inherent in the standard fixes available to DexCo. Table 9-2 looks at a specific set of remedies for one of the internal control problems identified in Table 9-1. If there is potential for users of the ERP system to override the controls and restate inventory figures, then DexCo can strengthen the internal control by implementing a more robust, centralized user access management system. In addition, the company can automate a process that correlates inventory data in the ERP system against other records in other systems, including those of its suppliers.

Alright, that sounds pretty good. If DexCo could implement a good user access control system, then it would improve its compliance. However, we have a problem. Figure 9-5 shows how the internal controls process at the accounting level and its supporting IT systems are far too slow to accommodate the rapid cycling of change that the flex-acturing process demands.

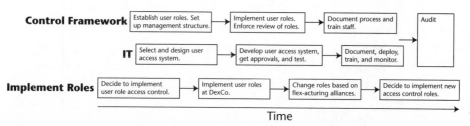

Figure 9-5 Mismatch between time frames of decision and deployment in user role access management and the controls and IT systems that support it

Table 9-2 IT Remedies to Internal Control Problem Matched with Inhibitors of Those Remedies

CONTROL OBJECTIVE	RISK	CONTROL PROCEDURE	DEXCO'S INTERNAL CONTROLS	IT/COBIT CONTROL FACTORS	REMEDIES FOR IT/ INTERNAL CONTROL PROBLEMS	INHIBITORS OF REMEDIES
Ensure that customer, inventory, and sales order information is accurately updated to reflect released and delivered goods.	Inventory information may be incomplete, inaccurate, or lost.	Inventory records are maintained based on shipping records and are periodically counted, costed, and compared to inventory control accounts.	Controls call for monthly counting and costing of inventory records and comparison to inventory control accounts.	ERP system enables counting, costing, and comparison of inventory documents. However, system users can override. ■ COBIT DS 11 issue, data quality	■ Centralized user access management system ■ Enforcement of security policy: only authorized users can override the system ■ Automated correlation of data from ERP system to other systems and paper documents	■ Cost and time required to implement access management system ■ Management issues involved in enforcing policy ■ Cost and time required to implement automated correlation of data

When DexCo senior management signs off on a set of user access roles that would enforce internal controls and end the practice of overriding the ERP system, the IT aspects of the implementation, as well as the procedural and documentation requirements that COSO demands would take another significant period of time to complete. At some point well before then, senior management would likely want to change the user role definitions and configuration again to accommodate the *flex* in flex-acturing.

If DexCo were to integrate with its vendors, who would be in charge of the controls? If DexCo were not careful—and let's face it, they have not always been so careful in the past—they might accidentally enable their vendor to override the system. This is the issue of IT governance, which is at the heart of COBIT. Who has the governance of the inter-company systems? Of course, thorough coding, testing, and documentation will make it work, but this is a slow and inflexible process. The more such connections are contemplated, the more complex the internal control and related IT governance issues become.

As shown in Figure 9-6, there are control points throughout the business process of flex-acturing. As is often the case, several of the control points overlap with an integration point between systems. Even if the integration is manual, the enforcement of the control is related to the IT involved. For example, if it is necessary for a clerk to enter the results of a customer credit check into the financial system, the internal control that calls for restricting sales from noncreditworthy customers will derive from how well the data from the credit check is handled when it gets to the ERP system through the interface. If the results of the credit check do not show up in the order management process, then DexCo might order goods it cannot or should not sell. If the manual process is too slow to keep up with the order management system in the ERP system, then the company faces the same credit risk for a different reason.

If DexCo starts to change manufacturing partners rapidly, as it intends to do in flex-acturing, the control points will not keep up. If each of the six control points identified must be evaluated and modified for a new partnership, the system will not remain compliant over time.

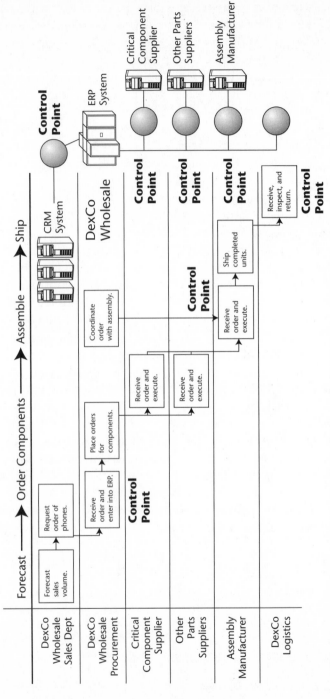

Figure 9-6 Connections between flex-acuring business process, IT systems, and control point

Answering Dale's Questions

Dale asked four questions about flex-acturing at the start of the meeting. Let's see how this particular business process did. As Dale draws Table 9-3 on the board, it's obvious that flex-acturing has gotten rather low marks. Not an utter failure, but certainly not very well in control today and not particularly flexible looking ahead.

Returning to the xyz diagram used earlier, Dale now plots the flex-acturing process on the grid and shows how it falls short of the optimum (see Figure 9-7). "I think it is important to know where we stand on a given situation before we get into a lot of detail on making it right. I don't want to talk about how we are going to make a process flexible if it isn't in control to start with. And I want to understand what's holding us up from being flexible if the process is already in pretty good control. I don't want to mess up the controls with the flexibility solutions."

Table 9-3   Summary of Answers to Dale's Four Basic Questions About Flex-acturing

	AGILITY/CONTROL CATEGORY	RATING (1–5)	COMMENT
1	Does it have effective internal controls from an accounting perspective, as is?	3	The accounting controls mostly exist, at least on paper, but deficiencies in IT, such as lax user management and access controls, compromise many of them.
2	Does it have effective internal controls from an IT perspective, as is?	2	Lack of integration between vendor systems and DexCo, as well as between DexCo's CRM and ERP systems, compromise internal controls.
3	Can the process be flexible in terms of internal controls from an accounting perspective?	2	Accounting internal controls cannot change rapidly enough to be flexible, because of IT dependencies.
4	Can the process be flexible in terms of internal controls from an IT perspective?	2	Remedies to IT control problems are impaired by time, cost, and management factors, slowing the change process down and reducing agility.

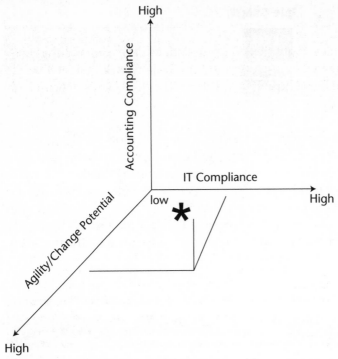

Figure 9-7 Flex-acturing as measured on the xyz scale of agility potential, accounting compliance, and IT compliance

What It Will Take to Flex

"What can we take away from this discussion?" Sebastian Harris asks.

"Open a bar and forget all about this sorry business," someone says from the back of the room.

"Well, you might have control issues there as well," Sebastian counters. "Let's put together a list of have-to-have features for the systems and controls that we will need to achieve flexible compliance." He adds a column to Table 9-1. For several of the control procedures, he writes in the kind of IT system and internal control framework it will take to be compliant but also agile. Table 9-4 shows the results.

Table 9-4   Requirements for Agile Compliance in Flex-acturing

CONTROL PROCEDURE	DEXCO'S INTERNAL CONTROLS	IT/COBIT CONTROL FACTORS	AGILE BUT COMPLIANT APPROACH TO THE CONTROL
Establish an approved supplier list and set up periodic review of prices, quality parameters, and service levels.	Controls call for use of approved suppliers only.	ERP system can track approved suppliers. ■ COBIT AI 1 in effect, automated system time cycle as changes in partnerships.	Must be able to change supplier role configuration in same
Establish proper cut-off procedures at the end of the month for all purchase orders.	Controls call for cut-off of purchase orders at end of period.	ERP system users can override period ending, mitigating effectiveness of the control. ■ COBIT DS 11 issue, data quality ■ COBIT DS 5 issue, security	■ Must have user access system that can interoperate with disparate systems and be reconfigured in same time cycle as partnership changes ■ Must have flexible integration with CRM to provide real-time updates to sales forecast and flow data through the ERP system
Inventory records are maintained based on shipping records, and are periodically counted, costed, and compared to inventory control accounts.	Controls call for monthly counting and costing of inventory records and comparison to inventory control accounts.	ERP system enables counting, costing, and comparison of inventory documents. However, system users can override. ■ COBIT DS 11 issue, data quality	Cannot allow system overrides by unauthorized users. User access system must be able to maintain policy enforcement even as it changes configuration and integrates with outside systems.

(continued)

Table 9-4   *(continued)*

CONTROL PROCEDURE	DEXCO'S INTERNAL CONTROLS	IT/COBIT CONTROL FACTORS	AGILE BUT COMPLIANT APPROACH TO THE CONTROL
Inventory control accounts are reconciled against the general ledger.	Controls call for monthly reconciliation of general ledger accounts.	ERP system generates inventory detail report that is used to reconcile the general ledger accounts. However, system users can override. ■ COBIT DS 11 issue, data quality System user management is not adequately implemented to guarantee this control. ■ COBIT DS 5 issue, security	Must be able to automate reconciliation of accounts and allow for changes in account setup and system configuration in same time cycle as partnership changes.

Sebastian now draws a simplified version of Table 9-4 and labels it Take-aways. "Let's summarize," he says. "What we need, in general, are the following control and system requirements:"

The requirements outlined in Table 9-5 are the generalized version of those needed to make flex-acturing a reality. They are not the complete set of requirements needed for agile compliance overall, but they are a start. As Sebastian says as he wraps up the session, "I wanted you to see an in-depth example of what it takes to be flexible and compliant—to enable agility but keep our internal controls in line to comply with Sarbanes Oxley. These requirements, and others that we will add to them as we go over other areas of DexCo's wish list, will form the basis for the discussion of any systemic changes that we plan to make at the company."

Table 9-5   General Requirements for IT Systems to Enable Agility and Compliance

User identity management system(s) must be able to change role configuration in same time cycle as business agility dictates.

User identity management system(s) must interoperate with disparate systems and be reconfigured in same time cycle as business agility dictates.

Table 9-5 *(continued)*

Must have flexible application integration with CRM to provide real-time data flow between systems that are necessary for maintenance of internal controls.

Cannot allow system overrides by unauthorized users. User access system must be able to maintain policy enforcement even as it changes configuration and integrates with outside systems.

Must be able to automate reconciliation of accounts and allow for changes in account setup and system configuration in same time cycle as business agility dictates.

Summary

This chapter takes a deep dive into the factors driving the potential for DexCo to achieve agile compliance in one specific instance, which is CEO Jim Wilde's vision of flex-acturing, or flexibly and rapidly developing new wireless products with a host of manufacturing partners. COO Dale Steyer, who presides over a second meeting of the executive team, first asks to establish a baseline of understanding about flex-acturing and determine if it has effective internal controls both from an accounting and IT perspective, and then whether the process can maintain its controls if it changes.

To answer these four questions, the accounting and IT teams lay out the business processes involved in flex-acturing, and then map them against the company's current IT systems and those of its partners. Part of the exercise is to gain an understanding of the analytical process involved in determining what it will take to achieve agile compliance in a given business scenario. The accounting and IT departments then go through an exhaustive set of steps designed to highlight the strengths and weaknesses of the internal controls in flex-acturing, as well as their capacity to be changed.

Overall, flex-acturing does not get high marks for either existing internal controls or potential to change and remain in control. However, those attending the meeting get a good overview of what it will take to enable agile compliance from a technological perspective. The meeting ends with a set of takeaways that include such core issues as having user identity management systems, control over system access and overrides, potential for interoperation between disparate systems both inside and outside the firm, and automated reconciliation of accounting data with order and inventory data—all of which needs to be changed systemically in a time frame synchronous with the tempo of the flex-acturing process.

CHAPTER 10

The Organization of Agile Compliance

Dale Steyer walks into Jim Wilde's office and throws a recently whittled branch of Tennessee Maple on the desk. Wilde picks up the piece of wood and looks quizzically at his COO. "Yeah?" he asks.

"I got you a stick," Dale says. Wilde nods again, unsure what this is all about. "So you can start shaking it."

"I got it," Wilde replies. "More trouble than I can shake a stick at . . ."

"This Sarbanes Oxley thing is a bear," Dale says. "At first, I thought it was a lot of auditor hoo-hah. Now, I can see that we have to get a handle on this, or we're going to be shaking that wood all day long." He takes a sheaf of papers out of his briefcase and hands them to Wilde. "Look at this one about Delphi. You know they just filed for Chapter 11. Well, the *New York Times* says that they 'sold problematic inventory to third parties for enormous sums of money' . . . 'Sham Transactions to Lift Profits.' They're being sued in a class action by shareholders, and the SEC is investigating. They're restating financials going back three years according to the *New York Times*. Plus, check this out." He opens a copy of Delphi's 2004 annual report and shows Wilde a highlighted section that reads, "Delphi management's assessment pursuant to Section 404 [of the Sarbanes Oxley Act] determined that Delphi had not maintained effective internal controls over financial reporting at December 31st 2004. In addition, management concluded that during such periods, Delphi's disclosure controls and procedures were also ineffective. Delphi has undertaken and is continuing to take such actions to address material weaknesses in its internal controls . . ."

"Yikes," Jim Wilde says. "I'd hate to be having to write that in our annual report.

"Right," Dale answers. "Especially because, as you can see, the problem is far from being solved. All they've really copped to is admitting that they have a problem. They're nowhere near a solution, as far as I can tell. Now, check this out." He shows Wilde an article from *Computerworld* magazine that provides accounts of how several large companies have complied with Sarbanes Oxley. 'SOX is a very expensive proposition. Viacom conducted 19,600 tests on 1,560 business controls and 540 on IT controls in 2004. The work covered 116 business processes and 75 IT applications.' Can you imagine what that cost them? Time Warner spent 350,000 person-hours identifying, evaluating, and testing its financial and IT controls. Dow Chemical tested 30,000 internal controls. Here's the capper: 'Because Section 404-related work consumed so much time and resources, many companies ended up placing a number of strategic IT/business projects on the back burner to meet the December 31, 2004 deadline . . .'" (*Computerworld;* September 28, 2005.)

"What are we in for?" Wilde asks. "We're a lot smaller than those guys."

"True," Dale says. "But still, proportionally, we may have to pay our dues, too. The problem, and this is what's really bugging me about all of this, is that I am not at all confident that we can get good advice about any of this. Look at this article I found in *CIO Magazine*. It begins, 'The dirty little secret of the first Sarbanes Oxley Audit [in 2004] is that no one really knew what they were doing. Not the auditors, not the consultants, not you.' The article describes how the CIO of a major chemical company watched as his auditors and SOX consultants argued in a 'constant tug of war' where they 'created, tweaked and clarified controls . . .' and seemed to be making up rules as they went along." (*CIO Magazine* July 1, 2005.)

"Right," Jim says. "After they tested tens of thousands of controls, did they actually accomplish anything, or did they just go through a hugely expensive set of motions of wills till it bites them in the . . . you know." Jim smiles and takes his new stick, shaking it at Dale. "Okay, boy, I'm shakin' it good now. Tell me what I need to do."

"Before we get into the overview, I think we have our own version of this kind of problem that we need to nip in the bud," Dale says, giving Jim a knowing look. They have discussed this matter before, but this time Jim can tell it's serious.

"What's going on?"

"Well, we had a suspicion about the practices going on at the wholesale division. Our internal Sarbanes Oxley audit uncovered some internal control deficiencies. Now, our regular auditor has done some digging. Our hunch was correct. Although we're not 100 percent certain, it looks as if Reggie Marchaldon's been doing a channel stuffing routine to pump his bonus up. Even without the audit, you could see something funny was going on. His cost of goods sold went way down in the fourth quarter of last year, which is his busiest season, and then shoots right back up in the first quarter of this year. His bonus is based partly on gross margin growth. It went from $290,000 in the fourth quarter to nothing in the first quarter. He was in a position to prime the pump for this year by pushing his costs up in the first quarter. He had the ability to arrange for buyers to give him fake purchase orders in the first quarter that he could then rescind in the second quarter. He could have had trucks taking merchandise out of warehouses over the weekend between the quarters and bringing it back the next week. He could have had suppliers take bogus POs to drive up cost of goods sold and then changed the orders in the next accounting period. The whole effect would have been to give him a heck of an increase in gross margin when he needed it to earn a nice bonus."

"Well that's just a dandy way to start my tenure at this company. Okay, he's fired."

"We don't know for a fact that this is going on. It just smells bad, Jim," Dale says. "But this is just the kind of situation we're talking about with all these Sarbanes Oxley meetings. Reggie's probably not the only one playing us like that and now the stakes are pretty darned high if we can't figure out what's going on."

Jim Wilde nods in understanding and says, "We have to confirm what happened, disclose as necessary, maybe do a restatement. Take our lumps with the SEC and the shareholders."

"Right, ethically, we have to show that we will not tolerate or cover up this kind of activity. Plus, we're doing what we're supposed to be doing under Sarbanes Oxley. We have identified a deficiency, and now we can remediate it."

"That's like saying we totaled our car but at least we know a good body shop. This cannot happen again," Jim says with determination.

"I agree," Dale says. "That's what we're working on with Linda's and Sebastian's teams."

Challenges to the Agile, Compliant Organization

"How is that process going, anyway?" Wilde asks. The impact of the news about his wholesale division is beginning to sink in. He's a glum cowboy all of a sudden.

"We're off to a good start. But the thing with Reggie Marchaldon shows me that there's a whole dimension to this SOX stuff that we have to figure out before we can do anything serious. Yes, it's about IT. Yes, it's about internal controls and accounting. But it's also about the company as a whole. The organization. The personalities. The politics. The incentives. Everything ties together. SOX seems to be as much an organizational issue as anything else."

"That makes sense," Jim replies. "There's a common denominator to all of the SOX control and agility issues. The problems, and the solutions no doubt as well, spring from organizational factors. That's where you ought to be focusing your teams."

"We are," Dale says. "It's providing its share of challenges, though. In some ways, the technological and accounting rules issues are easy. The organizational stuff is hard."

Tone at the Top Revisited

"For example," Dale says, "COSO describes a category of control known as control environment, or tone at the top. Control environment is a substantial, but troublingly vague concept that begs further definition. On one level, it's obvious that the ability of a company to achieve agile compliance is ultimately a matter of top management's style and substance. At the same time, it's quite difficult to define exactly what it is about top management that can have a real impact on the potential for agile compliance."

What follows is an account of Jim Wilde's and Dale Steyer's attempt to make sense of that question in a pragmatic way. What can they do at DexCo to make the company agile and compliant? How do their actions translate into the capacity for the company to move quickly, but also maintain internal controls? The subtext of much of their discussion was the failure of DexCo's internal controls to catch Reggie Marchaldon at his game of rigging the financials in his division. What organizational factors were at work to enable this kind of breakdown in control?

Jim and Dale agree that there is both a big picture to top management's role in compliance, as well as a little picture. Both are important. The big picture is that the ethics and control discipline of a company, even a very large one, will generally follow the ethics and control discipline of its leaders. As the situation at Enron showed, for example, if the top managers of a company are unethical, or at least willing to bend rules to achieve their objectives, then it is quite unlikely that any serious internal controls will work regardless of the effectiveness of their design. Of course, if there is outright crime occurring at the top, then internal controls may be a joke. As the WorldCom case showed, if the top managers are intent on violating internal controls, they can usually make it happen. "Okay," Jim says to Dale. "Are you a crook?"

"No."

"Good, me neither. Let's move on to the little picture." "Not so fast," Dale says. "I think we're getting good grades on ethics, but I believe that we may be exuding an indifference to control issues that could infect the rest of the company."

"Really?" Jim replies. "I thought we were taking this all very seriously."

"We are, but I think we are creating the impression that we want internal controls to shift in deference to our plans, without taking enough responsibility for the quality of the controls themselves." They agreed to work on modifying that impression.

The little picture is more subjective. It's a lot of little pictures, actually, Dale observes. First, there is the issue of incentive pay. As top managers, they both play a role in managing a compensation scheme that offers big payoffs for certain kinds of performance. To move ahead with agile compliance, DexCo's top management should try to make sure that any incentive pay programs are matched by agile, effective controls that mitigate against the temptations to game the system.

Change is a critical factor in incentive programs, too. As Dale points out, it is probable that at some point, Reggie Marchaldon was restricted from his tricks by a set of internal controls. However, as time went on, personnel came and went in the accounting and IT department, business rules changed, and various systems were not updated. Eventually, Reggie was able to aggregate enough control levers to have the ability to conduct his trade loading activities and hide the results.

Top management can also have an impact on compliance through the quality of the people they select to run the various departments involved. I spoke about this with the CEO of a multibillion dollar publicly traded company. He said, "Every quarter, I have to sign a letter, as does our controller, that says that everything here is to the best of your knowledge according to GAAP and according to the other rules that Sarb-Ox added on top of that. I have to look my CFO in the eye and say, 'Are these economics in fact correct and do they reflect the state of the business so forth?' Once he says yes, and I absolutely trust the guy, that's it. I have to take that as face value. Sarbanes Oxley puts a huge premium on the caliber of the people that you have in your organization more than anything else. It's not like I'm going to take a day or two out of a quarter to sit down and do somebody else's job for them with a fine tooth comb just so that I can stay out of jail."

Picking people forms a master set of issues related to top management's responsibility to shareholders to run the entire company. Top managers don't do the day-to-day jobs of the people they hire. They can't. However, if they choose the right people to do the job, and provide them with high-level guidance on what they expect when it comes to agility and compliance, they are exerting positive force on the situation. Unfortunately, the opposite is also true.

With understanding that their role is supervisory, top management is nonetheless responsible for setting the policies and organizational structures of both the IT and accounting departments, the two areas most concerned with agile compliance. And, top management is responsible for setting a tone of seriousness amongst line-of-business managers that internal controls matter.

For any of this to work, however, the IT architecture and business practices of the company must be set up to enable top management to have timely visibility into the activities going on all around them. When you hear about the importance of "real time visibility" in IT vendor pitches, one of the takeaways should be that you can enable top management to implement and govern agile compliance by understanding what is going on in the company they are charged with running.

Finally, top management needs to be willing to expend resources where necessary. Although Jim Wilde likes to say that "the buck stops with me," the reality is that the bucks actually start with him. He's got his hand on DexCo's checkbook. If he is not ready to spend money and time on agile compliance, he will handicap the company's efforts to attain this important goal. To be effective at this, the CEO has to have an understanding of the issues involved and the ability to evaluate when and where it is right to spend. The responsibility to keep the CEO up to speed on these issues is the responsibility of each major department involved.

The Accounting Organization

Although I'm not an accountant, I have some thoughts on the way accounting is organized at public companies and how the accounting organization can relate to the issue of agile compliance. For starters, there really isn't such a thing as an accounting organization. I mention this because many non-accountants (including myself at times) tend to think of the accounting branch of a corporation as a monolithic entity. It is not. A major public company will usually have an accounting department comprised of day-to-day payables and receivables, bank relationships, internal audit and budgeting, tax planning and preparation, reporting, and SEC disclosure and reporting. There is the external auditor, that is charged with auditing the books and assuring shareholders that the financial statements are accurate. There is also often a Sarbanes Oxley consultant—in some cases another major audit firm—who helps the company put its SOX house in order before the external auditor looks it all over.

To complicate matters further, many large companies have far flung and loosely connected accounting organizations at divisions and subsidiaries. This practice may be a necessity or a cost-cutting luxury. And, while it may work at some companies, it can also cause trouble. The crisis at Interpublic Group, for example, is largely a matter of dislocated and poorly integrated subsidiaries reporting problematic numbers.

At a structural level, the pieces of an accounting organization need to have a sufficient degree of internal coherence to achieve agile compliance. Each element of the accounting team should be able to communicate its internal control needs to the other relevant groups. To be agile, the elements of the accounting organization need to be able to move together in lockstep where necessary.

On a subjective level, the accounting organization needs to have a true understanding of the strategic and operational needs of the actual business in order to play a role in ensuring agile compliance. The relevance of this point emerges when one speaks with IT people and line-of-business managers who may feel the necessity to skirt internal control policies set down by accountants who don't get what's going on.

An example of this problem is segregation of duties. An accountant may establish an internal control based on segregation of duties but not examine exactly who is supposed to perform the segregated duties. Or, the accountant may simply be unaware that the structure of the organization has changed, or someone has been laid off, and so on, thus removing the person who can provide the internal control of duty segregation—because the accountant lacks proper visibility into the operations.

Bruce McCuaig, a Certified Internal Auditor (CIA) and Certified Information Systems Auditor (CISA) writing in *Internal Auditor Magazine* in 2005, comments with experienced insight on the issue of segregation of duties. "There is not a shred of definitive proof in the audit literature that segregation of duties is generally effective or worth its often significant cost. In fact, the preponderance of evidence indicates that segregation of duties is the most overrated and often least cost-effective control design option available. The real problem is lack of risk assessment, lack of a control environment that places emphasis on ethical standards and competence, and lack of monitoring when conflicting duties exist."

To bolster this assertion, McCuaig gives an example that could come right out DexCo's situation. "In an operating environment, a foreman may requisition the purchase of materials. They are purchased from an approved supplier by a purchasing agent. The result is often chaos—purchasing orders from the lowest bidder, the foreman does not get the material specified, or gets it late. What happens really? The foreman picks up the phone and orders the material directly from the supplier [in violation of internal controls that specify segregation of duties in purchasing] and purchasing prepares the paperwork after the fact. Time and again, honest, well-meaning employees, in the pursuit of legitimate business objectives, find themselves hopelessly encumbered by these controls while trying to do their jobs. Thus, they simply bypass or subvert and violate them." (*Internal Auditor,* April, 2005.)

In the case of Reggie Marchaldon, DexCo's internal controls clearly stated that the division General Manager was prohibited from rewriting purchase orders to suppliers once they had been entered into the system. In addition, the internal controls stated that shipments had to be validated by an individual separate from the one who originated the order. What happened in reality?

Over time, Marchaldon was able to fire or shift the personnel who were responsible for enforcing these separations of responsibility. He replaced them with people he could control, or who simply didn't know any better. The boss asked them to rewrite a PO and they did it. DexCo's manual of internal controls was not exactly a page-turner and few people read it thoroughly enough to understand that what the General Manager was asking them to do was against company policy.

I'm not trying to knock accountants here. Like so many well-meaning professionals, they have the potential to miss the major point of their activities in pursuit of specific policies. My goal in exploring this example of a disconnect between accounting practices and actual business processes is to show how an accounting organization can inadvertently foster an atmosphere that is inimical to agile compliance.

The IT Organization

Alas, like the largely fictitious "accounting organization," the IT organization is also a composite of many separate entities that operate in concert to a greater or lesser degree depending on the quality of their leadership. In terms of agile compliance, though, coordination of separate units of the IT organization is highly relevant.

To reiterate a theme I began to develop in Chapter 6, it seems that a lot of business people view those in the IT field as being a homogeneous lot. Nothing could be farther from the truth. IT people are not replaceable parts that lack unique characteristics. The fellow who helps replace your keyboard probably has a dramatically different educational pedigree and professional skillset than the person who designs the application architecture for a Fortune 500 company, even if you think of them both as nerds.

In general, an IT organization at a large company consists of several discrete entities that may have little do with one another. There is desktop services, which maintains the myriad PCs and printers in use at the business. The Network Operations or Infrastructure people make sure the networks are working—this keeps you online and communicating with file servers and enterprise applications that operate on the network. Developers write the software applications that the company uses, or customize commercial software packages. Database administrators manage the databases that underlie so many of the applications used throughout the enterprise. Architects are responsible for overall design and functioning of the enterprise information technology apparatus. Security people are responsible for ensuring privacy and integrity of data and systems, making sure they are free from intrusion and malfeasance. Security people are also responsible for defining and enforcing security policy, which covers Identity Management and dictates who can use or modify specific systems.

To make things truly confusing, the IT area is one where vendors often work inside the company, a practice known as *in-sourcing*. Or, the work itself is shipped off to a vendor, sometimes on another continent. This practice is known as *outsourcing* or *off-shoring*. In some instances, the work is done by a combination of internal staff, outsourced and in-sourced personnel, and separate vendor firms. Keeping track of who does what, and who is in charge, can be quite a challenge.

To attain agile compliance, then, the IT organization must achieve a level of unity where it can understand and implement the IT aspects of internal controls. The IT organization must have enough internal coordination, comprehension, and communication to be able to change the IT aspects of those controls as the company's agility requires.

None of this can happen without coherent management of the IT organization. This may seem obvious, but the reality of many large IT organizations is that they lack unified management. The application development organization may report to a lead developer. The architecture staff reports to a chief architect. A CTO or CIO may preside at the top, but in some cases, they cannot exert effective control over the staffs that roll up under them. CIOs often have short tenures. Like political appointees in Washington, they may be outlasted by more enduring employees lower in the ranks who may or may not implement the wishes of the current boss.

A significant aspect of the organizational coherence problem in IT is driven by personality. The common joke in the industry is that managing software developers is like herding cats. People who are good at slinging code may not be overly inclined to enjoy participating in large organizations. Another major issue is the actual design of the IT organization. To ensure security and compliance, a lot of IT organizations have strict separations between sub-departments and roles. Developers cannot access production-level systems, and so on. This is necessary. Unfortunately, it can also impede the kind of communication and coordination needed for agile compliance.

For example, if we look at identity management, a factor that emerges in our analysis of the baseline technological requirements for agile compliance, we can see several organizational challenges to making it work. Ideally, an identity management system keeps track of all system users and developers, whether they are inside the company or outside firms. No one can log onto a system to use it or modify it without being authenticated and authorized by the identity management system. Good. The problem is, who is in charge of the identity management system?

Consider the case of Thomas Coughlin, former Vice Chairman of Wal-Mart. In July of 2005, Wal-Mart sued Coughlin, who at that point was retired, accusing him of stealing up to $500,000 from the company through unauthorized use of gift cards and fake expense accounts. In his position at Wal-Mart from 1986 to 1992, he was responsible for investigating employee theft and abuse. Although it is impossible to know for sure, it seems a good bet that Mr. Coughlin, if he is guilty as alleged, was able to subvert whatever internal controls existed for identity management in the gift card and expense account software applications. His position of authority would have enabled him to do so (*New York Times*, July 28, 2005).

At DexCo, one reason Reggie Marchaldon was in a position to pull off a scam was that he acquired a complete set of usernames and passwords that gave him total control over the ERP system. With that level of access, he would be able to manipulate his quarterly results at will with few co-conspirators. Actually, as the SOX audit revealed, Marchaldon simply could have used the account identities of employees who had retired. The IT department had no centralized way of checking to see if all system users were current employees.

Territoriality, Silos, and Culture

"Seems like we have a serious problem with silos," says Jim Wilde. "Everyone belongs to some little club inside the department, and they don't even talk amongst themselves hardly enough let alone with the people in other departments."

"Right," Dale replies. "We need to connect the silos. We won't ever make them go away. Let's be realistic. We can't have any embedded fantasies of how things are going to be different just because we say so. However, we do need to get each group to say what it needs, be heard, and get what it needs to make its own contribution to agile compliance."

At this point, they invite Linda Fuller and Sebastian Harris into the office and initiate a high-level discussion of how they can achieve an organizational breakthrough for the sake of agile compliance. Dale leads off, giving his overview on the core issues at stake.

"My take on this," Dale says to his CFO and CIO, "is that you've got two essentially separate issues bound up in the organizational side of agile compliance. There's specific technical stuff like how your organizations and their respective silos manage their systems and enforce rules, and so on. As a first step, you have to enable your silos and organizations to communicate with one another, which is a matter of establishing a common language. That's quite a lot by itself. But the real issue, I think, is cultural."

"Yes," says Sebastian. "I've been thinking about this, too. If you look at the cultural context of these business-accounting-IT discussions that go on regarding Sarbanes Oxley, you see the differences in the groups right away. In IT, we're typically engineers, or at least working in an engineering mindset. We're problem solvers who get things done on a project-by-project basis. Accounting seems to be more rule-based and driven by periods of time. Business management is incentive based. I found a cartoon that brings this issue to life." He hands out the cartoon shown in Figure 10-1.

"Funny. Sad, but true," Linda Fuller says as she looks at the cartoon. "I can relate. It seems so often that we all see a problem in internal controls, and we all want to solve it, but we simply go after the challenges so differently that we have a heck of time getting anything done. I want to make sure we're compliant with GAAP and Sarbanes Oxley. The IT team wants to turn it into a set of engineering requirements, submit a budget, do it and move on. The business guys just want to know when it's going to be done and why it isn't done already. Plus, they've got ten other things they want done."

"It's kind of like this," Dale says as he maps out Figure 10-2 on the white board. "Taking another look at this familiar drawing, I see how the differences in culture and working process slow down both compliance and agility. The business managers want something done. The IT folks, who want to help, have to put the change order into their budget and project pipeline. That can take a while. Accounting may not get involved until the whole thing is built and ready to deploy. Why? Well, they're probably busy, may not know what is even going on until the IT project is finished, or, perhaps they only do an annual audit to see if these kind of things are in control."

Figure 10-1 A cartoon that captures the essential cultural differences between IT, business, accounting, and consultants

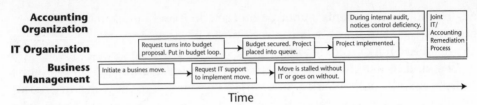

Figure 10-2 Organizational aspects of compliance and agility as affected by IT budget and project cycle

"It's like building a building and then inspecting the plans for code violations," says Jim Wilde.

"Right," Sebastian adds. "And then tearing half of it down, building it up again, and wondering why the place can't open for business sooner."

"Don't forget," Dale adds. "We've also got consultants in and around the whole mix. And they have their agendas as well."

Requirements for an Agile, Compliant Organization

"Is it fair to say, then" Dale asks, "that we can only tackle the organizational side of agile compliance if we can find a way to bring everyone together onto the same page, at the same time."

He erases some of the boxes on the board and drafts Figure 10-3 in its place. "This is how I see it. In the Army, we had officers called Liaisons. They would get together when the Army and the Navy needed to coordinate its actions. With a Liaison Officer, the Navy could shell the beach before the Army landed there. The Liaison would tell the Navy when and where to send the shells. Without the Liaison, well—there's a lady present so I won't say what we called it in the Army."

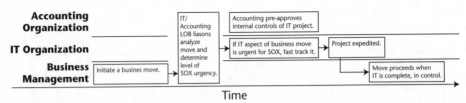

Figure 10-3 Modified IT/accounting/line-of-business process for delivering SOX-sensitive IT projects that are pre-approved by accounting

"Rhymes with 'buster' and 'duck'?" Linda asks with a wry smile.

"Just about," Dale says. "We need Liaisons between Accounting, IT, and Business. Not informal, but real, corporate mandated, and as non-bureaucratic as possible. Another difficult feat, but I think it can be done. The Liasons get together and review major business initiatives. They determine if they are material to compliance. If the initiatives are material to compliance, like our Flex-acturing process would be, then they recommend a fast track IT implementation that skips to the head of the line for project and budget status. And, the accounting people go over the requirements of the IT project and basically pre-approve it for Sarbanes Oxley and other compliance issues. That way, we don't have to wait six months until the whole thing is up and running to find out that we've got deficiencies in the setup and have to do it over again."

"I really like this," Linda says. "But, we're still missing two big pieces of the process. For one thing, we currently don't have any technological solution in place that enables us all to share information rapidly enough to implement the process shown in the diagram."

"What about e-mail?" Jim asks.

"Of course, we can e-mail each other," Linda says. "But if we are just throwing spreadsheets at each other on e-mail, there's no guarantee we'll get anything done. I think this kind of coordination and liaison activity needs to have a dedicated communication platform where we can work together online. And, these different groups need to be speaking the same language if they are going to have a chance of acting in a unified process."

"This is true," Sebastian adds, "At the very least, we seem to lack a common way of describing what we all need to do. Even if we all agreed to work together and break the silos down—a huge assumption—we would still find ourselves speaking in tongues."

"Perhaps we should hold a meeting and focus everyone on this issue," Linda suggests.

"Yeah, but is that a real solution?" Jim asks. "We aren't going to solve the organizational issues of agile compliance by forcing everyone to stare at a PowerPoint screen for an hour. Is there such a thing as a common language for IT, accounting, and business?"

"There's BPEL," Sebastian says. "Business Process Execution Language— it's a way that a business analyst can describe a business process in a way that is easy for a software developer to understand. And, an accountant can look at it too and map it back to controls."

"Sounds like a heck of an idea," Jim says. "Let's buy six of them."

"Sounds like a tool that will be useful if we can get everyone to agree that it's important," Dale responds. "I still think that our core challenge here is an organizational, interpersonal one. At some level, this revolves around tech, because tech builds the solution that the business and controls ride on top of. Yet, if we can't get the accounting and business people to be sensitive to the needs of tech, and vice versa, then we'll just have erected another set of obstacles to getting things done."

"So what do we do?" Jim asks. This is getting to be a long day for him, and it isn't even lunchtime yet.

"I say we do all of the above," Dale replies. "We move forward with the common communication platform, we establish the Liaison positions and group review structure, conduct some cross-training and sensitivity sessions, and keep gunning for this to all work out."

"Done," says Jim.

Summary

Jim Wilde and Dale Steyer review current events and catch up on just how important achieving agile compliance can be. Several major public companies are running into to legal hassles over compliance, and others are spending fortunes on SOX and will likely have to repeat the expenditure in the coming year just to stay on top of compliance. Finally, they realize that they may be facing a major internal controls problem of their own, as their SOX audit has revealed a breakdown in controls that may have enabled the General Manager of the wholesale division to manipulate his earnings and increase his bonus.

Wilde and Steyer come to the conclusion that organizational issues are at the core of attaining the goal of agile compliance. With issues ranging from organizational structures and process differences to cultural divides between the IT, Accounting, and Business executives involved in running DexCo and ensuring its compliance, the two top managers see how vulnerable the company is to problems in compliance that can dampen agility. The classic problem, they see, is that even if all groups want to work together, their incompatible respective work process and time frames keep compliance and agility at odds. For example, a business change may beget an IT project, which is then queued with other projects for some period of time. When it is complete, an audit may reveal that the IT work that has been done is not compliant. The result is a waste of time and a business agility problem, as well as a compliance headache.

Seeking to identify a solution, Wilde and Steyer, joined by their CIO and CFO, map out some ways that DexCo can avert the kind of compliance and agility trouble that has befallen other public companies. After agreeing that they need to break down the silos and territoriality between Accounting, IT, and Business—yet acknowledging that they will never eliminate them—they arrive at an operating solution. There will be a set of liaison executives who bridge the accounting, IT, and business groups. The liaison team will review major business initiatives and determine if an initiative will require fast-track IT attention and simultaneous pre-approval by the accounting staff for SOX issues. This way, the business people can get what they need rapidly, and the IT department can develop their solutions without worrying about internal controls.

To make this all happen, which everyone acknowledges will be a challenge, DexCo will have to initiate some cross-training of accounting, IT and business people in their respective fields. In addition, the company will have to deploy a common communication infrastructure where business, IT, and accounting issues can be reviewed and processed in a common language and rapid time frame.

CHAPTER 11

The Walk-Through

Writing this book has provided me with the dubious pleasure of seeing some striking examples of how diligent adherence to the Sarbanes-Oxley Act could have saved investors and corporate managers a lot of grief. The case of Refco, the failed commodities trading firm, shows some of the worst potential damage that can result from a lack of attention to compliance.

Refco disclosed that a company controlled by its CEO owed the company $430 million. This debt was not known to shareholders; the CEO had allegedly hidden it from them. According to published accounts, the CEO and others had hidden the debt from Refco's shareholders as a way to protect a large institutional client that had defaulted on its obligations to the company.

Within a few weeks of the announcement, Federal agents arrested the CEO for fraud. The company went into freefall, with many clients pulling their funds out of Refco accounts. The stock price tumbled and the company's very survival was thrown into doubt.

Refco had gone public just ten weeks before the revelation of this crisis. Prior to that, Refco had been funded by private equity firms. As the *New York Times* observed, "Some say that one advantage of private equity is that involved owners can keep a close watch on their investments without the costs imposed by the Sarbanes-Oxley Act. But the Lee firm [Refco's backer] did not. When it went public, Refco was forced by Sarbanes-Oxley to report significant financial deficiencies in its internal controls, including an inadequate finance staff. Investors did not care. It turns out that such deficiencies can be very real and very costly," (*New York Times,* October 14, 2005).

What cost internal controls? Refco's stock went public at $22 and rose to $27 before the news of the debt scandal was announced. After the news, the stock fell to around $10—a loss of $2 billion in market cap in two weeks. A week after that it was at 65 cents and the company had filed for Chapter 11. So much for those who would try to avoid complying with Sarbanes Oxley or taking it seriously.

For our purposes, the Refco case can be instructive regarding the importance of maintaining a functioning framework for compliance. Refco had little in the way of relevant internal controls, including a 100 percent improper *tone at the top*. Auditors reviewing the situation have noted that the kind of alleged fraud perpetrated at Refco is quite difficult to catch because it involved a collusion between two separate companies. Still, Refco shows us how critical it is for *someone* to care about what's going on when it comes to internal controls. The Refco case also shows how dangerous it can be to rely on high-profile executives to be responsible for policing their own actions. Most major executives are honest, or at least want to do the right thing. However, when it's your $2 billion on the table, perhaps you might want some verification of what's going on. I know I would.

Dale's Need for an Overview

Compared to Refco, DexCo at least has the makings of a control process and sincere interest in compliance at the highest levels of the company. Yet, as Dale Steyer reviews his situation, he feels the need to walk through the proposed agile compliance changes in technology, organization, and process that he and his team have been discussing.

Now that the IT and accounting departments have explored some basic changes in structure and approach needed for agile compliance, Dale wants to see the whole process as a holistic set of functions. As he explains, it is as if they were going to build an office, but before they put up any walls, he wants to walk through the space and see the chalk lines on the floor where the walls are going to go. It's a precaution against premature movement in the wrong direction. To this end, he has asked Linda and Sebastian to prepare a detailed presentation for him so he can evaluate the overall process of DexCo's agile compliance.

Agile Compliance—The IT Plan

With the requirement that they remain agnostic regarding specific vendors and technologies, Sebastian's staff presents a plan for participating in agile compliance to Dale. The plan consists of four central tenets:

- Use of business process management as a working process to develop applications, including Business Process Execution Language (BPEL).

- Establishment of a unified online vehicle for work planning and coordination inside the IT department and amongst other corporate groups: Apply COBIT management guidelines to key areas.

- Implementation of a centralized user access control and identity management system for DexCo: Apply COBIT management guidelines for security.

- Implementation of an application development and system integration process that takes business process and internal controls into account: Apply COBIT guidelines for data integrity.

Business Process Modeling and BPEL

When Sebastian's team starts to describe business process modeling and BPEL, Dale immediately jumps in and says, "Hey, I thought I asked you to avoid specific vendors and technologies. I didn't want this meeting to turn into a shoot-out over who's better than whom and why."

"Yes," Sebastian reassures Dale. "BPM is a general term for an approach to IT, and BPEL is an open standard. Nobody owns it, although several vendors publish their own version of it. So, our baseline requirement for helping out with Agile compliance is to model the business processes involved in a business initiative that affects internal controls. And, we propose using BPEL as a way to form a firm connection between the business process modeling that we do and the software development and systems integration activities that follow."

Sebastian now shows a slide resembling Figure 11-1. "As you see, BPEL is partly a visual language. It models business processes using a flow chart iconography that we're generally familiar with. However, the difference between a standard flow charting program like Visio and a real BPEL tool is that we can use the BPEL to map each process step to a real system that's either deployed at DexCo or in development."

"Why does that matter?" Dale asks.

"Okay, walk through this with me. One of our biggest problems to date is that when we get started on an IT project, we often lose sight of the ways that business processes correlate to underlying systems. Perhaps, we do a business process model at the outset of an IT project. Then, we go off and perform all the work and then present the business owners and accounting department with a finished application. At that point, someone is likely to ask, 'Hey what about the business process?'—which may have changed in the meantime anyway. There's a lot of potential for disconnects. With BPEL, however, we can keep a pretty constant link going between the business processes we're working on and the systems that we're adapting to fit those processes. BPEL is kind of like a common vocabulary for discussing business and IT at the same time. It keeps everyone on the same page. And, we will need to highlight areas where internal controls may be affected by changes in business process and system architecture."

"You're assuming that everyone wants to be on the same page," Linda says.

"That's a working process issue, and we'll get there in a minute," Sebastian replies.

Unified Online Workspace

"We'll only be on the same page if we actually build the page for everyone to look at," Sebastian says. "Assuming, of course, that people want to look at it." He shows a slide of Figure 11-2. "This is a hypothetical compliance portal for DexCo. It's an online vehicle for work planning and coordination inside the IT department and amongst other corporate groups.

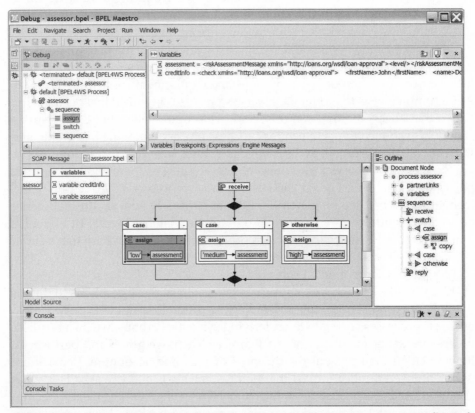

Figure 11-1   BPEL example modeling the process of authorizing customer credit. Each process step can be mapped to a specific software program or underlying IT system. (Courtesy of Parasoft.)

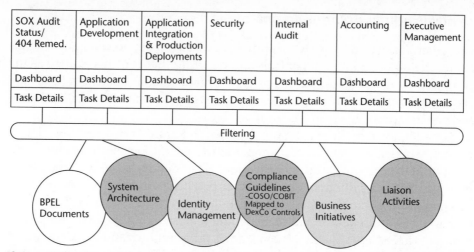

SOX Audit Status/ 404 Remed.	Application Development	Application Integration & Production Deployments	Security	Internal Audit	Accounting	Executive Management
Dashboard	Dashboard	Dashboard	Dashboard	Dashboard	Dashboard	Dashboard
Task Details	Task Details	Task Details	Task Details	Task Details	Task Details	Task Details

Figure 11-2 Proposed DexCo compliance portal that provides a unified online work environment for keeping track of compliance-related tasks amongst divergent corporate groups that relate to compliance

Using the principles of COBIT PO 10 (project management) and PO 11 (manage quality), the compliance portal connects each major group with the relevant aspects of work that need to be done for compliance. The primary purpose of the portal is to provide a real-time work space where compliance issues can get attention and follow up from relevant groups. The portal enables the SOX audit and remediation teams to have access to BPEL documents and system architecture plans that relate to the company's SOX 404 internal controls. Similarly, any group that needs to interact with identity management issues can view relevant information on the portal. Business management gets an overview of compliance-related activities and the status of its initiatives through the portal, which is also the main activity center for the departmental liaisons that were discussed previously.

The key to the portal is a set of relationships between departmental tasks. Managed by the liaisons, the compliance portal tasks extend to whatever corporate group is involved. For example, if a business initiative creates an identity management issue, then the Liaison group will create a task in the compliance portal that requires the security group to be notified and take action if necessary. The portal provides a way for the Liaison group to monitor whether the security people have done what is needed on the identity management issue. In this way, the company is able to stay on top of ongoing compliance matters and have some confidence that people are following through on their commitments to keeping the company compliant.

Centralized User Management

As earlier discussions revealed, control over system user access rights is critical for maintaining internal controls and ensuring that controls change as the company modifies its operating plan or organizational chart. As Sebastian shows in Figure 11-3, an access manager gives the company that ability to control system access rights on a centralized basis.

In the highly simplified example depicted in Figure 11-3, a user logs into a central access manager, which compares the user's log-in credentials with those contained in a central identity store. The identity store tells the access manager the user's role and specific access privileges. In this case, the user can be allowed access to Systems B and C, but not Systems A and D. The access manager passes an authorization credential to System B along with the user's request to access the system. System B accepts the authorization credential and grants the user access. Then, because the example shows a process that requires the use of two systems—a distributed computing situation that is common in corporate operations—the user also needs access to System C to complete the request. Working with the access manager, System B then passes the user's credential along to System C, which processes the request and returns the needed data to the user. The process is transparent to the user.

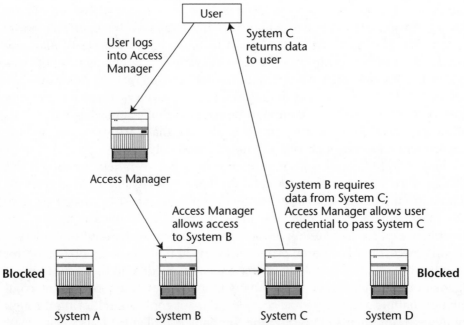

Figure 11-3 Schematic of access management at work enabling centralized control of system access—a component of internal control

The access manager provides two components of agile compliance. First, by providing central control over user access privileges throughout the company, the access manager ensures a high level of enforcement of access control policy. Assuming that the central administrator understands the requirements of the internal controls, and assuming the system itself is secure, then the access manager can enforce segregation of duties and protect information assets and financial systems from misuse. The central control also enables flexibility by creating a single point of control over multiple systems. As business processes and organizational roles change, the central access manager can modify, add, or eliminate users and their roles in a time cycle that matches the business process change.

Like other areas of IT, however, the matter of centralized user access management is a good deal more complex in reality than it is in a neat printed diagram. There are some serious challenges to its implementation. However, if the organization recognizes its importance, then the subject could get the kind of priority it deserves. Luckily for DexCo, COBIT DS 5 (ensure system security) provides some workable management guidelines for putting the user access management system into effect.

Application Development and Integration Process

DexCo's approach to developing software programs and integrating them into the overall production environment is the fourth tenet of the IT organization's commitment to agile compliance. Based on the assumptions that DexCo will be adopting BPEL, centralized identity management, a compliance portal, and an organizational structure of liaisons between corporate groups, the IT department can proceed with an application development process resembling the one shown in Figure 11-4. The new process puts compliance into each aspect of the application development and integration process.

Sebastian's application developers must now work with an underlying assumption that is new to them. Whereas before, the developers could take a set of business requirements and run with them, delivering a beta application and throwing it over the wall to the business users for approval or revisions, they must now work in a fairly constant state of connection with the business users, compliance liaisons.

This constant connection also now endures past the delivery of the application. As the organization evolves and makes business moves, any number of interdependent applications or links between applications may be affected. The new application development process is designed to keep the key stakeholders aware of changes and acting on them in the name of internal controls and compliance on an ongoing basis.

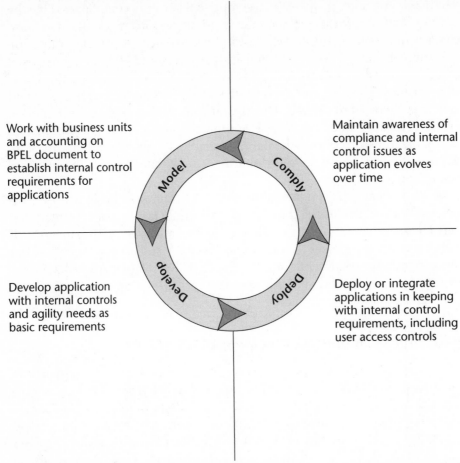

Work with business units and accounting on BPEL document to establish internal control requirements for applications

Maintain awareness of compliance and internal control issues as application evolves over time

Develop application with internal controls and agility needs as basic requirements

Deploy or integrate applications in keeping with internal control requirements, including user access controls

Figure 11-4 Proposed new application development and integration process that enables compliance by connecting development with business process modeling, identity management, and internal control requirements

Agile Compliance and IT—The Sum of Its Parts

Sebastian wraps up his initial presentation by showing the chart depicted in Table 11-1. The table shows the general requirements for agile compliance in the flex-acturing process and the impact that the IT department's proposed agile compliance would have on each of them. As Sebastian notes, the IT plan for agile compliance only works as the sum of its parts. BPEL alone won't ensure agile compliance. Nor will a compliance portal, identity management, or a new application development process. Each one alone will fail. Together, they have the potential to enable the IT side of DexCo's agile compliance initiative.

Table 11-1 Core Compliance Requirements Viewed in Context of the IT Department's New Agile Compliance Plan

COMPLIANCE ISSUE IN FLEX-ACTURING	IMPACT ON BPM/BPEL	IMPACT ON IDENTITY MANAGEMENT	CONNECTION TO COMPLIANCE PORTAL	IMPACT ON APP DEV PROCESS
User roles must keep pace with business process changes.	User role needs to be included in the BPEL documents.	User identity management systems must be able to change role configuration in the same time cycle as business agility dictates.	If role changes are related to internal controls, then relevant stakeholders must be advised of issue through the compliance portal.	If change in user roles has an impact on application design and deployment, stakeholders must be made aware.
User roles must be constantly in force, regardless of system makeup.	The need to pass credentials between systems may have to be reflected in the BPEL documents.	User identity management systems must interoperate with disparate systems and be reconfigured in the same time cycle as business agility dictates.	Administrators of the identity management systems need to be apprised of relevant changes in the operating environment that affect the identity management systems.	Developers need to be aware of ways that identity management systems can be affected by changes in application development and integration.
Must have flexible application integration with CRM to provide real-time data flow between systems that are necessary for maintenance of internal controls.	CRM/ERP integration needs to be in BPEL documents.	CRM/ERP integration needs to be accounted for in identity management roles.	Changes to CRM integration that have an impact on internal controls need to be highlighted to relevant stakeholders on portal.	Integration point that connects CRM to ERP systems must be maintained as both applications change.

(continued)

Table 11-1 *(continued)*

COMPLIANCE ISSUE IN FLEX-ACTURING	IMPACT ON BPM/BPEL	IMPACT ON IDENTITY MANAGEMENT	CONNECTION TO COMPLIANCE PORTAL	IMPACT ON APP DEV PROCESS
Cannot allow system overrides by unauthorized users. Access management system must be able to maintain policy enforcement even as it changes configuration and integrates with outside systems.	User authorization must be on BPEL documents.	Strict authorization role assignment necessary.	User authorization parameters need to be published to relevant stakeholders.	User authorization must change as application changes.
Must be able to automate reconciliation of accounts and allow for changes in account setup and system configuration in the same time cycle as business agility dictates.	Connection to account reconciliation process must appear on BPEL documents.	Accounting staff that transacts daily business may not have access to account reconciliation capabilities.	User authorization parameters need to be published to relevant stakeholders.	User authorization must change as application changes.

As Table 11-1 shows, there is a lot of detail and complexity to maintaining agile compliance. The trick, Sebastian says, is to make the tenets of the IT department's plan automated enough to enable them to be more or less built into every action that the IT department takes. If the IT staff has to stop what it is doing and update a compliance portal or BPEL document every time it does a project, and that updating has nothing to do with the actual project at hand, then this effort is doomed to failure. However, Sebastian hopes to make the compliance portal into the main IT project management portal. There will be no other way to manage projects at DexCo's IT department. That way, the IT staff will have no choice but to focus on compliance issues. Similarly, as all identity management flows to a central system, then the IT department will necessarily use it for all application and system controls.

Of course, the interdependencies shown in Table 11-1 will only work, as Sebastian notes, if the staff members involved in the work have an awareness of the importance of maintaining agile compliance. If they don't, the matter is too complex and esoteric to matter. To work on this challenge, Sebastian throws in a fifth tenet of IT's agile compliance plan, which is a training program to inculcate an emphasis on compliance and agility.

Agile Compliance—The Organizational Plan

After a few of these discussions, Jim, Dale, Sebastian, and Linda all mutually agree that there needs to be an additional person on the company's management team responsible for leading DexCo's compliance efforts. The position, which they refer to as Chief Compliance Officer (CCO), will be filled as soon as possible. In process maps, the CCO's staff will be known as the Compliance Office. Even without that executive in place, however, they continue to work through the details of the organization's plan for agile compliance.

After some tinkering, the group came up with the draft organization chart shown in Figure 11-5. The CCO will manage an ever-changing group of project compliance teams. The teams will consist of the liaisons between the business, IT, and accounting departments. In this sense, DexCo's plan for agile compliance calls for a matrix type of organization. Each IT project that touches on internal controls will have representative liaisons from accounting and the line of business that requested the project. The board of directors will designate a compliance committee that will have oversight over the new CCO's activities.

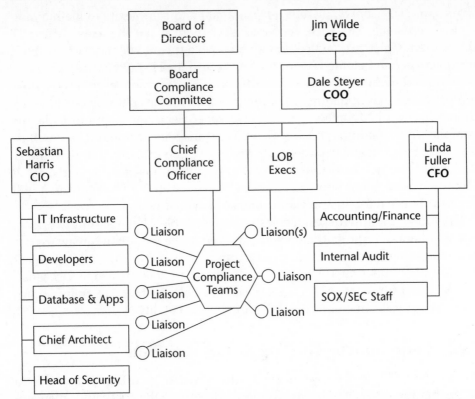

Figure 11-5 Proposed organization chart for project compliance teams that work in a matrix with IT, accounting, line-of-business managers, and the CCO

The project compliance teams will coordinate the activities of the IT department, accounting, and line-of-business groups using the compliance portal. Technical matters will be translated from one group to another using BPEL and related business-to-technology communications vehicles.

Tying it all together will be an online guide to compliance issues, written by an outside consultant, that the management group has dubbed the Compliance Bible. The Compliance Bible will be an evolving document that captures the prime guidelines, policies, and procedures necessary for ensuring agile compliance at DexCo. It is envisioned as a living online knowledge resource, the go-to place for information on how to make any IT project that relates to internal controls compliant.

The Agile Compliance Process Plan

Jim Wilde, who now wields what he calls his trouble stick wherever he goes, points it at the screen where the last set of figures has played out. "I don't know about all this," he says. "To me, this looks like the making of a major bureaucracy and it'll just tie us in knots. You've got a new department, basically, a whole lot of committees, matrixed goings-on, which can create its own problems, a new board committee. How does this make us agile? I see compliance, but I also see handcuffs."

"Yes," Dale says. "This has the potential to strangle us. But, we need to acknowledge that compliance already is strangling us. What we're talking about here is a proactive approach to getting a handle on compliance and trying to assure agility at the same time. There is one special ingredient, though, that we need to emphasize, or this entire organizational change and process is going to kill us."

"And?" Jim asks. "The suspense is killing me. What is it?"

"Selectivity," Sebastian says, stepping into what he has suspected will be a critical phase of the discussion. "Of course, if we tried to apply this agile compliance process to every single business initiative and IT project, we would never get anywhere. We would be neither agile nor compliant. In fact, we'd be a whole lot worse at everything. The key to making this work is to filter the projects that we consider and only put the full court press of compliance onto those projects that really can make a material difference in our internal controls."

"Give me an example," Jim says.

"Okay," Sebastian says. "This is one that came up this week. We are due for an upgrade in our CRM systems. We would like to consolidate our customer resource management systems. The first question I got asked was, 'What about Sarbanes Oxley?' because my project managers are starting to get hip to what we're doing here. And, they're already bracing for the budgetary and schedule fights that they think are going to ensue as we freight their task list with what they consider an unfunded mandate of compliance. I said, 'Don't sweat it. CRM has almost nothing to do with compliance.' As we have seen with flex-acturing, there are a couple of places where CRM touches the sales forecasting cycle, and in those little spots, we're going to need a compliance review like the one we've outlined here. For a general CRM project, though, the compliance office may take a look at it and wave it through without even setting up any compliance requirements. Because, what impact could CRM have on our bottom line?"

"Well," Linda says. "On one level, very little. However, what if someone steals our customer list? Isn't that a compliance issue?"

"Good point," Sebastian says. "But let me address that kind of problem."

"What you are talking about is a general security issue. Of course, DexCo needs to be confident that its proprietary customer lists remain secure and beyond the reach of hackers, including our internal staff. One of our basic goals with the compliance process is to institute general, company-wide, permanent changes in the way we do IT. That is also part of this process. However, as we inculcate these practices into our everyday IT business, we will not need a specific review process for every project."

"Now you're losing me," Dale comments. "How are you going to establish permanent guidelines without reviewing every project?"

"We're going to have to do some training," Sebastian replies. "Actually, we are going to have to do a lot of training, and continually re-up with more training and adoption of new practices. We're going to use the COBIT M1 guidelines to help us figure out the best practices for monitoring processes." He shows a slide of Figure 11-6 and says, "This is the essential process for maintaining agile compliance."

"Let's say that a line of business wants to make a change in its operations, and that change requires a modification of the IT systems that support the line of business. Based on our process, the first step is for the line of business to submit a plan to the Compliance Office. This will be accomplished through an automated form on the compliance portal. I estimate it would take a line-of-business executive ten minutes to complete the form. We want to keep this as simple as possible. The Compliance Office reviews the form and makes a decision. Is this business move related to internal controls and compliance? If it is not—like a basic CRM upgrade—then whatever IT project results from the business move will occur outside the purview of the Compliance Office."

"If the project does merit attention from the perspective of internal controls," Sebastian continues, "then the Compliance Office will assign the project to a liaison team that will work with the account, IT, and line-of-business project owners to arrive at a Compliance Plan. As we move forward, we hope to populate the Compliance Bible with enough data to enable the liaison teams to assemble a compliance plan rapidly for most IT projects. We see the Compliance Bible as a friendly minefield. You will know when you're tripping a fuse so you can jump on it. It will contain an index of all of DexCo's internal controls and ways to continue their implementation. It should be kind of a first draft of our SOX 404 report.

"Like we discussed, the project compliance team is going to ask the four basic questions every time they see a project. Is the business process in question in compliance now? If not, what will it take to make it so? Will it flex? If not, what will it take to flex? These are the guiding principles of a project compliance team."

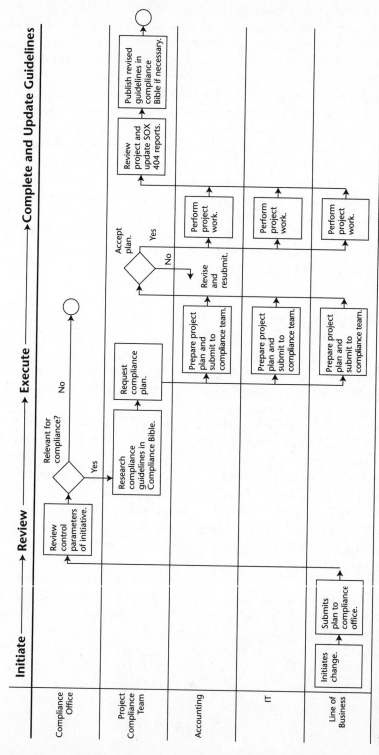

Figure 11-6 Proposed process for agile compliance connecting the Compliance Office, project-compliance teams, and any departments involved

"After the project compliance team has reviewed the project plans from IT," Sebastian goes on, "Accounting, and the line of business, they will either approve the plan or send it back for another iteration. We will have to set a time limit so things don't drag, but we need to work that out. It shouldn't be more than 30 days, however. After their plans have been approved, the IT, accounting, and line-of-business project owners go to work and perform whatever project requirements are needed to make the business initiative work. When they are done, the project compliance team reviews the work and endorses it for inclusion in the SOX 404 report for the year. If they don't approve it, they request rework. However, at least the company is aware of a potential control deficiency much earlier than they might normally be with a standard SOX audit conducted after all the work is done. And, the project team still exists to do the revision if there is a remaining internal controls problem. One big challenge we have seen when we have control deficiencies is to grab former team members who have moved on to other projects and get them to fix something from an old project."

Troubleshooting

"This looks like an awful lot of process steps, memos, and meetings," Dale says. "I can totally see people working around this system and making a hash of it. In my experience, people hate these kinds of mandated processes. They exist on paper and in practice they go to heck."

"I understand," Sebastian says. "This is a real challenge, but I think we can do it. The key to making this process agile and popular is to back it up with a number of company-wide changes in the way we do IT. For one thing, the compliance portal is also going to be the only IT project management portal that we use. Anyone connected with IT is going to have to use it for basic information on how to get their job done. The portal will be the control center for application development, testing, staging, deployment, infrastructure, quality control, and on and on. In these ways, it will be mandatory and difficult to subvert. Plus, we expect to implement some other universal systems that will simplify the process of agile compliance. For example, we expect to standardize on one central identity management system, which will automatically resolve a huge number of internal control issues. By default, the access control aspects of an IT project will be resolved in advance. With this kind of general move, and others that I will explain as we move forward, the whole process should move along nicely. If we have to invent the wheel every time we figure out the internal controls and compliance aspects of an IT project, we'll die.

"What about informal changes?" Jim Wilde asks. "Let's say someone makes a change but fails to notify the Compliance Office."

"Okay," Linda says. "That's a good question, and you know it's going to happen. One solution is training and awareness. If we can get people to understand that they are causing expensive hassles for upper management, or even serious liabilities, by being frivolous about this process, then we can probably make inroads against undocumented changes in business process. Furthermore, we still need to do an annual SOX 404 review from the top down. The Compliance Office is one pro-active step we are taking to be agile and compliant. But still, we are going to have an internal audit and an external audit of our internal controls. The objective, of course, is to reduce the cost and pain of these audits by having more documented processes in place. But hopefully, we will still be able to catch internal controls problems even if they evade the Compliance Office process."

"Alright," Jim says. "What about conflicts of interest? It seems to me that the really egregious internal control problems occur when someone is afraid to rat out the boss. In my experience, few people ever volunteered to tell the internal audit team that their division manager is messing around with the controls."

"Of course," Linda says. "You could have a problem like that, and our system is not totally bulletproof against collusion or abuses of power. However, I do believe that the more process that we can instill—as well as good tone at the top control direction—the more we will get out ahead of upper-level control malfeasance. On a practical level, too, we are demonstrating a firm commitment to internal control, so we will avoid the appearance of being lax about controls if a matter comes under scrutiny from the auditor or the SEC."

"Also," Sebastian says, "We're laying out a process in theoretical steps. Our plan is to implement the compliance portal and project compliance teams with enough built-in flexibility to adapt to reality as we go through our shakedown period. DexCo's actual business is going to throw us some curve balls, of that we are quite sure. Our goal is to build our agile compliance process in a way that moves with the company."

Summary

Having heard a generalized plan for agile compliance, DexCo's executives now receive a presentation that lays out a more detailed approach to this challenge. While staying vendor and technology agnostic, the CFO and CIO present their plans for establishing a workable plan for agile compliance.

From the IT perspective, the agile compliance process will rely on several fundamental technologies and tools. IT wants to standardize on Business Process Execution Language (BPEL) as a medium for transposing business requirements to underlying IT systems. BPEL has the potential to keep software application development and business processes tightly linked and adherent to internal control guidelines.

The IT department, accounting, and lines of business will share in a multifaceted compliance portal that will serve as a nerve center for all agile compliance-related issues. The portal will also be the de facto control point for all IT work at DexCo, even for projects that are not affected by internal controls issues. The compliance portal will contain an online index of internal controls and guidelines that will be known as DexCo's Compliance Bible.

The company plans to establish a standardized, company-wide user management system that will control access to all systems for all employees and partners. This technology is critical to enabling agile, rapid changes to systems while keeping them adherent to sound internal controls.

The software application development process will utilize a continuous model of compliance that forces developers, line-of-business project owners, and accounting to focus on a control-oriented project discipline.

From an organizational perspective, the CIO and CFO recommend that the company hire a Chief Compliance Officer and establish a Compliance Office that will oversee compliance project teams. The Compliance Office will review each business initiative for its relevance to internal controls. If the initiative touches on internal controls, then the Compliance Office will assign it to a compliance project team and monitor the work to ensure that the IT, accounting, and line-of-business aspects of the work conform to internal control guidelines. If the project does not relate to compliance, then the Compliance Office will not monitor its progress.

Broad and pervasive staff training is also considered critical to DexCo's overall agile compliance plan. In addition to providing COBIT training to the IT staff, DexCo wants to train all relevant people on COSO and SOX issues. Ultimately, they want to attain a degree of cross-training, where the accounting staff has a familiarity with IT issues, the IT staff has a sense of the audit work process, and so on.

Overall, the CFO and CIO see agile compliance as being the sum of its parts. No one aspect of these implementations will make DexCo compliant and agile. Together, however, the combination of organizational changes, new project processes, technologies, tools, and training has the potential to put DexCo on the track to agile compliance.

CHAPTER 12

The Pay Off

Jim Wilde fiddles with his trouble stick as he pores over the agile compliance PowerPoint decks and process flow charts that his staff has placed on his desk. Dale, Sebastian, and Linda sit around his desk in a semi-circle, watching him expectantly. Jim makes a face and looks up. "Alright," he says. "I buy what you're saying." Everyone breathes a sigh of relief. "But, because I'm a simple businessman I need to ask the one question that always comes to my mind when I look at all this kind of high-minded process stuff. What is this going to cost?"

"Fair question," Dale replies. "I just happen to have a back-of-the-envelope calculation handy." He powers up his laptop computer and opens a massive spreadsheet file.

"That's quite an envelope," Jim observes. Dale winks at him.

"The issue, of course, is only partly what it costs. This isn't going to be cheap. Yet, I always like to ask the other question: What is this worth?"

Investing in Agile Compliance

Dale's figures for DexCo's agile compliance plan reflect the realities of the company's specific situation. They may seem high or low to you, depending on your circumstances and experience. However, my goal in taking you through his calculations is to go through the exercise of valuing the relative differences between traditional management of internal controls and the potential for savings with agile compliance.

Dale splits investment into the agile compliance program into two parts: Startup costs, which include capital expenses and one-time costs, and ongoing expenses. As shown in Table 12-1, capital expenses are projected at $1.05 million; one-time costs are expected to be about the same amount. The total startup cost is estimated at $2.1 million.

"Is that all?" Jim Wilde asks with a sick grin.

"Actually, no," Dale says. "Let me go over the ongoing expenses. As we discussed, we're going to need a Chief Compliance Officer, a support staff, facilities, additional IT and Accounting staff, consultants, and continuing training. I'd put it all at about $1.6 million a year." He shows Jim Table 12-2.

Table 12-1   Estimated Startup Costs for DexCo's Agile Compliance Program

STARTUP COSTS	
CAPITAL EXPENSES	
Hardware	$150,000
Software licenses	$150,000
Portal development	$750,000
Total capital expenses	$1,050,000
ONE-TIME COSTS	
Consultants	$500,000
Training	$500,000
Recruiting of Personnel	$50,000
Total one-time costs	$1,050,000
Total startup costs	$2,100,000

Table 12-2   Ongoing Expense for Agile Compliance Program

	QUANTITY	COST	TOTAL
Software maintenance			$27,000
Chief Compliance Officer	1	$200,000	$200,000
Support staff for compliance office	2	$60,000	$120,000
IT liaison staff	3	$100,000	$300,000
Finance liaison staff	3	$100,000	$300,000
Consultants (first year)	1	$500,000	$500,000
Ongoing training	1	$150,000	$150,000
Total			$1,597,000

"Now, wait a minute," Jim says. "Linda told me the whole SOX thing cost us about a million and a quarter this year. You want me to spend over three million bucks over the next year, and another 1.6 million every year after that. Why? Let's just leave things the way they are. Pull in the horns, as we say on the ranch."

"Okay," Dale says. "I told you this wasn't going to be cheap. Now we know what it's going to cost. Let's try to figure out what it's worth."

Return on Agile Compliance Investment

Dale now goes through several different ways that DexCo can earn a return on investment with its agile compliance program. His overall point is to stress that agile compliance is a driver of increased profitability. He sees opportunity for improvements in profitability driven by the effects of agile compliance on three separate aspects of the company: compliance efforts, operations, and agility. In addition, there is a set of intangible, profit-enhancing benefits that come from agile compliance. Most relevant of these are the avoidance of non-compliance penalties. He draws Figure 12-1 on the whiteboard to show how he thinks that agile compliance provides four vectors of improved profitability that will justify the investment in the program.

Lower Cost of Compliance

If you've been paying attention, you might be wondering how Dale came up with the idea that agile compliance lowers compliance costs. At $1.6 million per year in ongoing expenses, he's way ahead of the estimated million dollars per year that Linda claimed she spent on Sarbanes Oxley compliance this year. Dale explains his compliance savings in several ways.

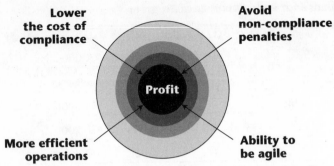

**Lower
the cost of
compliance**

**Avoid
non-compliance
penalties**

Profit

**More efficient
operations**

**Ability to
be agile**

Figure 12-1   Agile compliance as a driver of increased profit

For one thing, the million dollars that Linda spent on outside consultants for the SOX pre-audit work has now dropped to half a million, and it will continue to drop as time goes on. In addition, after several discussions with DexCo's external auditor, Dale is confident that he can reduce the company's overall audit costs by streamlining the process of preparing documentation on internal controls for the SOX audit.

The agile compliance program, if implemented properly, will reduce ongoing expenses for both outside SOX consultants and external audit. External audit and SOX consulting costs will likely go up due to inflation and other factors if left alone. Although the new program will be more expensive initially, it will cross over and cost less in the third year, as shown in Table 12-3 and Figure 12-2. By the fifth year, the agile compliance program should save the company over a million dollars a year.

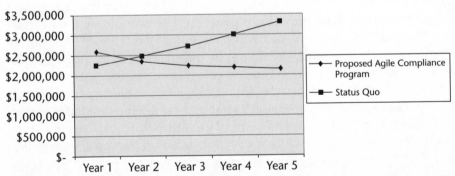

Figure 12-2   Line graph showing break inversion point where proposed agile compliance program begins to cost less than status quo

Table 12-3   Contrast in Compliance and Audit Costs Between Proposed Agile Compliance Program and Status Quo

PROPOSED AGILE COMPLIANCE PROGRAM	YEAR 1	YEAR 2	YEAR 3	YEAR 4	YEAR 5
SOX consultant costs	$500,000	$400,000	$350,000	$350,000	$350,000
Compliance office overhead	$1,097,000	$1,097,000	$1,097,000	$1,097,000	$1,097,000
Total compliance	$1,597,000	$1,497,000	$1,447,000	$1,447,000	$1,447,000
External audit cost	$1,000,000	$850,000	$800,000	$750,000	$700,000
Total proposed SOX and audit costs	$2,597,000	$2,347,000	$2,247,000	$2,197,000	$2,147,000
STATUS QUO					
SOX consultants	$1,250,000	$1,375,000	$1,512,500	$1,663,750	$1,830,125
External audit	$ 1,000,000	$1,100,000	$1,210,000	$1,331,000	$1,464,100
Total	$2,250,000	$2,475,000	$2,722,500	$2,994,750	$3,294,225

The saving calculation shown in these first displays, however, neglects a very salient detail that Dale believes will be a factor in costing out the true cost of compliance at DexCo over time. Remediation of deficient controls, often required under Sarbanes Oxley, will likely inflate both SOX consulting and external audit costs significantly. (They would also increase IT and other financial consulting costs, but for now, we will leave those out of the equation.) As Table 12-4 and Figure 12-3 shows, if DexCo has to undertake even just two remediations a year, with a cost inflation factor of 10 percent for each remediation, the cost differential between the status quo approach and the proposed agile compliance program could reach over one million dollars a year.

Table 12-4   Contrast Between Status Quo and Proposed Agile Compliance Factoring in Costs of Remediation of Deficient Controls

PROPOSED AGILE COMPLIANCE PROGRAM	YEAR 1	YEAR 2	YEAR 3	YEAR 4	YEAR 5
SOX consultant costs	$500,000	$400,000	$350,000	$350,000	$350,000
Compliance office overhead	$1,097,000	$1,097,000	$1,097,000	$1,097,000	$1,097,000
Total compliance	$1,597,000	$1,497,000	$1,447,000	$1,447,000	$1,447,000

(continued)

Table 12-4   *(continued)*

PROPOSED AGILE COMPLIANCE PROGRAM	YEAR 1	YEAR 2	YEAR 3	YEAR 4	YEAR 5
External audit cost	$1,000,000	$850,000	$800,000	$750,000	$700,000
Total proposed SOX and audit costs	$2,597,000	$2,347,000	$2,247,000	$2,197,000	$2,147,000
STATUS QUO WITH REMEDIATION					
Number of remediations	1	2	2	2	2
Cost inflation of a single remediation	10%	10%	10%	10%	10%
SOX consultants	$1,375,000	$1,650,000	$1,815,000	$1,996,500	$2,196,150
External audit	$1,100,000	$1,320,000	$1,452,000	$1,597,200	$1,756,920
Total	$2,475,000	$2,970,000	$3,267,000	$3,593,700	$3,953,070

Working with the assumption that the agile compliance program would result in fewer remediations (or no remediations), then it is a clear winner. When factoring in the intangible costs of remediation, the case for the agile compliance program becomes all the stronger. Remediation has the potential to stagnate progressive business activity, tie up accounting and IT staff, and potentially diminish the company's stock price.

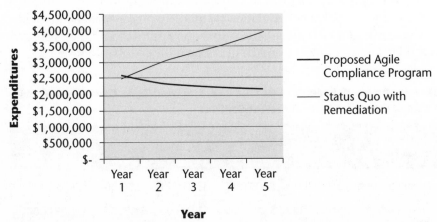

Figure 12-3   Line graph showing divergence between status quo with remediations and proposed agile compliance plan

Operational Savings

Dale wants Jim to understand how agile compliance results in operational savings. To illustrate his point, he chooses a hypothetical IT project that we saw earlier. With the staggered start, inefficient IT and controls process currently in use at DexCo, the project takes 7 months, as shown in Figure 12-4.

With the improved process of planning the controls and IT parameters of a project and then developing in parallel, as shown in Figure 12-5, the project takes five months. With the new integrated BPEL, development, and deployment model proposed in the agile compliance program, the project management results in fewer iterations of testing prior to deployment.

In addition, the more tightly focused project management methodology proposed for agile compliance results in a more efficient utilization of staff during the project itself. As shown in Table 12-5, this improvement in utilization reduces total project cost by 49 percent. Not only would DexCo get more work done in a year using agile compliance, it will enable them to save money on each IT project.

"What about FAST?" Linda asks. "I'd love to save money on that if I could." Sebastian elbows her in the ribs. "That's my baby," he says. "Hands off of FAST."

"My sense," Dale interjects, "is that we're going to spend that money either way. FAST, no FAST, modified FAST, I can sense that we are heading for an IT overhaul. We're going to invest in an access control system and COBIT programs. It will certainly add up. Let's leave that alone. Besides, even though I think I have already proven my point that agile compliance is a good business move, I believe the real meat is in the financial benefits of the agility we get."

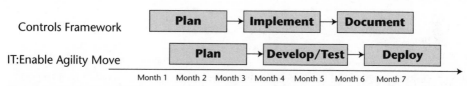

Figure 12-4 Timeline of an IT project and internal controls changes needed to implement a business agility move under existing conditions at DexCo

Figure 12-5   Timeline of an IT project and internal controls changes needed to implement a business agility move with proposed agile compliance program

Table 12-5   Timeline of an IT and Controls Project, Contrasting the Existing Project Methodology with the Proposed Agile Compliance Program

EXISTING PROJECT METHOD-OLOGY	MONTH 1	MONTH 2	MONTH 3	MONTH 4	MONTH 5	MONTH 6	MONTH 7	TOTAL
FTEs on project	4	4	3.5	5	5	3	5	
Cost per person per month	$12,800	$12,800	$12,800	$12,800	$12,800	$12,800	$12,800	
Project cost	$51,200	$51,200	$44,800	$64,000	$64,000	$38,400	$64,000	$377,600
Agile compliance project method-ology; FTEs on project	3	2	2	4	4			
Cost per person per month	$12,800	$12,800	$12,800	$12,800	$12,800			
Project cost	$38,400	$25,600	$25,600	$51,200	$51,200			$192,000
Savings	49%							

Agility

"If we tried to do flex-acturing without good internal controls, to use a familiar example, we would face a bunch of plain old financial problems, as well as compliance issues," Dale says. "As we are set up today, we would face a situation like the one I am looking at now." He shows Table 12-6. "With our current level of dislocation between systems and internal control implementation, we are not able to act on changes in forecast rapidly enough to cool down the supply chain in time. The way it would be set up today is to have a standing order for a certain number of units a month based on a forecast that we pull from our CRM system. The sales forecast translates into a set of standing POs for materials, assembly time, and so on.

"Then, if we revise the forecast up, based on a disconnected CRM system, we put through increased POs for supplies. In addition to filling the supply chain with a larger amount of work in process inventory, these POs trigger some overtime charges and setup fees.

"But then, as we have sometimes experienced, a major client cuts its order, defaults on an earlier invoice, or flunks a credit test. Then what? We cut the actual demand. Question: Are we fast enough to catch the revision or do we get stuck with a whole lotta stuff we can't sell. We would end up paying for a lot of materials and assembly line time that we couldn't use. We might even find ourselves in a net loss position on an item. Based on this example, we would end up in a net loss situation at a gross profit level. With marketing and overhead costs wasted on a discontinued product, it would be a whole lot worse. And, we might face some out of period charges that could mess us up in terms of financial reporting."

"In contrast," Dale says. "If you look at the way it could be if we had sound internal controls and were able to detect and act on changes in actual demand in time to make a difference in the supply chain, we could make a tidy profit on the same set of sales figures." He shows Table 12-7. "I think you can see now why it's worth investing the money into the agile compliance program. You get one bad quarter like we're projecting here and the whole thing would pay for itself. This isn't so much a matter of compliance as just sound business. The compliance is a side benefit."

Table 12-6 Effect of Forecast Changes on Flex-acturing Profitability in DexCo's Existing Internal Control Environment

	PER UNIT	MONTH 10	MONTH 11	MONTH 12	MONTH 13	MONTH 14	TOTAL
Forecast demand (completed units)		100,000	100,000	100,000	100,000	100,000	
Revenue	$75	$7,500,000	$7,500,000	$7,500,000	$7,500,000	$7,500,000	
Chip expense	$15	$1,500,000	$1,500,000	$1,500,000	$1,500,000	$1,500,000	
Other component expense	$10	$1,000,000	$1,000,000	$1,000,000	$1,000,000	$1,000,000	
Assembly expense	$5	$500,000	$500,000	$500,000	$500,000	$500,000	
Gross profit		$4,500,000	$4,500,000	$4,500,000	$4,500,000	$4,500,000	$22,500,000
Revised forecast		100,000	250,000	250,000	100,000	100,000	
Revenue from revised forecast	$75	$7,500,000	$18,750,000	$18,750,000	$7,500,000	$7,500,000	
Chip expenses incurred from revised forecast	$15	$1,500,000	$3,750,000	$3,750,000	$1,500,000	$1,500,000	
Other component expense—revised forecast	$10	$1,000,000	$2,500,000	$2,500,000	$1,000,000	$1,000,000	
Assembly expense; revised forecast	$5	$500,000	$1,250,000	$1,250,000	$500,000	$500,000	

Table 12-6 *(continued)*

	PER UNIT	MONTH 10	MONTH 11	MONTH 12	MONTH 13	MONTH 14	TOTAL
Gross profit; projected based on revised forecast		$4,500,000	$11,250,000	$11,250,000	$4,500,000	$4,500,000	$36,000,000
Actual demand	100,000	100,000	50,000				
Revenue from revised forecast	$75	$7,500,000	$7,500,000	$3,750,000			
Chip expenses incurred from revised forecast	$15	$1,500,000	$3,750,000	$3,750,000	$1,000,000		
Other component expense; revised forecast	$10	$1,000,000	$2,500,000	$2,500,000			
Assembly expense; revised forecast	$5	$500,000	$1,250,000	$1,250,000	$500,000		
Double shift penalties	$500,000	$500,000					
Gross profit; projected based on revised forecast		$4,500,000	$(500,000)	$(4,250,000)	$(1,500,000)		$(1,750,000)

Table 12-7 With Effective Internal Controls, DexCo Is Able to Cut Off Supply Orders in Advance of Downturn in Demand and Realize a Higher Profit with Greater Agility

	PER UNIT	MONTH 10	MONTH 11	MONTH 12	TOTAL
Actual demand		100,000	100,000	50,000	
Revenue from actual demand	$75	$7,500,000	$7,500,000	$3,750,000	
Chip expenses incurred from actual demand	$15	$1,500,000	$1,500,000	$750,000	
Other component expense; actual demand	$10	$1,000,000	$1,000,000	$500,000	
Assembly expense; actual demand	$5	$500,000	$500,000	$250,000	
Gross profit; actual demand		$4,500,000	$4,500,000	$2,250,000	$11,250,000

Realizing the Wish List

"Okay," Jim says. "I'm starting to get the picture." He pulls a folded-up piece of paper from his pocket. "What about this wish list we did? I hope you didn't forget about this?" He hands it to Dale, who starts diagramming the list items on the white board. The results look like Table 12-8. "This is a high-level view, of course," Dale says. "But, I think you get the idea. Not only can we use the agile compliance program to realize each aspect of the wish list, which is in itself a major business objective of the company, but we can also save money on almost every aspect of it at the same time."

Table 12-8 Summary of Return on Investment for Agile Compliance Program for DexCo's Compliance and Business Wish List

BUSINESS GOAL	AGILE COMPLIANCE RETURN ON INVESTMENT
Make moves at will	Cost to make move is less than with existing compliance program.
	Move will have less chance of producing a compliance problem.
Create products in rapid cycles, including flex-acturing	Agile compliance program results in controls that aid in accurate forecasting.
	Avoidance of internal control problems that could result in financial restatements or remediation.
Buy/sell companies	Integration of new company's business processes is faster, more streamlined (costs less than existing model of integration).
	Avoidance of internal control problems that could result in financial restatements or remediation.
Change org chart	Lower cost of IT aspects of implementing an org chart change.
	Avoidance of internal control problems that could result in financial restatements or remediation.
Make/break alliances	Streamlined, rapid cycling of alliances results in profitable agility. Lower cost of IT aspects of implementing or dissolving an alliance.
	Avoidance of internal control problems that could result in financial restatements or remediation.
Instant credit checks	Lower cost of IT aspects of implementing instant credit checks, and adapting instant credit check to constantly changing business processes (through use of BPEL and integrated development and deployment model).

(continued)

Table 12-8 *(continued)*

BUSINESS GOAL	AGILE COMPLIANCE RETURN ON INVESTMENT
Accurate, timely financial reports	Lower cost of IT aspects of implementing financial reporting, and adapting reporting process to constantly changing business processes.
	Avoidance of internal control problems that could result in financial restatements or remediation.

"The key to understanding the ROI of the wish list," Dale says, "is to see how we plan to lower the IT implementation cost and time frame of each item on the list. The agility comes from our ability to execute, especially on the IT side of the equation, rapidly. And, doing it without compromising our ability to generate accurate financial statements in the correct time frame, and remain on top of our Sarbanes Oxley 404 process in a cost effective manner."

"Well," Jim says. "This is great. I'm almost sold."

"Almost?" Dale says. "What else do you need me to do, tap dance on the desk?"

"Not anything so extravagant," Jim says. "All I want to know now is how we actually do all of this. We've been talking in generalities for weeks now. How do we make this happen. In the real world?"

Summary

Now that Jim Wilde has had a walk-through of the agile compliance process, he wants to hear an explanation of how much this whole project is going to cost, and why the investment is going to be worth it. Initially, he balks at the figures—millions to get started, and over one million a year in ongoing expense for agile compliance. Wouldn't it be easier, and cheaper, he asks, just to keep doing Sarbanes Oxley the way they did it the first year?

Yes and no, explains Dale Steyer. The agile compliance program is an investment, and it is likely to yield good returns for DexCo in hard dollars as well as intangibles. He proceeds to outline the ways in which agile compliance will pay off for DexCo.

Agile compliance, if implemented correctly, has the potential to reduce the firm's outlay for compliance and audit over time. Eventually, the firm will spend less on compliance and external audit than it currently does. In addition, it is probable that DexCo's audit and SOX compliance fees will rise in the future as the company expands and faces remediation of deficient internal controls. Agile compliance mitigates against this potential.

IT spending growth can be controlled by agile compliance, as the process improves the efficiency of many application development and system integration projects. Agile compliance can also reduce time wasted on rework and remediation of deficient internal controls.

Agility is where agile compliance offers the biggest pay off to DexCo. In just one example, Dale shows that a lack of agile compliance exposes DexCo's supply chain to a potential multimillion-dollar loss if the company cannot react quickly enough to a unforeseen change in demand. In contrast, if the agile compliance measures were implemented, the company could actually profit in the same scenario.

Finally, there are several substantial intangible payoffs to agile compliance, including avoidance of non-compliance penalties and SEC problems. Although it is impossible to predict the impact of agile compliance on DexCo's stock price, there is a clear advantage to guarding the company's stock against the negative impact of damaging SEC inquiries and material weakness remediation disclosures.

Actually Doing It— For Real

In all the fascinating revelations about the rapid collapse of RefCo, the high-flying commodities trading firm that went bankrupt ten weeks after its IPO amidst allegations that it had improperly masked $430 in debt from shareholders, a comment in the *New York Times* underlining the need to focus on the practicalities of agile compliance caught my. In describing how auditors failed to catch a recurring interest payment made between a RefCo subsidiary controlled by its CEO and the parent company (interest on a debt that the CEO was allegedly trying to hide from auditors and shareholders), an accounting expert made the following comment:

"The complexity of the transaction, the fact that it was carefully timed and that legitimate-seeming aspects of it could be verified made it hard to spot... 'This isn't a needle in a haystack...It's a needle in a pile of needles.'" (*New York Times*, October 24th, 2005).

This is our challenge: to enable auditors to find needles in a pile of needles. The question must be asked: How do you actually do it? If you want to achieve agile compliance in a real company in the real world, what are you going to do about?

This part looks at some practical issues relating to the Information Technology aspects of agile compliance. Although there are certainly many human elements to the puzzle, I will concentrate on Information Technology because IT often is the most complex and opaque entity to the business manager.

Although my intent is to be vendor agnostic, I will explore some concepts in this part that sound like vendor pitches. This is an unfortunate reality of our age—that vendor materials work their way into what ought to be a neutral set of discussions. My goal, however, is to give you some familiarity with the technological approaches to agile compliance that are gaining traction in the real world.

CHAPTER 13

IT Solutions for Agile Compliance

Jim Wilde wants to know how he can actually begin working toward the goal of agile compliance. His quest reminds me of the situation in my hometown of Los Angeles, where it seems that every waiter and legal secretary has a screenplay or headshot ready to show to the studios. In Los Angeles, there is a saying that's apt in the world of Sarbanes Oxley. "Everyone," the saying goes, "has two businesses: their own business and show business." So it goes with compliance. All of us in the business world have two businesses: our own business and the IT business.

Like all of us who are involved in compliance, Jim is going to have to become a quick study in some in-depth technical issues. If Jim isn't happy with that idea, I'm sorry to say that the other Hollywood classic comment, "Who do I have to @$%!$@ to get off this picture?" does not apply. A Gartner report from August of 2005 affirmed the centrality of IT as the solution to many Sarbanes Oxley 404 material weaknesses. For example, with references to material weaknesses in accounting policies, Gartner suggested that companies look into "IT-enabled solutions [that] include e-learning to provide consistent internal auditor training and updates on control procedures; audit automation tools that provide for account procedure alignment with financial controls; and workflow, records management and financial close automation."

With regard to internal controls, Gartner says, "IT-enabled solutions for internal controls include financial compliance process management and document management to provide improved oversight and visibility of the compliance process." The report also says, "IT-enabled solutions for IT material weaknesses include segregation of duties, IT change and business process management tools, and document management, as well as defined compliance architecture" (Gartner, "Examine Sarbanes Oxley Section 404 Weaknesses and Use IT as Your Solution" August 2005, by John Bace, Carol Rozwell, French Caldwell).

The Gartner report validates one of my main arguments, which is that the Sarbanes Oxley weaknesses can be remediated through the proper use of information technology. Got that? Sounds simple, kind of like the way proper diet and exercise can reduce the risk of heart disease or flossing can reduce tooth decay, and so on. It appears to be a simple solution, but it's not. Implementing agile compliance is going to involve you in some pretty heavy-duty IT. And not just plain old IT, either. To achieve agile compliance, you will probably have to begin working with some of the newer forms of system and application architecture.

For example, what exactly is *compliance architecture*? There is surely no consensus as to the definition of this concept, or even consensus that there is such a thing. However, working as I do in the enterprise software field, I have an idea of what might work, and that is the emerging paradigm of the service-oriented architecture (SOA).

Disclaimer time: I make my living as a marketer of SOA software products. SOA is an approach to computing that uses open standards (IT specifications that no one owns, like HTTP) to empower software programs written in different languages and running on different operating systems to work together without the use of proprietary interface software. It is a new field, one with great potential, but it is also immature enough to generate controversy and lack overall validation in the world of IT. When I began writing this book, I was cautioned not to appear to be an overzealous advocate of open standards in computing or the overall SOA paradigm. In an attempt to put you at ease about my potential partisanship in the IT field, allow me to make several comments about the subjective, complex topic of IT in the world of compliance.

Open standards, and SOA, one of its more popular current incarnations, have a great deal of potential to enable agile compliance. However, it is not an absolute essential. Despite my occupation, I believe that it is possible to achieve agile compliance in any number of IT scenarios. English is still an excellent business process modeling language. Disciplined project management and sound integration of business process and IT will work regardless of platform. You can use a single vendor proprietary architecture to achieve agile compliance. You can develop custom code in a proprietary language to achieve agile compliance. Yet, I think you will also be making life harder for yourself if you do.

Of one thing I am certain, however, and that is you will find the world of IT— the developers, architects, vendors, consultants, analysts, and journalists—to be a fractious, opinionated bunch. I include myself in this collection, so I hope I'm not offending anyone. In IT, opinion matters, and we should be proud to state what we believe passionately. However, we sometimes forget that it can be confusing and irritating to have to listen to our fractious opinionating.

SOA is merely a tool that can be used for the achievement of agile compliance. There is absolutely nothing within the SOA that guarantees, or even offers, compliance unless it is executed properly. I would even say that SOA, if implemented poorly, can do great harm to compliance efforts.

So, with the caveat that SOA is not the only solution to SOX, and the warning that SOA done wrong is worse than useless, I will now discuss how SOA can form the IT basis for agile compliance. I truly believe SOA is the best solution for SOX. Furthermore, if you are involved in any IT project right now, you are going to be hearing a lot about SOA anyway. I am not the only one involved in describing SOA as a potential solution for business IT issues, including compliance. SOA is at the heart of Microsoft .NET technology, Oracle Fusion Middleware, the BEA's Aqualogic platform, the IBM Web-Sphere brand, SAP NetWeaver, and on and on. Everyone, it seems, is now in the SOA business. Let's take a look at how an SOA works.

Defining SOA

In an industry known for fingernail-on-blackboard acronyms and jargon, the notion of service-oriented architecture has got to be one of the worst offenders. It has no inherently comprehensible meaning that a non-technology person can divine. Even those in the tech field have trouble figuring it out. When combined with such related terms as "Web services" and "SOAP," it gets even worse. Let me try to explain what all the fuss is about so you can understand why SOA can be a relevant IT approach to agile compliance.

First, some background. Most corporate computer systems are *distributed*, meaning that more than one system and piece of software is often required to accomplish a specific task. For example, at DexCo, the ERP system tracks inventories and manufacturing schedules while the general ledger system handles the bookkeeping and financial reporting for the business. The process of doing business at DexCo is therefore distributed between the two systems.

There is nothing new about distributed computing. For almost as long as there have been computers, the IT industry has offered various ways to enable one computer to "speak" with another. Whether it is for the purpose of exchanging data ("Here's a price list, remember it . . . ") or issuing functional commands ("Here's a dollar figure, now give me the equivalent in pounds"), owners of enterprise computer systems have had several options for connecting machines together.

For years, it has been possible to connect systems in a distributed environment using either custom-coded software or proprietary software packages as *middleware* that can send, receive, and translate messages back and forth between distributed systems. Figure 13-1 lays out a standard, if highly simplified, version of this kind of traditional proprietary middleware approach to application integration in a distributed environment. We have four systems (and software applications) that support each of fours steps in a business process. Three separate, incompatible proprietary middleware packages connect the four systems. In order to complete the business process, the four systems must exchange messages at least once. Factoring in the middleware that sits between the systems, there are actually six message steps involved in completing the business process. Each message step is technologically distinct in terms of message transport protocol and connectivity; for example, Message One might connect a Java application to a Tibco interface over HTTP, while Message Three might connect a Microsoft C++ application to a WebMethods hub over FTP, and so on.

There is absolutely nothing wrong with this proprietary approach to connecting distributed systems. It has been proven to work and it will continue to be in effect in myriad enterprise architectures for a generation to come. However, IT managers have learned over the years that it can be quite costly and time consuming to modify proprietary middleware in a distributed environment. If the middleware connects more than one company, it can be that much more challenging and expensive.

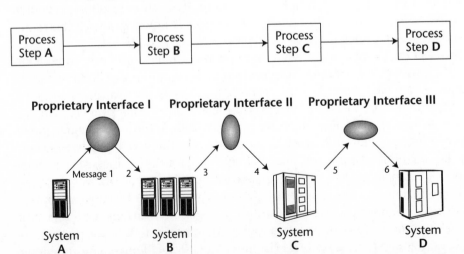

Figure 13-1 A traditional application integration setup: Three proprietary middleware packages connect four separate systems to support a four-step business process. There are six message steps involved in getting from System A to System D.

To understand why a proprietary application is costly and slow, consider what will happen in the example shown in Figure 13-1 if one of the proprietary middleware packages is replaced or upgraded. That change will likely require modifications to the message format and software configuration of the other two middleware packages used in orchestrating the business process, and it may also require changes to the underlying applications themselves. A change in the business process will have a similar effect. As the Gartner report notes, "Changing business models were also a contributing factor to [Sarbanes Oxley 404] problems." Each change will probably generate an IT project, and we know how slow those can be.

If you are involved in application integration in support of multistep business processes you may have seen a chart that resembles Figure 13-2. Inspired by a slide from my friends at IBM, it shows the classic hairball of tangled, interconnected processes that can drive any serious IT manager completely insane. If you are going to start orchestrating incompatible software programs and middleware packages in the middle of this kind of thicket, you are going to run into trouble very quickly. The interdependencies and brittle connections quickly overwhelm the application integration process, and it grows lengthy and costly to complete. (Or even impossible to complete.) Keeping on top of compliance while remaining agile in such a mess is quite a challenge.

The hairball has been around for decades, so it has been a long-term vision of the IT industry to devise simple ways to connect applications that support business processes. The idea of an SOA is to enable some flexibility, efficiency, and cost effectiveness in dealing with the hairball. Several well-intentioned attempts at achieving such open interoperability between incompatible systems, including the Common Object Request Broker Architecture (CORBA) and Component Object Model (COM) failed to gain true industry-wide success. The industry was left with a grand goal but no technological basis for solving the problem of streamlining application integration.

Then, as the Internet and World Wide Web grew in popularity in the late 1990s, due in large part to its reliance on open, non-proprietary standards such as HyperText Transport Protocol (HTTP) and HyperText Markup Language (HTML), IT industry leaders began to wonder if they could achieve a similar rate of growth in software use by opening up the middleware connections between distributed systems. Thus the vision of an SOA based on open standards gained in stature.

In an ideal SOA, any piece of software in the world can access the functionality or data of any other piece of software in the world by communicating over the Web using a common, public language known as Extensible Markup Language (XML). In other words, every piece of software in the world can be invoked as a *service* when needed, or *on demand*. Software then would become known as a web service (software, available as a service, over the Web) and enterprise architecture would then be based on such services. Thus, you have a *service*-oriented architecture.

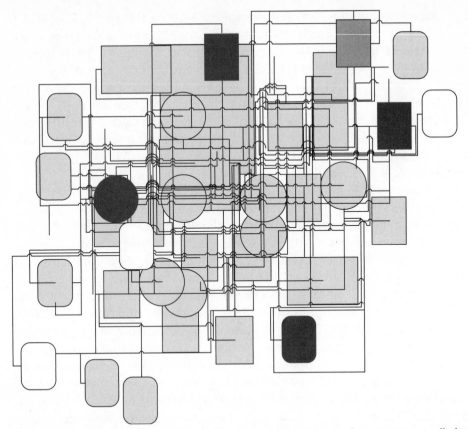

Figure 13-2 The business process hairball—what interconnected processes actually look like at a real company

In 2001, all the major global technology players—Oracle, IBM, Microsoft, HP, BEA and others—agreed to standardize on several key SOA technologies to enable truly open interoperability amongst computer systems and software applications, regardless of their operating systems and programming languages. This was the beginning of the modern, viable SOA that we are seeing today in such products as IBM WebSphere and Microsoft .NET. The open standards that were ratified included SOAP (Simple Object Access Protocol), a format of XML that provides a standardized way for systems to exchange data and operating instructions. SOAP is now one of the most common XML message formats used in the SOA. There are others, such as ebXML and ACORD XML, which is used by insurance companies, but the principle is the same. Heterogeneous systems can take advantage of a common, non-proprietary message format (that no one owns) to achieve simpler, more flexible, and more cost-effective interoperation (see Figure 13-3).

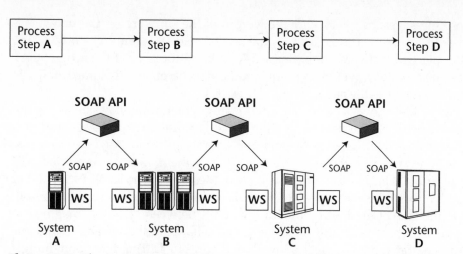

Figure 13-3 The same four-step business process as enabled by SOAP and web services

Web services and SOA do for computers what the phone did for business people 125 years ago. Whereas prior to the invention of the phone, telecommunication relied upon mail, telegrams, couriers, smoke signals, and carrier pigeons, when the phone came into existence, people could speak to each other over long distances in real time. Doing business got a lot easier. If you throw in a common language, as English is today in so many business situations, commerce gets all the more streamlined. So it is with SOA. SOA has been likened to a dial tone that connects disparate software applications.

The parable of the three blind men and the elephant gets trotted out frequently when discussing new paradigms in the IT field. The scenario where one man thinks the elephant is a wall, the second man thinks it's a tree, and the third a snake is quite apt when getting people to embrace a subjective and complex new idea. The joke in SOA circles is that if you really want people to comprehend SOA, you need 4 elephants and 12 blind men. Indeed, there is a great deal of market noise, hype, and confusion about what an SOA is, what it can be today versus tomorrow, and what it might actually look like at your company. To stay focused, let's look at some current configurations of an SOA and how they relate to today's business needs.

Enterprise Service Bus

In the real world, one of the first challenges that a company must overcome if it wants to develop an SOA is the incompatible communications protocols it uses on its networks. Although virtually all computers are connected by networks, the ways that messages travel across those networks and the formats of those messages, can vary widely. Even if all the software on the network is exposed as web services, and is potentially able to communicate with any other piece of software on that network, it does little good if the actual SOAP messages cannot travel from point A to point B because of incompatibility in what is known as the *message transport layer*.

Figure 13-4 shows a typical large company with numerous systems operating on a network that uses three different and incompatible message transport protocols for the exchange of data and operating instructions between systems. Machines, and the software that runs on them, may be connected on a point-to-point basis, or in loops, using Java Messaging Service (JMS), HTTP, or TCP-IP. This message transport hairball within the hairball further complicates the goal of modifying integration points between systems. Imagine trying to negotiate both the business process hairball shown above and the message transport conflicts shown in Figure 13-4. The time and budget required to make changes to applications could get unmanageable.

As a solution to this message transport Tower of Babel, a number of software companies have developed a software architecture known as the enterprise service bus (ESB). (In tech talk, a bus is a device or program that carries communication signals.) The ESB is essentially a vast set of connectors that translate message transport protocols back and forth as messages travel across the network. As shown in Figure 13-5, the ESB forms a common message transport layer through which all systems can communicate with each other.

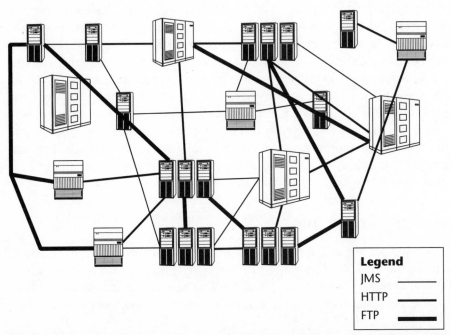

Figure 13-4 Typical heterogeneous message transport protocols at a major company

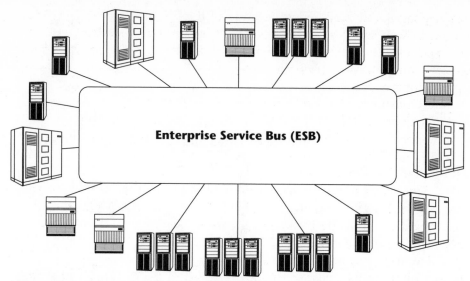

Figure 13-5 Schematic of an ESB that provides a common message transport layer through which all systems can communicate with each other

Of course, the example I have shown here is a simplistic one. In an actual enterprise, there are a number of hurdles to deploying an ESB, including security, routing, actual physical infrastructure, and the management of the service levels of the multitude of message sending entities. Yet, ESB is an ingenious approach to putting the power of an SOA to work. To take advantage of the potential of web services and an SOA to enable efficient interoperation of systems, you need to solve the message transport incompatibility issue. Even if you don't use an ESB, you will have to tackle the problem. As you will see shortly, ESB can have a lot to do with achieving agile compliance.

SOBA

SOBA stands for service-oriented business application. Like ESB, SOBA is a practical application of the principles of an SOA in the business context. A SOBA is a piece of software that realizes the fulfillment a business process by invoking a selected set of web services in an orchestrated sequence. Figure 13-6 shows a simple SOBA that affects a four-step business process by invoking four separate web services that exist on a large ESB.

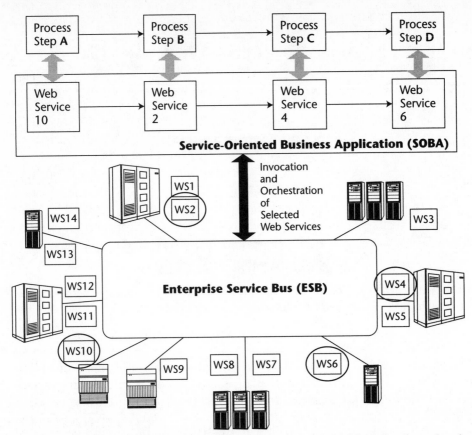

Figure 13-6   SOBA orchestrates a business process by invoking selected web services in a sequence dictated by the business process.

SOBA solves a basic problem in SOA. That is, after you have opened up your software programs and enabled them to communicate with other software programs regardless of their location, operating system, programming language, and message transport protocol, then what? Are you really achieving much by exposing all of your applications to one another if you cannot implement specific business processes in a controlled way? That is the problem solved by SOBA.

For example, let's say that you have a business process in place to do credit checks on new customers prior to shipping an order. Before SOA and SOBA, you would implement the process by building a business application that used a proprietary interface to link the credit database with the order system. The user of this application, an order processing clerk would query the credit database and either release or hold the order based on the results of the query.

With SOA, you could expose the credit database and order processing systems as Web services and connect them to the ESB so they can be invoked from any application that can communicate with them using SOAP. You could deploy a SOBA that invoked the credit check web service and the order system web service in the order specified by the business process (BPEL).

Now, you might be thinking that sounds like a lot of effort to achieve the same result. You've built an ESB, exposed the web services, and integrated them with a SOBA—all this to achieve a result you already had, which was the ability to check a credit record and approve an order. That is true. However, think about what happens when you want to start changing the systems around, or outsourcing either your order processing or credit checks to other firms.

As you can see in Figure 13-7, the SOBA is built to enable quick changes to the Web services that support the business process. The SOBA can be easily configured to invoke new web services that support the business process defined for the operation. If the company changes its system configuration for credit checks, the SOBA makes it a great deal easier to adapt to the change. SOBA is a potential enabler of agile compliance.

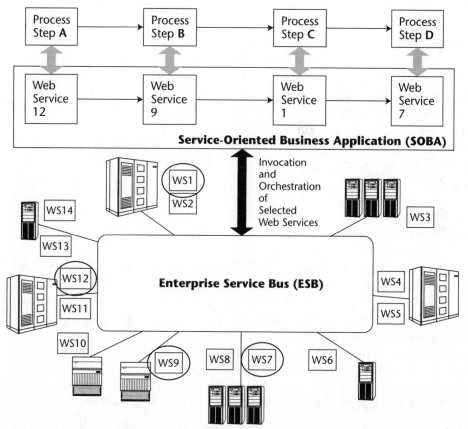

Figure 13-7 As underlying systems and web services change, the SOBA keeps the orchestration of the business process constant and simple to monitor.

As you survey the marketplace for software these days, you will see a number of emerging SOBA vendors in specific categories. For example, there is now a SOBA vendor that helps health insurance companies connect with hospitals using web services. And, there are a growing number of SOBA platforms, or software programs that help you develop your own SOBA for your specific business process needs.

On-Demand Software

The concept of on-demand software, which can be invoked when needed, on demand, without regard for specifics of infrastructure, network, hardware, or software, is a corollary of an SOA that has grown in popularity in the last few years. Also known as *software as a service* (SAAS) or *application service provider* (ASP), the on-demand model is perhaps best exemplified by Salesforce.com. Salesforce.com is a sophisticated piece of customer resource management (CRM) software that users access through a web browser. Salesforce.com handles all the complexity and expense of managing a massive datacenter operation and provisioning a high-functioning software to hundreds of thousands of users simultaneously. Users pay an annual fee for the right to use Salesforce.com as a service on demand. The user does not have to install any special software or hardware to run it. In addition, Salesforce.com provides a web service, known as *Sforce*, if you want to make Salesforce.com part of a SOBA.

On-demand software provides several of SOA's advantages without some of its major hassles. On-demand software can be modified centrally and the updated version of the software is instantly provisioned to all of its users without the kind of specific machine software upgrades that traditional software requires. This has great applicability to agile compliance. I consider on-demand software and SAAS relevant to the discussion of SOA and agile compliance because the success of the model shows how the use of open standards can lead to flexibility, rapid change potential, combined with centralized control.

The important thing to remember about on-demand software, as well as its cousins grid computing and utility computing, is that it won't work very well unless you have an architecture that takes advantage of open standards as an SOA does. If you want to access software functionality on demand, you will have a hard time making it happen if you have to adapt constantly to shifting proprietary standards amongst the machines and infrastructure elements that you are trying to tie together to support the on-demand capability.

The Promise of SOA for Agile Compliance

Okay, now you may be thinking, "This SOA stuff is totally fabulous, and I kind of see the connection to agile compliance, but how is it really relevant?" I will explore this in detail Chapter 14; for now I'll look at some overview issues to try to connect the dots and see how SOA has the potential to enable agile compliance.

As I have mentioned throughout this book, the IT change management process can be a killer of agile compliance. While the business climate demands agility and rapid change, the IT and internal controls process can slow the process down so much as to dampen the performance of the business or mitigate the effectiveness of the controls. This has negative ramifications for SOX compliance.

SOA has the potential to do several things to enable speed and agility in the IT change management process. With SOA, a company can make changes to the IT systems that power business processes and internal controls with relative ease and cost effectiveness. With ESB and SOBA, it becomes possible to modify software applications without having too great an impact on the business process models that they support.

SOA also potentially allows a greater degree of flexibility in integrating applications, which can benefit internal controls. Linking financial systems, CRM, and ERP, for example, which may be necessary for effective controls, is made easier by SOA, at least in theory.

SOA makes possible the kind of enterprise-wide sharing of information and learning that is also considered necessary for Sarbanes Oxley. As I posited in the DexCo case, a flexible compliance portal could make it possible for the company to conduct its internal controls work in plain sight of the various departments that had to cooperate on the process.

Even a Magic Bullet Can Kill You

You could be agile and compliant without an SOA, but an SOA has the potential to make the job a lot easier than doing it with proprietary technology. Yet, charging blindly into an SOA without considering a number of serious security and infrastructure factors could be a big mistake. Advocates, and vendors, may want to portray SOA as a magic bullet that can save your business from all kinds of trouble. Sometimes, however, even a magic bullet can kill you.

Security issues are paramount in an SOA. By exposing enterprise applications to functions in XML, a text-based open standard language, you are potentially opening up your software to unwanted prying eyes. In contrast to earlier IT systems that achieved security through obscurity, where it was almost impossible to find a piece of software even if you could gain illegal access to a company's network, with an SOA the locations of much of the company's software is actually published. Whatever SOA work you do, you need to consider security issues as you move forward. If you do not, you will compromise the security of your enterprise applications, which will set you back in terms of Sarbanes Oxley compliance and COBIT maturity.

Management and governance of an SOA is also a challenge. Because of its openness, an SOA tends to bring people from different divisions and roles together in ways that they have not been associated before. That can be a great thing, or a terrible situation depending on what your company does and who works there. Line of business managers may find themselves with a much greater IT responsibility with SOA than they had in the past. It is important to map out the management and system governance issues brought on by an SOA prior to its deployment. If these issues are not adequately addressed, then you may find yourself contending with a fresh set of internal control deficiencies brought about by exposure of enterprise systems to poor oversight.

I bring these issues up because there is a tendency in the IT field to look at emerging trends as potential saviors without assessing their downsides properly at the outset. I do believe that an SOA has unique potential to enable agile compliance if implemented properly. That can be a big *if*, however, if you and your organization are not up to the task of listening knowledgeably to hype-prone vendors, technology advocates, in-house champions, and consultants.

Summary

True agile compliance means digging into some pretty heavyweight IT issues. Based on what is happening in the IT industry, I recommend that executives who are interested in agile compliance look into the emerging paradigm of the service-oriented architecture, or SOA, as an approach to solving some of the IT challenges posed by agile compliance.

Although SOA is far from the only workable solution to agile compliance, I believe it warrants serious attention because of its potential to enable broad interoperation of systems and software programs without the same heavy investment of time and money that traditional application integration methods have required.

SOA, which relies on the open (non-proprietary) standard of the XML language, provides a basis for any piece of software to exchange data or operating instructions with any other piece of software by communicating in a common language over a common protocol. Thus, each software program is available as a service, invoked on demand, over the Web. Web services is the term that refers to this model.

SOA has the potential to enable agile compliance because it solves, at least in theory, some of the cycle time challenges of matching the software change management process to the business agility requirements of a corporate entity. And, by nature of its openness ability to act as a universal dial tone of sorts amongst software programs, SOA can streamline the process of connecting systems required for maintenance of internal controls.

SOA is being realized in different forms, including the enterprise service bus, or ESB, a common communication platform that powers the actual web service message between systems. The service-oriented business application, or SOBA, is a type of software that manages the orchestration of invoking web services to support a business process. The SOBA and ESB working together form a powerful tool for agile compliance.

At the same time, an SOA is far from being a magic bullet for agile compliance. If implemented incorrectly, an SOA can actually compound internal control problems and COBIT maturity. With the warning that even a magic bullet can kill you, I encourage the savvy executive to get a firm grip on SOA, cutting through vendor hype, phony industry visionaries, and under-trained IT departments.

CHAPTER 14

SOX Software

The DexCo management team convenes for another session. This time the agenda calls for a review of Sarbanes Oxley software. It's Ramesh's turn to talk, but this time everyone is paying close attention. Ramesh is the naysayer who works for CIO Sebastian Harris. Sebastian has asked him to prepare a presentation on software packages that are specifically designed to help with Sarbanes Oxley Section 404 compliance.

Taxonomy of SOX Packages

Ramesh leads off by stating that the whole Sarbanes Oxley area is so new, and prone to change, that any software he discusses will probably be obsolete in a few months. For that reason, he is going to avoid discussing specific vendors. However, he had done enough of a review to be able to go over the basic categories of SOX compliance packages. The categories, and the ways that certain types of SOX packages work, will probably remain constant even as the specifics of the software and the law itself continue to evolve.

As an overview, Ramesh breaks SOX packages into five main groups. The terms he uses are not official, they merely reflect his (and my) view of what the major packages actually do. There are applications that create a shared workspace for compliance staffers to use in compiling lists of controls, testing controls, and preparing SOX certification documents and letters. Then, there are documentation management applications, which help companies establish and maintain documentation of internal controls and controls testing procedures. Financial coordination packages help companies with numerous general ledger accounts and financial systems maintain accurate, up-to-date reports on the state of internal controls that reside within the general ledger systems. Exception monitoring software helps accounting managers and auditors detect transactions that are exceptions to internal controls. These packages often monitor more than one ERP or financial application at the same time and correlate the data that is produced in order to detect problems or internal control failures. Finally, Vadjdpai notes that the major ERP and financial software packages are beginning to include built-in internal controls management modules to ease SOX compliance for their users.

Shared Workspace

As Ramesh explains, the Sarbanes Oxley Act requires coordinated efforts amongst many separate groups of people inside and outside of a public company. To conduct an effective SOX compliance effort, the accounting, line-of-business, and IT folks need to coordinate their activities and work within tight deadlines. On top of this internal coordination challenge, both an external auditor and compliance consulting firm will also need timely access to information about the firm's compliance effort.

To solve this problem, several software packages have come on the market that enable all these separate groups of users to share compliance-related tasks, assign responsibility, and enforce deadlines. For example, an internal auditor might use the shared workspace software to delineate a list of internal controls. Then a SOX compliance manager could pick up that list and assign controls documentation tasks to a different line of business people within the company. Those responsible for documenting the controls would receive their assignments and deadlines over the workspace software. When the process was completed, the software could be used to compile the reports that support the SOX attestations required by the law.

Documentation Management

SOX documentation management programs provide a tool that helps accounting departments assemble internal controls reports, documentation of controls, attestation letters, and so on, that conform to the standards set out by the PCAOB and regulatory bodies. These packages help compliance staff put together the proper documents that the auditors will need to inspect.

Document management packages are often bundled with a shared workspace feature because compliance typically involves so many disparate people and organizations. It can be a struggle to generate and maintain accurate, correctly formatted sets of internal control documentation when there are multiple authors, scattered and inconsistent revision cycles, and an overall lack of clarity about the entire process. A common complaint heard in SOX circles is the chaotic effect of multiple spreadsheet files—each of which is formatted differently—being hurled across e-mail networks as compliance staffs scramble to meet filing deadlines. Documentation management programs can solve this problem, provided that users can agree on a standard protocol for their use.

Financial Coordination

To help overburdened audit staffs, financial coordination software packages set up task management and shared workspace for the completion of specific compliance audit processes. For example, one area of internal audit where many public companies fall short on follow-through is the process of account reconciliation. Audit rules dictate that a company reconcile its general ledger accounts at the end of the period. This is a standard practice where the auditor will check accounts, such as receivables, inventory, and so on, for mistakes or inconsistencies.

Most accounting packages provide basic account reconciliation functionality. Where things get messy with SOX is the requirement that auditors have a complete, company-wide view of what's going on with account reconciliation even if there are multiple general ledger systems in use. For a business with separate subsidiaries, this task can be quite a challenge unless the internal auditors have a tool that helps them coordinate their account reconciliation tasks and deadlines.

Some packages offer a feature set that allows for compliance benchmarking, wherein the compliance staff can use the software to establish parameters for internal controls that they would like to see implemented throughout the organization, complete with documentation. In addition, packages may offer users the ability to track year-to-year and period-to-period compliance results and related analytics.

Exception Monitoring

Exception monitoring software helps accountants catch situations where internal controls are being violated. Based on rule sets, these software packages monitor ongoing transactions and alert accounting staff when a situation arises that breaks a rule. A broken rule is also known as an *exception* in accounting and IT circles. For example, an exception monitoring package might establish a rule that catches situations where goods are shipped from a warehouse without the proper approvals from both the sales manager and warehouse manager. The software is set up to check that both approvals be present before a shipment goes out. If the shipment leaves without approval (assuming that there is a logistics software program operating that monitors shipments), then the exception monitoring program sends an alert to a member of the accounting staff, who can then investigate and correct the problem.

Internal Controls Modules

As SOX compliance efforts have begun to consume a large proportion of IT and accounting department time, the major finance and ERP software vendors have introduced internal controls modules to their enterprise applications. Meant to enable identification of internal controls that exist within the ERP or financial application, these modules have the potential to simplify the laborious process of Section 404 control documentation.

Realizing the Potential of SOX Software

All of these packages are new, so it's not known whether they will do much to help with SOX. Software vendors have perceived a need to help their clients with SOX, and they have thus taken advantage of the market demand by creating compliance applications and control modules for existing applications. What Ramesh wants to emphasize in his talk, however, is that it is easy to get confused by software vendors who promise to "do it all" for a company's compliance process. As far as Ramesh can tell, no one package has anywhere near the breadth of functionality to take care of everything involved in compliance.

It is also tempting, he notes, to think that a company can buy some software, install it, and then be SOX compliant. That is highly improbable, even for a very small company with simple compliance needs. Furthermore, he wants the executives in the room to be wary of software packages that claim to be SOX compliant, as if the PCAOB and SEC were issuing a sort of Underwriters' Laboratory stamp of approval that makes anything you do with the software automatically kosher for SOX. Today, there is no such certification of SOX software.

As far as I can tell, most of the products available have been developed with sincere attention to getting SOX programs on track at companies that use them. However, like so much else in IT, the ultimate success depends on the proper implementation, user training, and usage. Your compliance staff and consultants will be able to use a documentation management package only if they understand the goal of SOX 404 internal controls documentation. They will benefit from a shared workspace only if they understand what they are meant to accomplish. An exception monitoring application can work only if the internal controls have been documented well enough to instantiate the rules that need monitoring. You get the idea.

To be effective even at achieving basic SOX compliance, these software packages will need to work together, or at least be worked together. Because their functionality covers some, but not all, of the SOX 404 requirements, your compliance team will have to plan and implement a way to make a suite of packages work in concert. This can be done either through application integration or coordinated separate use of different packages. Neither is easy, but given the lack of a total solution, it is probably necessary. The alternative, which is to use no software except e-mail and spreadsheets for SOX compliance, is surely less than optimal.

There is a difference, too, Ramesh explains, between using SOX software to help people work together and connecting and correlating internal controls on multiple systems. The latter requires a far higher degree of technical investment and systemic rigor.

Putting the SOX Packages into a Compliance Architecture

Ramesh is on the hunt for the elusive compliance architecture. "It is reminiscent," he says, "of seeking advice for a wayward toddler. Every child is different, say the childcare advice books. So too, every family is different, every therapist is different, every day is different . . ." How can one find sound advice? Not easily, seems to be the conclusion. So it goes with discovering the right compliance architecture for your company.

Assuming you even want one. Now that the term has come up in industry forums, I feel compelled to write about it. However, the concept is a little misleading. You are probably never going to have a compliance architecture. That is, if you are involved in running an IT department that supports a going concern, you will simply lack the time and focus, or even the necessity to build a complete infrastructure just to support compliance. It is more likely that you will build compliance into the enterprise architecture that you have. So, when we talk about a compliance architecture, we are really talking about compliance functions built into whatever enterprise architecture already exists.

What Ramesh wants his colleagues to understand is how compliance in architecture must be based on a workable application integration model. If a company approaches compliance by installing one or more software packages that themselves require custom or proprietary integration with the software that they are supposed to be monitoring, then there will be trouble. If you add a layer of incompatible software on top of your existing architecture in order to achieve compliance, you will be slowing down all of your IT processes. You will probably get neither compliance nor agility out the solution.

Figure 14-1 shows a simple example of a four-step business process that is supported by four underlying systems. If you were to install an exception monitoring application to monitor the internal controls involved in this four-step process, but rely upon a proprietary integration approach to achieve the monitoring, you will have a brittle set up. A change to the underlying systems or the connections between them would probably necessitate a change to the interfaces connecting the exception monitoring application. In real life, this means an integration change project would arise for the exception monitoring software every time a change occurred in the underlying systems. Given the way IT departments work, the odds are that the changes to the exception monitoring software would be deferred or at least not done synchronously. The result would be an impairment of the exception monitoring for an interval of time that may actually become permanent.

Let's look at the Refco disaster for an example of what I am talking about. As an auditor commented, the alleged fraud at Refco would have been difficult to detect, like finding a needle in a pile of needles. If Refco had installed an exception monitoring application, it would have had to have been smart enough to detect receipt of an interest payment that was too high for the outstanding loan balance held by the interest payer. (A Refco subsidiary was allegedly hiding an undisclosed $430 million loan.) To detect this irregularity, the exception monitoring system would have to be aware of the loan balances of each Refco account and the interest payments due. It would have to be able to correlate these sets of data and alert accounting personnel if a transaction appeared to be in violation of the internal control that dictated a matchup between interest payment and loan balance.

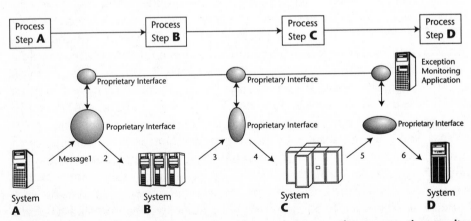

Figure 14-1   Difficulty caused by proprietary integration connecting an exception monitoring application to a set of distributed applications

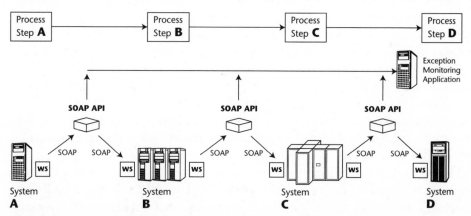

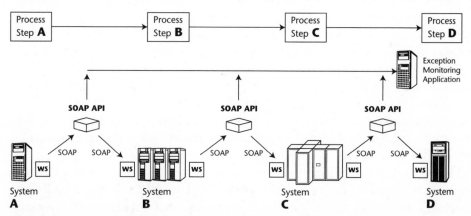

Forgetting for a moment that Refco did none of these things, consider how complex this kind of internal control enforcement can be. Refco had hundreds of clients and its business rules were constantly changing. If the company had installed an exception monitoring application for SOX, it would only work, realistically, if it could be integrated, modified, and re-integrated with an ever-expanding set of underlying systems on a rapid basis. Realistically, this means service-oriented architecture (SOA).

Figure 14-2 shows what this integration would look like. The exception monitoring application would be integrated with the underlying systems using web services. All the data that the exception monitoring application needs to perform its correlations and alerts regarding internal controls would flow to it as SOAP messages. As a result, changes in the underlying systems would not beget change projects to the exception monitoring software. Because the SOAP interface is based on open standards and the messages travel across the network using web protocols, the complexity involved in adapting the exception monitoring software to a change in the underlying system is greatly reduced. The end result is an exception monitoring package that can be up, running, and accurate virtually all the time.

If you are only going to use SOX software packages that establish an online work environment for sharing documents and tasks, then your need for an SOA is not urgent. However, if you are linking these packages with any existing applications, as would be the case if you needed a SOX package to retrieve a chart of accounts automatically from a financials application, you will be badly compromised if you don't have an SOA.

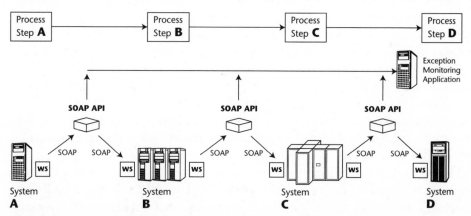

Figure 14-2 Connecting an exception monitoring application to underlying applications using an SOA and web services

The requirement that compliance efforts take advantage of SOA is not a big problem for the SOX applications themselves. Being new, they are invariable SOA based or SOA compatible. However, most enterprise architectures are still evolving, and while many companies are embracing an SOA, it is still way too early to assume that a company's compliance efforts will be based on an SOA.

SOX Packages and the DexCo Agile Compliance Plan

The question for Ramesh, then, is what SOX package would he recommend for DexCo? He answers by saying that DexCo must approach SOX software decisions on two levels. First, the company has to perform its annual Section 404 internal controls review and documentation in order to prepare for its external audit and 404 attestation. Then, as we have discussed at great length, DexCo wants to implement an agile compliance process to stay compliant without compromising any strategic or operational agility.

Ramesh, who has been working intensely on this subject with both Linda and Sebastian, states that DexCo, like any public company, must assess its readiness for the various SOX package options and evaluate their appropriateness based on its overall compliance objectives. He lays out a readiness grid for each type of SOX software and rates each one for its suitability for DexCo both today and in the future.

Based on his analysis, as shown in Table 14-1, Ramesh believes that DexCo needs a document management system designed for the SOX 404 process, and a SOX-shared workspace package. He does not feel that DexCo's enterprise architecture is mature enough for exception monitoring, although he recommends that the company consider it when it is ready. As for internal controls modules for ERP packages, he also wants to wait and see, because DexCo is likely to make major changes to its enterprise architecture for the sake of efficiency, agility, and compliance. Only after these changes have been made will it be practical for DexCo to get involved in installing exception monitoring, internal controls modules, or financial coordination packages.

Of course, the compliance portal itself is a shared workspace, but Ramesh wants to make sure that the portal contains SOX-specific task flows and work processes. He shows a new portal design, as depicted in Figure 14-3. To make it all work, Ramesh suggests the development of a correlation engine, a piece of SOA-based custom software that will enable portal administrators to link specific tasks and the SOX 404 attestation process with supporting BPEL documents, systems designs, and so on.

Table 14-1   Evaluation of DexCo's Readiness for SOX Software Packages

SOX PACKAGE TYPE	DEXCO READINESS	COMMENT
Shared workspace	Company needs it now, can use it now	Should integrate with compliance portal.
Documentation management	Company needs it now, can use it now	Should integrate with compliance portal.
Financial coordination	Not quite ready for it now	Should not buy this software unless it will integrate with compliance portal. Must fit into overall enterprise architecture plan.
Internal controls modules for existing applications	Not ready for it yet	Even if DexCo can buy it now, integration issues remain unclear. DexCo does not want islands of compliance data separate from the portal.
Exception monitoring	Not quite ready for it now, but it is a desirable feature once overall enterprise architecture has been worked out	Should not buy this software unless it will integrate with compliance portal. Must fit into overall enterprise architecture plan.

"Sounds complicated," Dale observes.

"It is," Ramesh replies. "But far less so than trying to do this without a compliance portal or correlation engine. In that scenario, we are all working blind."

"Now for the multimillion dollar question," Jim says. "What are we going to do with FAST?" He is referring to DexCo's huge application integration project, which has been on hold for several weeks while this whole compliance issue has been under discussion.

"Honestly," Sebastian says, "I don't know."

"What the heck kind of answer is that?" Jim demands. "Are you serious?"

"Yes and no," Sebastian says. "We are preparing a recommendation at this time, but we want to go over our methodology for selecting those aspects of FAST that we should keep and those that should be killed. Our decision-making process is based on compliance, agility, and the suitability of an SOA in each major systemic area.

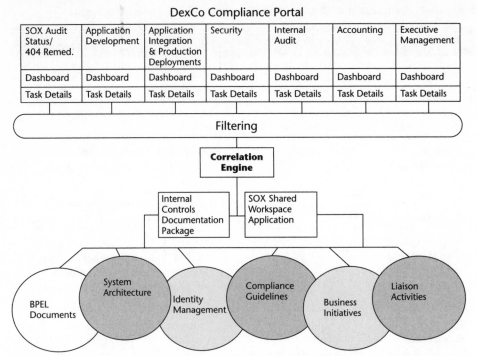

Figure 14-3 Design of DexCo's compliance portal, including an internal controls documentation package, a SOX-shared workspace application, and a correlation engine that enables portal administrators to match pending internal controls issues with documents and other data related to identity management, BPEL documents, and so on.

Summary

In the last two years, a number of promising software packages have come on the market to help with compliance efforts at public companies. Despite suggestions that some of these programs "do it all" or are out of the box SOX compliant, the reality is somewhat different. Acknowledging that the state of the art is constantly changing in this new area of software, we now see five basic types of SOX software. In some cases, their functionality overlaps, so please consider the following categories to be general and fluid.

Shared workspace applications enable compliance staffers to compile lists of controls, testing controls, and preparing SOX certification documents and letters. Documentation management applications help companies establish and maintain documentation of internal controls and controls testing procedures. Financial coordination packages help companies with numerous general ledger accounts and financial systems maintain accurate, up-to-date reports on the state of internal controls that reside within the general ledger systems. Exception monitoring software helps accounting managers and auditors detect exceptions to adherence to internal controls. Major ERP and financial software packages are beginning to include built-in internal controls management modules to ease SOX compliance for their users.

As with so many aspects of compliance, the full effectiveness of these software programs can be realized only when they are deployed amidst a complete compliance process. Indeed, the concept of "garbage in, garbage out" is especially apt when contemplating poorly implemented SOX software. SOX packages need to be used in the context of a well-designed compliance organization and work process.

In IT terms, SOX packages have the potential to actually make things more complex and less agile if they are not designed for simple integration. If installation of a SOX package requires use of more layers of proprietary integration software, its effectiveness will be mitigated by the added workload needed to support the extra integration. SOA has the potential to streamline integration of SOX packages with other applications. Most SOX packages have SOA features anyway, because they are new on the market today. The challenge is to match them with SOA integration points in existing architecture.

DexCo conducts a review of SOX packages and determines that it wants to integrate a document management and shared workspace–type application into its compliance portal. The company's systems are not mature enough, and too prone to change, to merit the use of an exception monitoring or financial coordination package.

CHAPTER 15

FAST or Slow?

"Why do I get the feeling," Jim said to Dale, Sebastian, and Linda, "That I am about to hear some very bad news. That we have to scrap the FAST IT plan and start over again. I don't have the stomach for that, nor the budget." He points his trouble stick at Dale. "I want answers. You go first."

"Well," Dale replies. "My IT colleagues have taught me a basic principle of technology change in large organizations. It seems we typically overestimate what we can do in a year, but underestimate what we can do in ten years. Though I admit that this looks quite scary, the prudent course we will take provides for us to be selective in what we transform into an SOA for the purpose of agility and compliance. We do not have to do everything at once. For one thing, we couldn't even if we wanted to. But even if we could, it would not be the best course of action. I'm going to let Sebastian explain how he suggests we approach the matter of FAST and the transition to SOA."

SOA for DexCo's Agile Compliance

Sebastian and Ramesh man the white board and begin to lay out the SOA vision for the FAST program. FAST, they remind everyone, stands for Future Applications and Systems for Transactions. The goal of FAST had been to achieve a high level of integration between back-end systems and existing and new management software, including management portals. FAST was intended to enable improved operations and management visibility into day-to-day business transactions. In addition, the system was envisioned as a way to help cut costs in managing operations and procurement.

Even without compliance issues factored in, FAST was going to have trouble living up to its potential. The proprietary nature of the integration was problematic, as it might stand in the way of cost-effective and streamlined change management as DexCo exerted its need to be agile. Figure 15-1 compares DexCo's existing enterprise architecture with the vision of FAST.

"There's good news and bad news about FAST," Sebastian says.

"Give me the good news," Jim says. "I need to hear some good news."

"The good news is that we did a lot of serious thinking about how we can use IT to improve our operations. That thinking was not wasted. Not one bit. The vision that we have come up with from FAST—a vision that includes management portals and combining of selected systems to simplify our back office processing—that's all very worthwhile. The money for the FAST consultants to help us was not all spent in vain."

"And more good news—we think that the concept of FAST, with its vendor portals and connected CRM, ERP, and financial systems, will be to the benefit of compliance."

"Dale," Jim says. "Do you sense the approach of a massive 'but'? What's the bad news?"

"Alright," Sebastian says. "FAST isn't going to work the way we thought it would. The proprietary EAI approach is just too inflexible, both from a business agility and compliance standpoint."

"So," Sebastian continues. "Let's make an assumption—one that I admit may be at least partly wrong—which is that web services and service-oriented architecture are DexCo's best bet for business operations, strategy, and agile compliance. In my estimation, SOA enables agile compliance."

Ramesh diagrams Figure 15-2 on the board. "The idea," Ramesh says, "is to build an enterprise service bus that will enable universal connectivity and communication between any set of applications we use. We will expose back-end systems as web services, and build connections to those web services to front-end management portals and other integration applications. Of course, we will need a centralized user identity management and access rights management system to power this whole thing, or else it won't work."

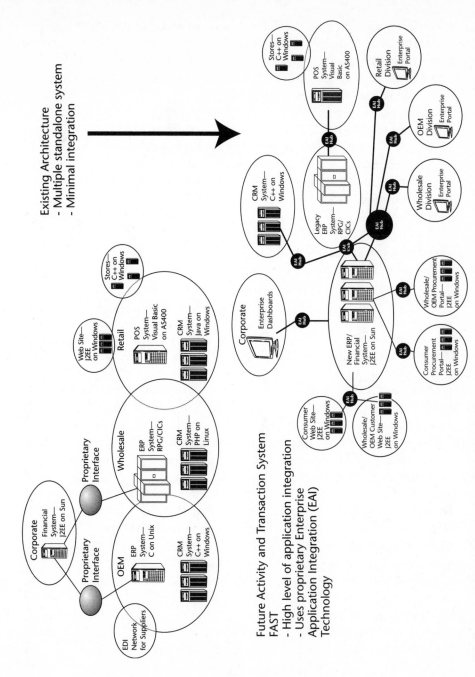

Figure 15-1 Recap of FAST's goals for DexCo's IT architecture: High level of integration is intended to enable improved operations and management visibility into day-to-day business transactions. In addition, the system is envisioned to help cut costs in managing operations and procurement.

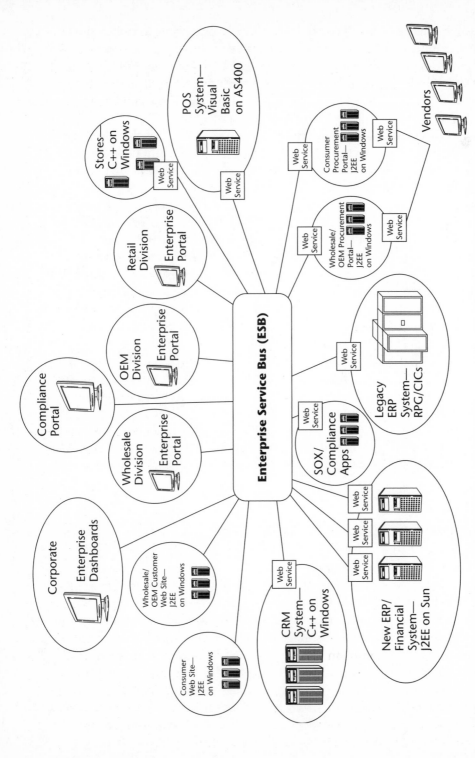

Figure 15-2 SOA for DexCo using an ESB. Back-end systems are exposed as web services and are able to communicate with front-end portals and other applications using the universal connectivity of the ESB.

"And," Sebastian says, "We achieve agility by being able to switch the integrations around with relative ease to match changing business processes. We can then work through compliance issues and perform our SOX 404 documentation of internal controls without the same kind of hassle we had before."

"This is the good news?" Jim asks. "Dale, tell me this is the good news. I feel like I'm looking at stereo instructions. This can't be cheap."

"You're right, Jim," Dale replies. "If we had to do all of this right away, we would go broke. And besides, we couldn't do it all right now even if we wanted to. What you are looking at is a five-year objective, and we may never actually implement every aspect of it."

"So why am I looking at it?"

"To give you an idea of where we are headed. As we move forward, our new SOA will give us the ability to make changes to the systems that support our business processes without taking too long or spending too much. That translates to agility. To the extent that we rely on those systems for the definition and enforcement of internal controls, our SOA will make compliance with Sarbanes Oxley a simpler matter to keep up with. If we want to get fancy and start using exception monitoring software or controls modules from our ERP vendors, it will all work better on an SOA."

"You didn't really answer my question," Jim says. "What are we actually going to do? I love fancy diagrams as much as the next guy, but I want to know what we are going to do right now and how much it's going to cost. How in the world do we know where to start?"

"Luckily for you and me," Dale replies, "we've got some pretty smart people here who can help us figure that out. The trick is to be selective. Sebastian and Linda are going to walk us through a process for determining which areas need to be converted to SOA first."

The Agile Compliance Scorecard

Linda joins Sebastian on the floor. Remarkably, they have become real friends through this whole experience. "Before we get into how to evaluate which areas of the business deserve the most attention for SOA conversion," Sebastian says, "let's state for the record that there are numerous parameters that one can use to determine a software program or business process's suitability for conversion to SOA. Compliance is just one factor, and in some cases it may not be the most compelling issue at hand. SOA-influencing factors include software code reuse potential, overall fit with enterprise architecture plan, system performance issues, security, and so on. For our purposes today, however, let's hold that all non-compliance factors are equal. We will measure suitability for SOA based only on compliance factors." (See my book, *Understanding*

Enterprise SOA [*Manning, 2005*], for an in-depth analytical process for determining optimal software candidates for exposure as web services in an SOA).

"This will be a two-stage process," Linda says. "First, we will compare the six basic business process groupings we have at DexCo and rank them in order of importance for SOA conversion for agile compliance. Then, we will look in depth at one of them and decide which of the supporting systems involved is most critical to expose as a web service for the purpose of agile compliance."

Scoring the Business Processes

They proceed to go through a score carding process, shown in Table 15-1. They have divided DexCo into six business process groupings—inbound and outbound transactions for each of the company's three divisions. Based on their knowledge of the company and the internal controls that reside in each business process group, Linda and Sebastian are able to assign scores to the groups. The idea behind the scorecard process is to identify which areas of the company are most likely to undergo change. Then, with the probability of change estimated, the scorecard measures the impact of a change on internal controls.

Although the scorecarding process is rather coarse grained, it does yield a helpful ranking of the business process groupings. Which one should be given immediate attention with regard to agile compliance? Obviously, the company does not have the time or money to do all of them at once, a project that in itself would be impossible even if it were desirable.

Table 15-1   Scorecard for Measuring the Importance of Converting Different Business Process Groups at DexCo to SOA for the Purpose of Achieving Agile Compliance

BUSINESS PROCESS GROUP	LIKELIHOOD OF CHANGE IN NEXT 2 YEARS	IMPACT OF CHANGE ON INTERNAL CONTROLS	SCORE*
Retail Inbound	2	5	7
Retail Outbound	4	5	9
Wholesale Inbound	4	7	11
Wholesale Outbound	6	7	13
OEM Inbound	2	3	5
OEM Outbound	6	7	13

*Each process was measured on a ten-point scale for the likelihood of it changing in the next two years, and the impact of a change on the process group's internal controls. A score of 1 means a low probability of change and impact on controls. A 10 is the highest level of probability of change and impact on controls.

Retail inbound business processes, those that relate to customers walking into stores and buying goods or patronizing the DexCo consumer web site, face a relatively low likelihood of major change. The business processes involved in selling merchandise to consumers are pretty much fixed, at least for the short term. Thus, Sebastian and Linda assign it a score of 2 on a scale of 1 to 10, with 10 being the highest probability of change in the next two years. If there were a change, however, that would have a definitive impact on internal controls. DexCo has many internal controls in the retail side of its business, so a change in the retail inbound business process scores a 5 in terms of impact on internal controls. Adding the two numbers gives the Retail Inbound transactions business processes a total score of 7, which makes it the second-lowest scoring group. Retail Inbound, therefore, deserves less priority in SOA conversion than another group, such as Wholesale Outbound.

The Wholesale Outbound transaction business process group, which covers procurement and strategic sourcing alliances for the wholesale business, scores higher than Retail Inbound for SOA conversion. Let's look at the reasons why. Because of the CEO's interest in improving DexCo's sourcing relationships, including ambitious programs such as flex-acturing, the Wholesale Outbound group receives a score of 6 on the likelihood of changing in the next two years. And, because of the complex, inter-dependent sets of internal controls contained within the procurement function, a change in the business process scores a 7 on the impact of change on internal controls. Thus, Wholesale Outbound receives a score of 13. As a result, it deserves a higher priority.

I have kept the example simple here for the purpose of illustrating the process. Your company is no doubt a great deal more complicated. However, the core issues will likely be the same. Some areas of your business are more prone to change than others, and when they do change, they will have a greater or lesser impact on your internal controls than others. If you are interested in agile compliance, my suggestion to you is that you look to begin your transition process with the areas of your business where change is likely and will have an impact on your controls and Sarbanes Oxley process.

One final comment on this topic—I have seen several articles and presentations about companies that invested heavily in establishing Sarbanes Oxley compliance for systems and processes that had nothing to do with internal controls. For example, the web server on the company's marketing web site is quite peripheral in terms of compliance. It is, at best, a vestigial issue when it comes to internal controls. I am not sure why these companies undertook these substantial projects for no particular reason. Perhaps their IT managers did not understand the concept of internal controls and felt they had to make every system under the roof "SOX compliant." I definitely encourage you to avoid this extra work. SOX compliance should be only for those systems that have a firm bearing on internal controls and financial reporting.

The Next Level: Scoring the Systems

Now that Linda and Sebastian have identified two high-level business process areas that deserve priority for SOA conversion for the sake of agile compliance, they turn their attention to scoring the IT systems that power those processes. Using flex-acturing, with which the management group is already familiar, they score its component systems as candidates for SOA conversion.

Flex-acturing, the situation where DexCo develops wireless products and brings them to market rapidly through an ever-changing set of alliances with manufacturers, is a business process that is supported by several distinct IT systems. As Figure 15-3 shows, each step in the process, which may involve more than one department or separate corporate entity, maps to a set of systems and correlates to several internal control points.

Where will these systems break upon flexion? What impact will a business process change have on these systems, and what will that mean to DexCo's ability to identify, document, and enforce internal controls for the purpose of Sarbanes Oxley as well as general business management goals? These are the questions that Sebastian and Linda are going to try to answer to determine which underlying systems are most suited for SOA conversion and which deserve the highest priority—in the name of achieving agile compliance with flex-acturing.

As Linda and Sebastian point out, to make any real sense of how an SOA is going to affect agile compliance, you have to look at the control points that link the systems that support the business process and see how they will fare under flexion. Using the same scorecard approach I used to look at the business process groupings of the company as a whole, Linda and Sebastian now score each of the control points that supports flex-acturing for their likelihood of flexion and the impact of flexion on the system's ability to support sound internal controls. This scorecard is summarized in Table 15-2.

The CRM to ERP link, which communicates the sales estimates used to plan production and procurement, scores fairly low because it is a simple connection that is not likely to change much once it has been instantiated. If there is a change in the business process, the CRM to ERP link is simple enough that the flexion would probably not have that big an impact on its ability to support effective internal controls.

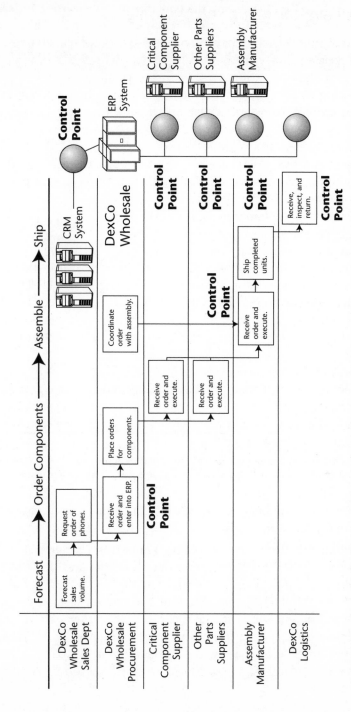

Figure 15-3 Matching IT systems, with business process for flex-acturing, along with internal control points

Table 15-2 Scorecard for Measuring the Importance of Converting Different Business Process Groups at DexCo to SOA for the Purpose of Achieving Agile Compliance

CONTROL POINT	LIKELIHOOD OF FLEXION	IMPACT OF FLEXION	TOTAL SCORE*	COMMENT
CRM to ERP link	2	3	5	When established, this link will remain essentially fixed
DexCo ERP to critical component vendor ERP	8	4	12	Very likely to change, but affects only one area of internal controls
DexCo ERP to other component vendors' ERPs	6	2	8	Likely to change, but will cause less impact on internal controls because of flexible nature of business relationships
DexCo ERP to assembly vendor ERP	3	5	8	Less likely to change, but will have an impact on internal controls because of contractual nature of business relationships

* Each process was measured on a 10-point scale for the likelihood of its changing in the next two years, and the impact of a change on the process group's internal controls. A score of 1 means a low probability of change and impact on Controls. 10 is the highest level of probability of change and impact on controls.

In contrast, the connection between DexCo's ERP system and that of the critical component supplier is almost guaranteed to change. That is, in fact, the whole point. DexCo wants to be agile enough to change critical component suppliers at will. Linda and Sebastian give this an 8 for likelihood of change. The impact of change on internal controls, too, will be great, because each alliance will probably have different contractual terms, which in turn could mean a different set of internal control parameters, risks, and objectives. For this reason, this control point receives a score of 12. This is a high priority to move to SOA to enable a more streamlined approach to integration and thus enable a greater degree of control to match the agility required in the process.

Back to Reality

"I like this process," Jim says. "We score the processes and the control points, and bingo, we know just what to do."

"Yes, but," Sebastian says. "Let me just show you one more thing." He displays Figure 15-4 on the screen and lets Jim, Dale, and the others take it in. "I realize this is a complex drawing," he says. "But what you should see is that there are three basic migrations involved in turning the flex-acturing process into an SOA, based on how we have architected our SOA."

"Number one involves exposing the ERP systems as web services so they can integrate easily with whatever systems need their data and functionality. Number two is the CRM to ERP link. Number three is the use of web services and SOA to connect our vendors' ERP systems with our own.

"Problem is," Sebastian adds, "not all SOA migrations are created equal."

He shows them Table 15-3.

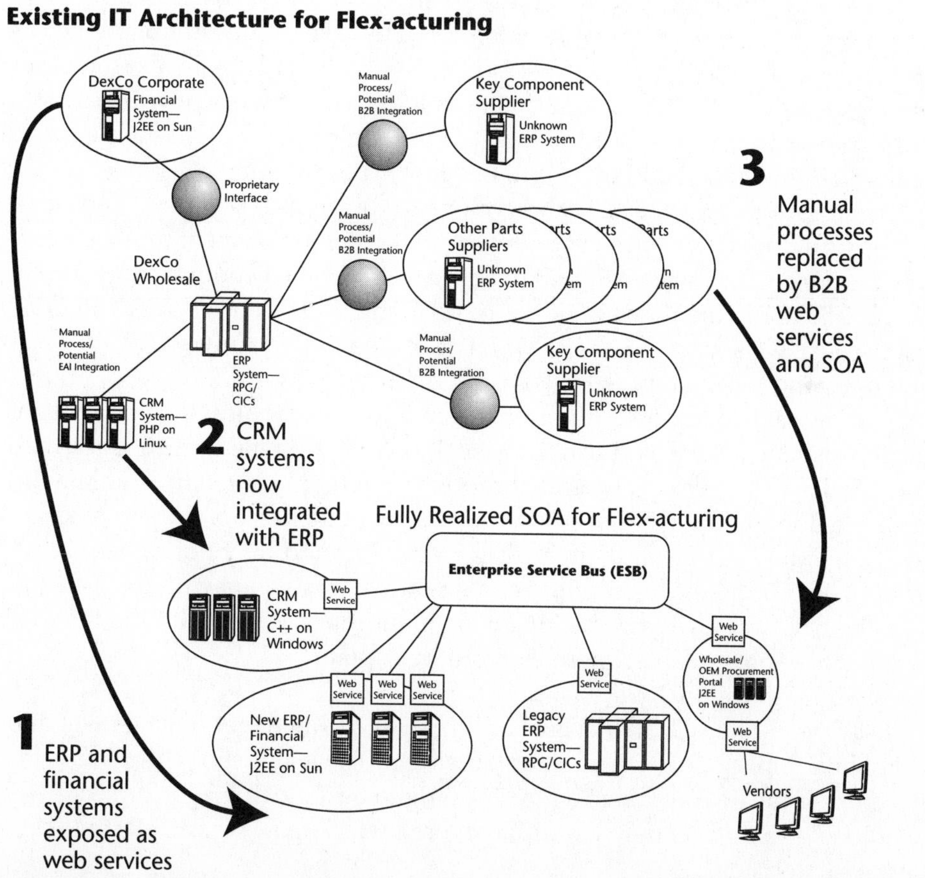

Figure 15-4 Migration of existing IT architecture used to support flex-acturing to the SOA envisioned for DexCo

Table 15-3   Scorecard for SOA Migration of Systems That Support the Flex-acturing Process

MIGRATION	DEGREE OF DIFFICULTY	BARRIERS TO IMPLEMENTATION	IMPORTANCE TO INTERNAL CONTROLS	TOTAL SCORE
1. ERP and financial systems exposed as web services	8	2	7	17
2. CRM to ERP link	3	2	3	8
3. Vendor ERP links	8	8	8	24

"Connecting ERP and CRM is relatively simple. It won't cost a lot, and there are no major barriers to its implementation. However, it doesn't really get us much. We won't die in SOX if we can't get that link made agile. On the other hand, exposing the ERP and financial systems is a lot of work. It will be costly and complex to migrate, but the benefits will be great. We will gain a lot of agility in our controls, and there will be few barriers to adoptions."

"If you look at connecting with vendor ERP using web services," Sebastian says, "it's a doozy. It's complex and very challenging, but the internal control benefits are great. However, it will not be easy to get the vendors to buy into it. We can't just assume they are going to go along with web services and SOA just because we say so. If we were a giant company like Sony, we could pressure our vendors to adopt SOA. We can't do that."

He shows a diagram of Figure 15-5. "Here's a way to look at the vendor connection issue. We have a critical component vendor. Maybe we can work with that vendor to go SOA. The other component vendors are too much of a wild card. We don't know what systems they use, whether or not they're ready to go SOA. Frankly, some of them are bigger than us and may not care what we want to do. The assembly vendor is an unknown, but we may be able to work with them. Overall, we'd be making a big assumption if we just think that our vendors are going to all cooperate on our SOA plan."

"So what do we do?" Dale asks.

"I say we do our CRM and ERP link first, as a way to get our feet wet and learn something about SOA as an organization. Then, let's start chipping away at exposing the ERP systems, which is going to be a much bigger project."

"Okay," Jim says. "I'm ready for an overall wrap up so we can start making some real decisions."

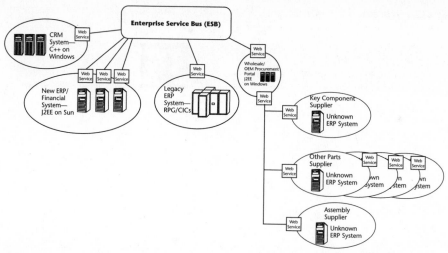

Figure 15-5   Detail of migration issues involved in exposing systems that support vendor connections in flex-acturing

Summary

The DexCo team now needs to make some decisions about its FAST program, which was designed to revamp the company's IT architecture for greater integration between systems and increased visibility for management. After discussion, the team reaches the conclusion that the goals of FAST, integration and visibility, are worthwhile, but the method is not workable. The proprietary enterprise application integration packages envisioned for FAST will not change easily or cheaply enough to enable effective operations or agile compliance.

SOA is a viable approach to FAST's integration goals. However, migration to an SOA all at once is not possible or even desirable. The question, then, is where to start? To figure out which business process and supporting systems deserve the highest priority for SOA, the team looks at a process of scorecarding. Business processes and their supporting systems are ranked based on the probability that they will change, and the impact that a flexion of business process will have on the internal controls involved in the business process. The highest scorers should go first because they will be the ones most likely to break upon flexion, which would endanger DexCo's agile compliance.

Drilling deeper down, the team discovers that migrating systems to an SOA is not itself that simple. Within one set of systems, for example, there are numerous complexities and challenges involved in migrating to an SOA for the sake of agile compliance. The team must make judgment calls regarding where to start on the SOA-based agile compliance plan.

CHAPTER 16

Conclusion

After writing this book, I tried to explain my overall concept to a colleague who comes from the audit profession and currently specializes in helping public companies prepare for their Sarbanes Oxley audits. She told me she felt that my idea—that SOX compliance could help businesses run better—was a hard sell. Compliance was a costly process that delivered little more than, well, compliance.

I had to say that I agreed, for it would be absurd to argue that there is an upside to filling out forms, compiling documentation of internal controls that may or may not exist in reality just to satisfy an auditor that may or may not really understand what's happening inside a business. Indeed, if you have come away from reading this book thinking that compliance alone will help your business, then I have failed rather spectacularly. Instead, I believe that improving the actual effectiveness of internal controls, while maintaining agility, can make a real difference to the success of a business. Compliance with SOX is really a side benefit of the whole process.

My goal with this book was to take you on a journey of thought. We have gone through the process of understanding how compliance and agility can co-exist in a business, and even provide the basis for improving a business. To get there, we have learned about Sarbanes Oxley, COSO, COBIT, IT, Service-Oriented Architecture, auditing, business process modeling, and more. We have seen an organization struggle with the issue on the technological, business process, accounting, and interpersonal levels. I am quite sure that you must feel a lot smarter than you did before you began reading. Let's see how our story ends.

Consensus

We have gone on this journey of thought with the DexCo team. Now, they have to make some decisions. "Alright," Dale says. "Let's summarize what we plan to do about Sarbanes Oxley. He gives each person in the room a handout. "When we go through this, we are going to agree that this is our action plan for Sarbanes Oxley and agile compliance. This is your opportunity to say no. If you're with me on this, you're with me. Speak now or forever—you know what I mean . . ."

The handout forms a basic plan of action for DexCo's total compliance plan. It summarizes the steps the company is planning to take in compliance. The major sections of the handout include:

- **Compliance portal:** DexCo will create a compliance portal that will serve as the nerve center for the company's ongoing Sarbanes Oxley 404 work as well as a clearing house for all proposed business process changes and their impact on supporting IT systems. The compliance portal will bring together many different groups of people involved in the company's compliance efforts and link them to sources of information they will need to keep DexCo agile and compliant.

- **Organizational changes:** The compliance portal alone will be useless without a set of significant organizational changes.

  - Basic compliance efforts: DexCo will undertake to train all of its managers in compliance issues, including internal controls. The company will invest in training senior managers, providing them with in-depth knowledge of SOX, COBIT, and IT.

  - The company will hire a Chief of Compliance, who will oversee all compliance efforts.

  - The Chief of Compliance will supervise a team of liaisons, who will represent the accounting, IT, and lines of business entities that are involved in internal controls for both the basic SOX 404 compliance process and the evaluation of proposed business process changes.

  - The liaison teams will use Business Process Execution Language (BPEL) as a way to communicate complex business processes and their IT components amongst themselves.

  - The liaison teams will review each IT project, but will put a full compliance analysis and status tracking process into effect only if it appears that the system in question has a bearing on internal controls and compliance.

- DexCo will undertake several major COBIT initiatives company-wide, including improved information security and IT change management procedures.

- DexCo will change the way it formulates its internal controls, attempting to put the accounting organization into more pragmatic contact with operations and IT.

- The twin goals of agility and compliance will be invoked for virtually every IT and business process change under consideration at the company. Some projects will get intense scrutiny for compliance, while others will not.

- **Systemic and architecture IT changes:** DexCo will undertake a gradual implementation of a service-oriented architecture (SOA), based on web services and an enterprise service bus (ESB) that will provide relatively simple and inexpensive interoperation between all of the company's disparate IT systems and software applications. In addition to enabling greater business agility, the SOA has the potential to provide open access to exception monitoring and internal controls management software that monitors ongoing IT systems in support of business processes.

- **Phase in:** To make this all work, DexCo needs to identify suitable candidates for conversion to SOA as a first step toward its overall goal of agile compliance. Using a scorecard system, the IT and accounting teams can rank business processes and their supporting systems to arrive at a workable plan of action for implementing the SOA and agile compliance program.

  - In the first year, the SOX 404 effort will take place in parallel with the development of the agile compliance plan. There is not enough time to implement the compliance portal and the whole agile compliance plan before the upcoming SOX 404 certification deadline.

  - In the second year, they will merge, and all of DexCo's compliance efforts will stem from the agile compliance program.

- **Benefits:** Executing agile compliance will not be cheap, but the investment in the program will pay dividends far outweighing the initial outlays.

  - Reduced audit and SOX certification preparation costs are two immediate savings that will amortize the investment in agile compliance.

  - Reduction in risk of running afoul of the SEC, a problem that can have a major negative impact on stock price, is a benefit of agile compliance.

- Improved business operations will result from the ability of IT to support business processes accurately and change in the same cycle time as they do.

- The ability to be agile, which means you can enter into partnerships and make changes to business processes in a rapid cycle time, will enable DexCo to remain profitable, competitive, and strategically healthy.

Jim reviews the handout and puts his trouble stick down. "Go for it," he says. "You've proven your point. Now, let's do this."

This is an end and a beginning for DexCo. We have covered the discussions that were necessary to get the management team on board with the agile compliance concept and then analyze it through its practical application. Now, they must do the painstaking detail work of laying out a functional agile compliance plan that will serve all of their needs. It will take them many hours of hard work. Alas, that's a story for another book.

Compliance, especially agile compliance, is a vast and complex subject. Although I have gone on and on about it in these pages, I feel as if I have barely scratched the surface. In so many places, I have had to say, "This is a just a simple example. Your business may be different, or more involved." I hope you have drawn some worthwhile lessons from my narrow examples.

The Future

This book was written in 2005, a year that was notable for a number of emerging corporate scandals, such as Refco, and the conclusion of several others, such as WorldCom and HealthSouth. The SEC has a new head, a man who is reputed to be opposed to rigorous use of the Sarbanes Oxley Act.

The future of SOX is unclear. It may be repealed. It may be watered down. Even if it is not taken off the books, it is somewhat clear at this point that it is not the Department of Justice's prosecutorial weapon of choice. The Refco case is being prosecuted as a matter of financial fraud, though it appears that the Sarbanes Oxley law was also violated.

In my opinion, it does not matter what happens with SOX. The impact of increased SEC scrutiny, combined with ever more aggressive domestic class action litigation, has forever changed the way public companies operate and disclose to their shareholders. As the crushing, global market presses American companies toward greater agility, the regulatory bodies force compliance. Agile compliance is the only way for a public company to survive. I have tried to lay out an essential foundation for you to use in thinking through your company's need for agile compliance.

Finally, researching this book and putting it all together has led me to a thought regarding the entire approach that the business world takes to compliance and operations management. I have come to believe that the fields of accounting, business, and IT need to change if they are to have a chance of attaining agility and compliance. There is a great need, I believe, for all of the disciplines involved in business operations and compliance to come together and reach a mutual understanding as they never have before. The stakes are simply too high for them not to.

The experience of telling DexCo's story has made me see that IT folks need to form a far more nuanced and detailed understanding of business operations and accounting if they are to be true enablers of strategic, agile business. Accountants, for their part, must undertake a much more comprehensive understanding of how IT works, and how it actually powers internal controls and business operations. Business managers, who are often the least knowledgeable of the lot when it comes to internal controls, IT, and accounting, are due for a major upgrade on their knowledge of compliance issues.

We all have to learn to work together if we can hope to work at all. This is no small task. Yet, as John F. Kennedy said, we do these things, " . . . not because they are easy, but because they are hard, because that goal will serve to organize and measure the best of our energies and skills . . ." This is the challenge of our generation of business leaders.

Glossary

The following definitions have been crafted to serve the needs of a general business reader trying to understand the role of IT in the SOX compliance process. For more in-depth information about these terms, please refer to the resources listed in Appendix B.

access management software   Software applications that manage access rights to other software applications. For example, an access management software package will determine whether a specific user can access a specific system. In large organizations with many users and software packages deployed, these provisioning issues can be quite important for security and data integrity.

accounting organization   A corporate group that is responsible for managing the accounting function.

agency problem   Conflicts of interest that arise between shareholders of a company and its management, the agents who account on behalf of the shareholders.

agile compliance   An approach to complying with SEC laws that provides a high level of accountability and compliance, but also preserves the ability for the business to change its strategy or operational tactics in a rapid cycle time.

agility   The ability of a business to change operations or strategy within a rapid cycle time.

application development process   The set of technological, organizational, and business tasks associated with developing a software program. Typically, an enterprise software program will go through an iterative process of requirements gathering, initial development, and revision until launch.

application programming interface (API)   A set of routines, protocols, and tools for building software applications. A good API makes it easier to develop a program by providing all the building blocks. A programmer puts the blocks together.

audit   A process wherein an independent CPA reviews records and other accounting data to check the accuracy of a company's financial reports.

business process   A series of steps, both manual and technology-based, that are necessary to attain a desired result in a business. For example, checking credit score.

business process execution language (BPEL)   A software language that uses symbols and text to model a business process and map the process to IT systems and manual processes.

business process modeling (BPM)   A technique that uses visual symbols and written descriptions to develop a model of a business process that can then be matched to supporting IT systems and manual processes.

COBIT   Abbreviation for Control Objectives for Information and Related Technology, a set of guidelines for achieving IT governance and improving internal controls through IT, from the IT Governance Institute (ITGI) and Information Systems Audit and Control Association (ISACA).

COBIT heat map   An approach to COBIT that suggests that a company undertake COBIT only in areas that are most relevant to internal controls and material financial reporting issues.

COBIT management guidelines   A set of performance parameters that help an IT organization attain a specified level of maturity in certain areas of IT management, such as security and data integrity.

COBIT maturity model   A measurement scale that an IT organization can use to determine how well it is implementing COBIT management guidelines.

compliance   The practice of making sure that a company is abiding by various laws that govern it, such as securities laws, environmental laws, and so on.

compliance architecture   A hypothetical construct that combines issues of compliance with enterprise architecture. For example, how does a business comply with SOX and other laws through the use of its IT architecture?

control components   Internal control areas defined by COSO, including control environment, risk assessment, control procedures, information and communication, and monitoring.

control environment   The overall tone at the top of the organization that affects internal controls. For example, are the senior managers honest and setting a good example for the rest of the company?

control point   A place (either physical or virtual) where an IT system, or set of IT systems, is responsible for enforcing an internal control. For example, a link between an ERP system and a vendor's financial system.

control procedures   COSO control component that covers specific steps that management must take to implement internal controls.

COSO   Abbreviation for Committee of Sponsoring Organizations of the Treadway Commission, which developed the standards for internal controls used in Sarbanes Oxley compliance.

customer resource management (CRM) software   Software that helps a business manage data about its customers and sales leads for purposes of marketing and sales.

distributed computing   An approach to enterprise computing that involves using more than one computer to accomplish business process. Also, an approach to information technology that relies on numerous computers running enterprise applications, in contrast to a mainframe approach, which centralizes processing on large machines.

enterprise application integration (EAI)   A software discipline that uses specialized software programs to enable more than one software application to work together with others.

enterprise resource planning (ERP) software   Enterprise software application that manages production operations, supply chain, logistics, and other key areas of operations.

enterprise service bus (ESB)   An IT architecture that uses specialized software to connect any number of heterogeneous systems across multiple communications protocols. For example, dial tone for multiple computer systems and software programs.

exception monitoring   A software program designed to catch exceptions to internal controls and business rules. For example, alerting management if a shipment leaves a warehouse without payment or credit being secured.

external auditor   A CPA firm, independent of a public company, that conducts an audit of the company's financial statements for purposes of disclosure to the SEC and shareholders.

financial reporting   The process by which a public company reports its financial results to shareholders. For example, the 10K report.

financial software   Enterprise software application that contains general ledger and other financial data for a business.

GAAP   The set of standards that govern how most businesses manage their accounting.

general ledger   The main financial records of a company (the "books"); typically a software program.

hairball   A large number of overlapping business processes, IT systems, and internal controls that can resemble a hairball when diagrammed graphically.

identity management software   Software applications that store information about system users at a business, particularly the access rights.

inbound transaction   A business transaction that results in a company earning revenue.

information and communication   COSO Control Component that deals with management's ability to collect accurate information on its internal controls and other factors that can impact reliability in financial reporting.

information technology (IT)   The field of computers, software, and networks that supports business.

internal auditor   An accounting staff member or group that conducts audits of internal financial process and reporting inside a business.

internal control   A process, effected by an entity's board of directors, management and other personnel, designed to provide reasonable assurance regarding the achievement of reliability in financial reporting, among other objectives.

internal control deficiency   A situation where an internal control is too weak to be able to ensure the financial accuracy result that it was intended to perform. For example, an unlocked cash register.

internal control documentation   Written document that describes how an internal control is designed and enforced.

IT architecture   A technological and business discipline wherein an IT architect designs and sets standards for the software, hardware, network, and integration of IT systems of an organization.

IT change management process   The series of working steps and processes, both technological and organizational, that are required to make a change in an IT system.

IT governance   The set of business rules and policies covering systems management, infrastructure usage, change management, application development, and security that determines how an IT organization should be run.

IT organization   The corporate group responsible for the operation of a business's IT systems, including application development, security, network, infrastructure, IT vendor management, desktop services, and so on.

magic bullet   A technology that can solve all problems; typically hype.

mainframe computer   A large, powerful computer that is typically used to run major business applications.

material weakness   A serious deficiency in internal controls that can result in materially significant financial reporting problems. For example, a lack of segregation of roles that results in a billion dollar earnings overstatement.

monitoring   COSO control component that refers to management's ability to monitor internal control to be confident that they are working as intended.

non-compliance penalties   Fines and other punishments carried out by the SEC or Department of Justice for companies that fail to comply with the securities laws. Under SOX, this can even include criminal prosecution for top executives.

on-demand software   Class of software programs that are available for use through a web browser. For example, `Salesforce.com`.

online workspace   A web-based software package that provides a way for multiple people to share tasks and divide and coordinate subcomponents of tasks.

operations   The area of a business that is involved in producing the business's product or delivering the service from which it derives its revenues. For example, a factory.

outbound transaction   A business transaction that results in a company spending money.

PCAOB   Public Company Accounting Oversight Board; an organization established by the Sarbanes Oxley Act to oversee the audit firms that audit public companies.

propriety interface   A custom or proprietary (that is, commercial, non-standard) software program that connects more than one software program or system with another.

remediation   The process of fixing an internal control deficiency, typically involving internal accounting staff, IT, and outside compliance consultants. The external auditor must sign off on the success of the remediation.

risk assessment   COSO control component that covers management's responsibility for evaluating the risks it faces in its business that can affect the reliability of its financial reporting.

Sarbanes Oxley Act (SOX)   2002 Federal Securities Law that adds numerous governance requirements for public companies, including the need for management to certify the effectiveness of internal controls.

scorecard   An approach to evaluating systems and business processes with the goal of assessing which one is a candidate for a particular action. For example, measuring the impact of a change in business process on an IT system to evaluate whether or not it should be changed to a web service or whether the change should be deferred so that another, higher scoring system should get the attention first.

Section 404   The section of the Sarbanes Oxley Act that requires management of a public company to establish internal controls and attest to their effectiveness.

Securities and Exchange Commission (SEC)   Federal Government body that oversees the securities industry.

securities laws   Federal and State laws that govern companies that sell stock or debt on the public markets.

service-oriented architecture (SOA)   An approach to enterprise IT architecture based on technologies that enable any computer system to interact with any other computer system anywhere, regardless of message protocol, software language, data format, application, or operating system.

service-oriented business application (SOBA)   Software program comprising multiple component web services that have been orchestrated to perform a business process.

silo   an insular approach to technology or corporate knowledge, where one group of people, or system users, have a deep grasp of a data set or business process, while others are excluded. For example, users of particular ERP system know everything that is going on in that system, while others in the company have no way of finding out. Similarly, others have no easy way to integrate with the silo system.

SOAP   Simple Object Access Protocol; a standardized format of XML that is used for web services, a basic building block of a service-oriented architecture.

SOX audit   The process wherein an independent CPA reviews management's documentation of internal controls and tests controls based on its own framework in order to identify any control weaknesses and issue their own report on internal control.

SOX software   Software applications that help businesses comply with Sarbanes Oxley.

standards   Software, computer, and communication specifications that are public (non-proprietary), and created by a standards body for the purpose of enabling open interoperations amongst disparate systems. For example, HTTP, HTML.

tone at the top   COSO concept that refers to the senior management's approach to compliance and ethical business conduct.

transport protocols   Technical specifications used to send and receive messages on a network. For example, HTTP.

web service   A piece of software that can be invoked over the Web using standards-based language and communication protocols. For example, XML over HTTP.

XML   An open standard (non-proprietary) software language and data format that can describe data and operating instructions that can be universally understood.

Resources

If you want to know more about Sarbanes Oxley legislation and how it affects you, you might find of the following resources helpful.

Government Bodies and Organizations

Committee of Sponsoring Organizations of the Treadway Commission (COSO): www.coso.org

Financial Accounting Standards Board (FASB): www.fasb.org

Information Systems Audit and Control Organization (ISACA): www.isaca.org

Institute of Internal Auditors (IIA): www.theiia.org

IT Governance Institute (ITGI): www.itgi.org

Public Company Accounting Oversight Board (PCAOB): www.pcaob.org

Securities and Exchange Commission (SEC): www.sec.gov

Audit Firms and Analysts That Publish Sarbanes Oxley Research

Deloitte & Touche: www.deloitte.com

Ernst & Young: www.ey.com

Forrester: www.forrester.com

Gartner: www.gartner.com

KPMG: www.kpmg.com

PriceWaterhouseCoopers: www.pwc.com

Online Resources

BPM Basics: www.bpmbasics.com

SarbanesOxley.com: www.sarbanesoxley.com

SOX Online: www.sox-online.com

XML.org: www.xml.org

Yahoo SOX Group: http://finance.groups.yahoo.com/group/SOXTalks/

Bibliography

Books

Green, Scott. *Manager's Guide to the Sarbanes Oxley Act.* Hoboken, N.J.:
Wiley, 2004.

Lander, Guy P. *What is Sarbanes Oxley?* New York, N.Y.: McGraw-Hill, 2004.

Nagel, Karl. *Internal Controls Primer.* Huntington Beach, Calif.: Karl Nagel
& Co., 2003.

Pulier, Eric and Hugh Taylor. *Understanding Enterprise SOA.* Greenwich,
Conn.: Manning Publications, 2005.

Ramos, Michael. *How to Comply with Sarbanes Oxley Section 404.*
Hoboken, N.J.: Wiley, 2004.

Articles

Chan, Sally, "Mapping COSO and CobiT for Sarbanes Oxley Compliance,"
IT Audit Magazine, October 1, 2004.

"Delphi Uses Sham Sales to Lift Profits, Lawsuit Says," *The New York Times*,
October 6, 2005.

Dubie, Denise, "HP to Release Mgmt Barrage," *NetworkWorld*, June 6, 2005.

Dubie, Denise, "IT Pros Share Their Tales of Making ITIL Work," *NetworkWorld*, September 26, 2005.

Edelstein, Sid, "Sarbanes Oxley Compliance for Non-Accelerated Filers," *The CPA Journal*, July 2005.

Hoffman, Thomas, "Execs Describe Sarbanes Oxley Compliance Lessons Learned," *Computerworld Magazine*, September 28, 2005.

"Interpublic Group Announces Restated Results for 5 Years," *The New York Times*, October 1, 2005.

Leech, Tim, "Will the SEC Admit It Got It Wrong?" *Global Risk Regulator Magazine*, June 2005.

Markham, Robert and Paul Hammerman, "The Forrester Wave: Sarbanes Oxley Compliance Software Q1 2005," Forrester Research 2005.

McCuaig, Bruce, "A Panacea of the Profession," *Internal Auditor Magazine*, April 2005.

Mooney, Laura, "Compliance, a Catalyst for Change," *BIOS*, August, 8, 2005.

Musoff, Jay and Brian Newman, "Criminal Provisions of Sarbanes Have Yet to Make an Impact," *New York Law Journal*, July 19, 2004.

Pasley, Keith, "Sarbanes Oxley (SOX)—Impact on Security in Software," *Developer Magazine*, March 3, 2004.

Popkin, Jan, "Improving Regulatory Compliance with Business Process Modeling," *Business Integration Journal*, June 2005.

Putrus, Robert, "Lessons Learned—COSO, CobiT and other emerging Standards for SOX Compliance," *California CPA Magazine*, July 2005.

Rasch, Mark, "Sarbanes Oxley for IT Security?" *The Register*, May 3, 2005.

"Refco Imposes a Partial Moratorium as Customers Seek to Close Accounts," *The New York Times*, October 14, 2005.

"Sarbanes Oxley and Information Technology," *Java Developers Journal*, June 2005.

Scannell, Ed, "HP Weaves SOA Into Openview—Company issues new SOA and compliance management software," *InfoWorld Magazine*, June 6, 2005.

Schwartz, Ephraim, "Security Lessons Learned," *InfoWorld Magazine*, July 4, 2005.

"SEC Could Sue Goodyear, Ex-Finance Execs," *CFO Magazine*, August 17, 2005.

Taub, Steven, "ERP Implementation Deflates Goodyear's Earnings," *CFO Magazine*, November 21, 2003.

"Top Regulator Says Sarbanes Oxley Act Audits are Too Costly and Inefficient," *The New York Times*, December 1, 2005.

"Wal-Mart Sues Ex Ex-Executive," *The New York Times*, July 28, 2005.

Wayne, Rick, "Service With a Smile," *Software Development Magazine*, July 2005.

Worthen, Ben, "How to Dig Out from Under Sarbanes Oxley," *CIO Magazine*, July 2005.

Zeller, Tom, "Mastercard Says Security Breach Affects 40 Million Cards," *The New York Times*, June 17, 2005.

Reports and White Papers

Deloitte & Touche. "Sarbanes Oxley Section 404: 10 Threats to Compliance." 2004.

Enron Annual Report 1999.

Financial Executives Research Foundation. "What is COSO?" April 2003.

Institute of Internal Auditors. "WorldCom: Internal Audit Lessons to be learnt." July 2003.

IT Governance Institute. "IT Control Objectives for Sarbanes Oxley." April 2004.

PriceWaterHouseCoopers. "How to Use Identity Management to reduce the cost and complexity of Sarbanes Oxley Compliance," PWC Advisory 2005.

PriceWaterhouseCoopers. "Internal Audit Sarbanes Oxley Survey." 2004.

PriceWaterHouseCoopers. "IT Investment Portfolio Management."

The Goodyear Tire & Rubber Company Form 8-K, February 11, 2004.

Index